PRAISE FOR RA*L*

"Many people think that some of us are _____ not. 'Not so!' says Kim Chestney. We are *all* bo _____ ....u to train ourselves to use it. In *Radical Intuition*, _____ your very own intuition coach, helping you understand intuition, develop practice routines, and maximize your skills. The result is liberating and life-changing." **— Christine Hassler**, author of *Expectation Hangover*

"Have you ever had a feeling that pops up inside you and speaks truth? That's called *intuition*. It wasn't until I read *Radical Intuition* by Kim Chestney that I understood it on a different level. What I enjoy most about this book is it's designed to allow you to pause and put intuition into practice." **— Jamin Olivencia**, pro wrestler and ambassador of positive change

"Finally, a book that speaks to the innate power of intuition in a modern and accessible way! If you want to awaken and radically amplify your intuitive superpowers, do yourself a favor and read this book." **— Katie Brauer**, founder of The Yoga Professional

"I am often asked the question: 'How do I hear my inner guidance?' I will now answer that question by recommending this book. In *Radical Intuition*, Kim Chestney provides an extraordinarily clear pathway into the art of listening to your intuition so you can find deep peace and lasting happiness." **— Corinne Zupko**, award-winning author of *From Anxiety to Love*

"*Radical Intuition* takes the mystical and makes it practical for everyone. In every word, I could feel Kim Chestney's wisdom, love, and guidance to elevate my spirit and empower my life. Rich. Warm. Powerful." **— Marla Mervis-Hartmann**, creator of Love Your Body, Love Yourself

"Follow Kim Chestney's guidance in *Radical Intuition*, and you'll tap into the universal enlightenment accessible to each and every one of us. It will change the way you see — and relate to — humanity itself." **— Tim Bickerton**, technology professional and IntuitionLab Certified Intuition Practitioner

"Kim Chestney is a gifted teacher on a mission to demystify intuition and weave it back into the fabric of our daily lives. Anyone seeking to increase personal power and do away with overthinking will find an abundance of support and guidance in *Radical Intuition*." **— Anita Scaglione**, owner of Power of Touch Wellness

"Provides a step-by-step process to gain a deeper understanding of how to best participate in and create our own lives. When we learn to listen deeply in this way, we have more power and capacity to heal, love, and evolve." — **Jillian Pransky**, author of *Deep Listening: A Healing Practice to Calm Your Body, Clear Your Mind, and Open Your Heart*

"It goes without saying that we are constantly overwhelmed and often frozen by an avalanche of data. Kim Chestney has crafted a very practical and brilliant guide to how we can cut through and see beyond the accumulation of facts and tap the interior creativity we all possess. This is not newfound wisdom, and Kim has cited the greatest visionaries of history to demonstrate how each of us, in similar fashion, can unearth the genius within." — **James Denova, PhD**, vice president of the Claude Worthington Benedum Foundation

"This book has it all, from the basics of what your inner voice is and how to recognize it in your life to how to trust, cultivate, and benefit from it. The perfect guide for anyone wanting to take their way of living to new levels." — **Neysha Arcelay**, founder and CEO of Precixa and author of *The Little Blue Book*

"I absolutely love Kim Chestney and everything she creates and shares. When I'm out of balance and seeking answers from a peaceful and calm place, I always go back to Kim's teachings. She is an extraordinary teacher." — **Gabriela Delgado Lopez**, yoga and intuitive movement teacher at www.gabrieladelo.com

"Kim Chestney recognizes the shift we're making from an information age to an imagination age and provides the tools to help you thrive in these exciting times." — **Audrey Russo**, president and CEO of the Pittsburgh Technology Council

"Wow, what an amazing read! Kim Chestney's book and training offered the tips, tools, and experience for me to learn and hear my own intuitive voice. Thank you, Kim, for sharing this with the world!" — **Meagan Grant**, MBA, PMP, IntuitionLab Certified Intuition Practitioner

"With *Radical Intuition*, Kim Chestney presents a truly new vision of our intuitive nature. Disrupting traditional conceptions about the way we think, create, and evolve, this book takes us deep into the mysteries of consciousness itself — where we discover what it really means to be human." — **Chip Walter**, author of National Geographic's *Immortality, Inc.: Renegade Science, Silicon Valley Billions, and the Quest to Live Forever* and *Last Ape Standing: The Seven-Million-Year Story of How and Why We Survived*

RADICAL INTUITION

RADICAL INTUITION

A REVOLUTIONARY GUIDE TO USING YOUR INNER POWER

Kim Chestney

Foreword by Kim Moses

New World Library
Novato, California

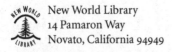 New World Library
14 Pamaron Way
Novato, California 94949

Text design by Tona Pearce Myers

Library of Congress Cataloging-in-Publication Data

Names: Chestney, Kim, author.
Title: Radical intuition : a revolutionary guide to using your inner power / Kim
    Chestney.
Description: Novato : New World Library, 2020. | Includes bibliographical references. | Summary: "Discusses the role of intuition in business, relationships, health, and the arts. The author maintains that intuition is a higher cognitive ability that all people possess and that it can be developed with effort and mindful attention. The book includes exercises and self-assessment quizzes." -- Provided by publisher.
Identifiers: LCCN 2020030379 (print) | LCCN 2020030380 (ebook) |
    ISBN 9781608687145 (paperback) | ISBN 9781608687152 (epub)
Subjects: LCSH: Intuition. | Cognition. | Self-help techniques.
Classification: LCC BF315.5 .C44 2020 (print) | LCC BF315.5 (ebook) |
    DDC 153.4/4--dc23
LC record available at https://lccn.loc.gov/2020030379
LC ebook record available at https://lccn.loc.gov/2020030380

First printing, November 2020
ISBN 978-1-60868-714-5
Ebook ISBN 978-1-60868-715-2
Printed in Canada on 100% postconsumer-waste recycled paper

 New World Library is proud to be a Gold Certified Environmentally Responsible Publisher. Publisher certification awarded by Green Press Initiative.

10   9   8   7   6   5   4   3   2

To anyone who has walked their own path —
to the free spirit who travels on the wind,
to the artist who is true to their muse,
to the pioneer who forges the new trails,
to the truth-liver who is proud to be their authentic self,
to the outlier who owns what makes them different,
to the genius who believes in their vision,
to the innovator who works to make the world a better place,
to the peacemaker who unites all people,
to the modern-day mystic who transcends it all,
to the way-shower who follows their intuition to lead others,
to anyone who was told it was impossible and did it anyway —
to anyone who has never given up on themselves —
this work is dedicated to you.

For it is intuition that improves the world,
not just following the trodden path of thought....
Intuition is the father of new knowledge,
while empiricism is nothing but an accumulation
of old knowledge. Intuition, not intellect,
is the "open sesame" of yourself.

— ALBERT EINSTEIN

CONTENTS

FOREWORD

As an executive producer and director of seven hundred hours of premium content (half a billion dollars of production), I have a front-row seat to the thrashing and chaos of Hollywood's process of cherry-picking winners, aka choosing which TV shows are green-lighted into production. Which shows will attract a loyal audience depends on an unknowable web of possibilities, and anyone who claims to be able to fully predict this is owning madness.

Once, while we were shooting actor tests for a new series, the studio asked if I wanted to take over the sets of a show they were pulling the plug on before it even aired, because the network did not believe that the series — *Grey's Anatomy* — would attract an audience. Seventeen seasons and three hundred sixty-four episodes later, Shonda Rhimes's award-winning medical series reigns supreme as ABC's number one program of passionate, loyal viewers and key demographics.

Nobody knows anything in Hollywood — and especially if it's never been done before. J Moses, my partner at Optin Studios (www.optinstudios.com), and I spent the past six months meeting with studio/platform executives, agents, managers, and potential strategic partners, trying to help them embrace the integration of technology into entertainment content in a way that reflects our daily lives. We met with a great deal of gatekeeper resistance. Why? Fear. White spaces, fresh ideas, new approaches — that's scary stuff to decision makers. Rare is the decision maker who does not want to be first second.

But that's not just Hollywood, that's in most businesses, right? So whether I'm prepping a series with a fresh creative approach or you're getting ready to present an innovative business concept to your boss, fear is the greatest obstacle. It is the killer of dreams and innovation. Well, there are two ways to go with fear: forget everything and run or face everything and rise. I don't know about you, but I choose to own my power and rise up. I do it purposefully — with intuition and rigorous discovery. These tools guide me in transcending fear, maximizing creativity, and making the best decisions for my businesses, my family, and myself.

I'm pretty confident that most of you have mastered discovery. But how in touch are you with your intuition? Unless you've used it, you may not understand the power of intuition. In order to make our best decisions, we need to bridge the gap between instinct and reasoning with rational thinking — and that's where intuition plays a key role.

With *Radical Intuition*, Kim Chestney expertly took me through the awesome journey of developing and integrating intuition into my life and work. I was fascinated to discover how intuition searches the past, present, and future, enabling us to connect with our hunches and feelings in nonlinear ways. It goes way beyond the limits of the thinking mind to clarify our inner voice. My *Radical Intuition* process allows me to bring true instinctual awareness into my daily life so that I can operate confidently. I may not be able to fully predict what projects will develop into hit shows, but I have eliminated the giant obstacle of fear that gets in the way of creativity and process — freeing me up to make bold choices that lead to success.

While producing a drama series in Pittsburgh, I had the great pleasure of working with Kim Chestney. She does groundbreaking work as founder of IntuitionLab, where she is an innovative leader in the tech sphere. Simultaneously, Kim was on the path to discovery, traveling the world as a thought leader, exchanging information with others operating at her level, and beyond.

There is no better person than Kim Chestney to show you the way to tap into your intuition when you are facing business and personal decisions usually embedded with fear. You can either forget everything and run or use *Radical Intuition* to face everything and rise. So what's it gonna be?

– **Kim Moses**, executive producer, director, and cofounder of Optin Studios

INTRODUCTION

THE INTUITION
REVOLUTION

A revolution is underway. You may not have noticed it yet —
because this is a revolution that starts on the *inside*. To join
it, you don't need to gather arms; you don't need to learn bat-
tle strategies. You don't need to *do* anything — except reclaim a
power that you lost long ago.

Real change is possible when, at last, you become aware that
the world is not what you *think* it is. When you realize that the
world has only shown you a half-truth — only taught you how
to become half the person you are made to be — then you are
ready to know the real truth, which is this: *You have an untapped,
underutilized intuitive faculty within you that the world has tried to
convince you doesn't exist.*

You and I are living on the tail end of centuries of psychological conditioning, taught that intellect and reason are the only
viable ways to navigate reality. Today, we are on the threshold of
a new, intuitive way of understanding the world. The philosophy
of *Radical Intuition*, along with scientific and technological inno-
vations, is crucial to that understanding. By turning to our "inner
genius," and going beyond the limits of our thinking mind, we
have the opportunity to expand our consciousness and bring the
world together like never before.

What could this mean for the world? Devoting over two decades of my life to exploring the intersections of spirituality, creativity, and innovation, I have been following my own intuition to find out. As an artist — starting my career with a degree in oil painting — I never expected to find myself working with some of the top tech innovators in the world. I never expected to witness a word like *intuition* being coveted by big business or leading-edge science — unifying the once-divided factions of left-brainers and right-brainers. But that is exactly what is happening today.

Everywhere I turn, I discover the most brilliant people talking about intuition. This is the holy grail everyone is trying to figure out: *What exactly is intuition? How can we get better at harnessing its power?* Extraordinary men and women have been asking these questions for centuries. Great leaders like Einstein, Steve Jobs, Marie Curie, Jonas Salk, Tesla, Paramahansa Yogananda, Mooji, Picasso, and Oprah — all fervent intuition advocates — are testaments to the pervasive power of intuition, whether we are artists, teachers, scientists, CEOs, or anything in between. History has shown us, time and again, that true greatness is defined, not by how *smart* we are, but by how *intuitive* we are.

When I began to develop the ideas of *Radical Intuition*, I wanted to answer the big questions: *What role does intuition play in the expanded potential of humanity? How can we foster intuition to make our lives and the world better?* I wanted to know if intuition is something that, like the intellect, can truly be cultivated with training and practice. This is why I started up IntuitionLab — to incubate intuition itself. I wanted to hack it. I wanted to learn everything there is to know about it and how we are designed to use it in our lives. Most of all, I wanted to create a practical framework to help people understand and trust it. Like all work at the threshold, a lot of people didn't get it. A lot of people still don't get it. But once they do — once they experience its power for themselves — everything changes. Life is different — more meaningful and filled with a new sense of wonder.

The ideas and practices I offer in *Radical Intuition* are radical in the truest sense of the word. They challenge the fundamental nature of consciousness as we know it. They invite you to open your mind — to step into the mystery and discover a revolutionary, new reality. Most of all, this book shows you *how to do those things*. It shows you what that mysterious "something" really is and how to touch it yourself — so that you can free your mind, once and for all, and reclaim the power that awaits inside you.

GETTING STARTED WITH *RADICAL INTUITION*

Radical Intuition provides a supportive framework for your journey of intuitive discovery. As you prepare to become radically intuitive, know this: This is an *experiential* book. You will have the opportunity to experience your intuition for yourself — to immerse yourself in its life-changing wisdom and power.

To enter into this work, you don't need to subscribe to any particular knowledge system, as intuition is implicit in all religions, philosophies, and worldviews. This book is not a defense of intuition; though I talk about the scientific theory that supports intuition, my goal is not to prove that it exists. If you have experienced it, you already know it does. The only agenda for this work is to open space for you to develop a powerful, personal relationship with yourself and the inner truth that you hold.

Just as every individual life journey is unique, every intuitive journey is unique. There is no one prescribed route to discover higher awareness. You start where you are and move forward, step by step. Your own intuition will guide you to incorporate these teachings into your life in your own meaningful way.

The goal of *Radical Intuition* is, simply, to help you know and trust your intuition, so you can live the extraordinary life that you are made for. Reading this book will:

- Help you answer the fundamental questions: Who am I? What is my purpose?
- Provide you with simple practices to awaken and enhance your intuitive perception.
- Unlock the dimension within yourself where higher consciousness arises.
- Show you the way to your highest, happiest, authentic state of being.

HOW TO USE THIS BOOK

To get the most out of this book, I recommend that you read it sequentially, from start to finish. Each chapter offers insight and practices to develop your intuition in a step-by-step process. You may want to take breaks between chapters to do the work as you go, or you may want to read the whole book, then go back and work on the areas that resonate with you. Either way, just be sure to supplement your learning with real-life practice.

The secrets of intuition are only revealed through *experience*. You can't become intuitive by reading about intuition. You need to practice it, get to know it — make it a way of life. The more attention you give to your intuition — the more you honor it and follow it — the more alive it will become within you.

What's Inside

Radical Intuition provides the knowledge, practices, exercises, tools, and inspiration that will bring your intuition to life.

Intuitive development practices: Not only will you learn the fundamentals of intuition theory, every step of the way you will be guided with interactive work to help you put what you learn into action. In a variety of workshops, you will receive all-new intuition development techniques, along with insight-empowering meditations, mantras, intentions, and daily practices.

Intuition affinity evaluations and self-discovery practices: The key to knowing your own intuition is understanding how it works uniquely within you. Using a variety of self-discovery exercises, you will have the opportunity to explore your own intuition — how you have already been using it in your life and the potential next steps you can take to awaken it more powerfully. This includes an intuition affinity quiz, a self-assessment that shows you what "kind" of intuitive you are naturally.

Radical Intuition Tips: Throughout the book, "Radical Intuition Tips" provide special guidance that will assist your intuitive growth.

Radical Insights: "Radical Insights" highlight the key points of each chapter. When you see one of these, I invite you to pause for a moment and reflect on its wisdom.

Insight leaders – extraordinary insights from extraordinary people: To honor the many perspectives that make up this new understanding of intuition, I invited a group of extraordinary new-thought leaders — or rather, *insight leaders* — to share their experiences and understanding of intuition. Each person stands, in their own way, as a monument to the power of living the insightful life. Each of these world-renowned intuitionists — from artists to doctors, from Hollywood producers to video game designers, musicians, writers, and spiritual teachers — offers us a glimpse into how intuition made them who they are today.

Preparing for Intuition Work

As you get started, consider gathering or creating some of the things below to support your new intuition practice:

A journal for recording insights: Think of your journal as an intuition receptacle. All your practice, inspiration, and uncensored thoughts can flow here. An intuition journal is a valuable tool, as you often record insights that become powerful validations in retrospect.

Tools for developing your intuition: You can access a variety of *Radical Intuition* tools at www.kimchestney.com/toolbox, including downloadable Insight Cards and DIY Intuition Billet templates. You can also use my free interactive Insight Card deck at www.kimchestney.com/insight-cards.

A sacred workspace: When you work with your intuition, it's important to be in an uplifting place. A peaceful, bright room, in or close to nature, is ideal. Setting up a dedicated intuition and meditation space, where you feel good and comfortable, can enhance your practice. Feel free to incorporate ambient lighting, aromatherapy, artwork, pillows, blankets, bells, candles, beads, or anything that moves you.

WHAT'S AHEAD:
INTUITION AWAKENING AND ATTUNEMENT

No matter where you are on your inner journey, this book is designed to take you to your next step. If you are just beginning to explore your intuition, you can take your first steps now; if you are already highly intuitive, this book will show you new ways to fine-tune your gifts.

The work of this book is twofold:

1. It imparts the wisdom and understanding that is necessary to awaken your intuitive awareness.
2. It provides practices that empower the unfolding and expansion of that awareness.

When you awaken your intuition, you set in motion the greatest process of self-discovery. As you gain awareness of new truths and ways of experiencing the world, your perception of life naturally expands and evolves in tandem with your consciousness.

Intuition Workshops for Your Personal Growth

Four chapters are workshops designed to help you personally attune your intuition, so that you can receive insight with clarity and assurance. Each workshop focuses on one of the four specific types of intuition, and consists of three separate parts:

Part 1 – Intuition attunement: Each workshop begins with lifestyle tips and practices to open up a specific intuitive pathway. Following these practices will help you to energetically align with your flow of insight for greater intuitive clarity.

Part 2 – Intuition meditation: Each workshop includes a specific meditation to empower its type of intuition.

Part 3 – Intuition practice: Most importantly, each of these workshops includes practices that you can do on your own, as often as you like, to help you to better recognize and understand the way each type of intuition is alive within you.

Ultimately, *Radical Intuition* will help you create a lifestyle of "insightfulness," where you are guided in all things, at every moment, by your inner wisdom. By the end of the book, you will have everything you need to own the extraordinary power within you. To continue to deepen your practice of insightfulness, you can join the *Radical Intuition* community for live workshops, online courses, and retreats at www.intuition-lab.com.

THE *RADICAL INTUITION* MISSION

Truly, you are about to embark on a journey into one of the most powerful mysteries of existence — a journey that ends with a return to the *real you*. To get there doesn't always come easy. You have to want it. You have to persevere. It may take a day, a week, or a year — but when you are fueled by the passion of higher self-discovery, life has no limits.

You have the opportunity now to participate in the true mission of insightful work: *to live in this world, guided by the wisdom that is beyond it.* To live every day with the ease of illuminated awareness, aligned with your true path and purpose, is the greatest joy of life.

To be true to yourself — this is the most revolutionary act. To overthrow your conditioning, overthinking, and what everyone else tells you to do — to pledge allegiance to your own, true inner voice — this is a powerful rebellion. These are the choices that forge great lives, blaze new trails — and ultimately, unbound our spirits.

CHAPTER 1

THE WORLD'S
BEST-KEPT SECRET

This is our birthright — the wisdom with which we were
born, the vast unfolding display of primordial richness,
primordial openness, primordial wisdom itself.
— PEMA CHÖDRÖN

I may not know you yet, but I know one thing about you: You
are extraordinary. Deep within, you hold a spectacular, hidden
power — a power that holds the greatest wisdom and reveals the
deepest mysteries of existence: intuition. This power is the secret
to discovering every truth you seek; it is the key to a whole new
way of understanding the world. Intuitive ability is part of your
intrinsic design; it takes you to your truth — to the law above all
laws and to the real meaning of your life.

Do you know who you *really* are?

Do you know what you are *really* made for?

Your intuition does.

To answer these questions for yourself, all you need to do
is follow it. For most of your life, a part of you has been asleep.
Your body is awake; your mind is awake; hopefully, your heart is

awake. But what about your intuition? What about *the real you* behind the social roles, labels, and years of conditioning? You may have known it as a child, in the dawning of creative imagination, while your mind was still free. You may have felt it from time to time, throughout your life, in the sparks of joy, creativity, or new beginnings.

But somewhere along the way, "reality" set in. The rational, thinking mind took over and told us that the subtle, imaginative world of intuition wasn't real, or at least, it couldn't be trusted. With the mind fully in charge, the sensitivity of our once-vibrant intuitive nature began to pale in comparison to "concrete" thoughts. Repressed, denied, or relegated to the shadows, our intuition slowly atrophies. We forget how to use it, if we even remember that we have it at all. The thinking mind reinforces its position in our culture every day. It tells us:

"Intuition isn't real."
"Intuition is crazy."
"Intuition is dangerous."

We are not taught these things because they are true; we are taught these things out of fear. The revolutionary power of intuition is a threat to the limited, thinking mind. It is a threat to any established system of control in our lives. Our free-spirited, intuitive nature often stands in direct opposition to the societal orders and knowledge systems of established society. This is because intuition's job is to break through anything false — anything that separates us from our higher power — so it can free us with truth.

The biggest secret the world has kept from you is the power you hold within. Intuition is the gateway to that forgotten, transcendent dimension of your being. If you are brave enough to follow it, you will discover the extraordinary power that is waiting for you there. If you are ready to follow your intuition beyond the limits of your mental constructs, you will come alive. This is the real business of intuition — to bring you into the unimaginable potentiality of life itself. Here in the untamed wilderness of intuitive discovery is where you make the most extraordinary discovery — the discovery of the real you.

YOU ARE MADE FOR SOMETHING MORE

Have you ever noticed the nudge of a still, small voice inside you? It is a voice that whispers only to you and knows you better than you know yourself. It guides you; it protects you; it inspires you; and it leads you to the open doors that change your life.

It says: *Trust yourself.* It says: *Something more awaits.*

This inner guidance system has been silently running in the background of your life since the day you were born. Every once in a while, it slips into your conscious awareness, reminding you that something bigger is at play in life. These moments of intuitive insight connect you to the larger purpose of your life and the ineffable knowingness that waits behind your thoughts, quietly, for your attention.

The gut feelings and the times when you *just know* things, even without having all the facts — these are the first calling cards of your intuition. The more you invite your intuition in — the more you get to know it and honor it — the more you will witness the subtle nudges of intuition becoming clearer, stronger communication. What begins with a whisper ends, after time and practice, with an assured calling to recognize and choose the best in your life.

The existential angst so many of us feel today is due, in part, to our habitual and seemingly inescapable overreliance on our thinking mind. We have so much information to process, so much to figure out. We are bombarded, each day, with an endless stream of input from our electronic devices. The return to intuition is the way out of that din, an inner retreat from the chaos of the world. It calls us away from the frenetic distractions of obsessive thinking and back to the richness of life itself — the vitality of presence in the human experience.

We all crave intuition. The stress, the gnawing ache of an empty place inside of us, the feeling that something is wrong, but we don't know what — these are symptoms of dislocation from our intuitive, inner being. When we learn to recognize and follow our inner guidance, it reconnects us with the fullness of our intended existence. In this way, intuition is not only our line to higher awareness but the cure for our pains — our imbalanced bodies, worried minds, broken hearts, and defeated spirits.

RADICAL INSIGHT
Somewhere inside, we all crave intuitive connection.
A part of us knows that it is the missing piece of our life.

We often live our lives with a sense that we are incomplete. Though we may set this feeling aside or cover it up with activities, ambitions, and worldly pursuits, on a deeper level we know that we are more powerful, with more potential than we realize. When we turn to intuition, we step into that power and into the potential it holds. We rise above the fear, the disappointment, and the confusion of the human experience.

You are made for a different kind of life. You are made to be complete, to be joyful, to be inspired and fulfilled. You are made to use your extraordinary inner power to create the life of your dreams. This is what your intuition is calling you to do, right now.

How will you answer this call? How can you open lines of communication between two very different worlds? How do you touch this ineffable dimension of reality? No teacher, no guru, no quest or drug can take you there; you only get there by following your intuition. What is on the other side of that "call" is nothing less than life itself — the Ultimate, the Supreme, the Absolute, the all-knowing, omnipresent Being. We can call it God, Spirit, or our Source — whatever we name it, we are all part of it. We are intrinsically embedded within it, and it within us — united by intuition.

"NEW-SCHOOL" INTUITION

Forget everything the world has told you about intuition. Gone are the old days of crystal balls and fortune-telling; today, we live in a different kind of world. And we are beginning to see intuition in a radical, new way. To embrace this new vision, we can no longer think of intuition as anything less than a vital, natural part of our human design — a part that we have not fully understood because, until now, we had not reached the full understanding of life that mastering it requires.

We are at the dawn of a new era where the traditional view of a cause-and-effect universe has been surpassed by the once-inconceivable wonders of a new, multidimensional quantum reality. Today, "old-school" conceptions of occult intuition don't apply to the world we live in. We understand the world in a way that we never have before, and part of that new vision includes the acceptance of our untapped intuitive potential as human beings. All we need now is a new language to talk about it and to foster its growth in our lives.

Tapping into your intuition means tapping into a new dimension of awareness — a kind of *quantum thinking* where you can connect with information that exists beyond this moment in temporal space and time. With traditional thinking, we can process information from our immediate physical, emotional, and mental experiences only. We think, subjectively, from our little place and time in the universe.

With intuitive thinking, a higher part of our mind is aware of all information, no matter where or when we exist in the world. We intuit, omnipresently, from the part of us that is connected to all things. This process is a natural, everyday function of human consciousness — one that we use in work, play, art, science, and just about everything we do. It is a mark of greatness — of genius.

What intellect is to the physics of yesterday,
intuition is to the physics of tomorrow.

In this way, we are able to know things that we once thought were impossible to know. We can see a reality that the world once told us wasn't real. This revolutionary quantum model of thought cuts right through the boundaries of limited thought, giving us immediate awareness of information that is unreachable by the thinking mind. When we use our intuition, we don't have to work to figure everything out the hard way, when we can, instantaneously, intuitively touch into the truth we seek.

Your intuition is a direct line to the ever-present data of the cosmos — data that exists as if in "the cloud" of universal storage. We know that, beyond our personal experience, the universe is timeless, changeless. All the data of existence is out there, available to us, intuitively. There are no physical boundaries for the intuitive mind. All the information of life exists always, available from anywhere, and ready to download as insight to the intuition-attuned mind.

While your intellect thrives in the linear, three-dimensional world, your intuition thrives in the higher, nonlinear, and relativistic dimensions of reality. With each new scientific discovery, we are coming closer to the understanding of intuition as a transdimensional, physio-energetic connection that gives a new dimension to the power of the mind. We don't need to fear it. We don't need to repress it. Instead, only by embracing our intuitive capacity will we fully utilize the human potential within us.

Using intuition, then, is a kind of evolution. It connects us with something higher. It elevates us, takes us beyond. It expands our consciousness and invites us into the timeless expanse of existence — where everything that has ever happened, or ever will happen, has already happened. This is the leap that will define a new era of living in the world.

DO YOU HAVE THE INTUITIVE GIFT?

The more you witness the power of intuition, the more you realize how awe-inspiring it truly is. You might be wondering how "normal" human beings can actually participate in such an incredible process. You might be wondering how — or if — you, yourself, have the capacity to do such extraordinary things.

You might have said to yourself: *What if I don't have intuition? I don't seem to have any special gift.* How do you know if you have intuition? Are there signs? What if you aren't born with any "superpowers?" What if you are just a regular person? To find out if you have the intuitive gift, take this quick test:

Step 1: Check your pulse.
Step 2: Do you have one?

If you answer yes: *You have the gift of intuition!*

Sometimes, people talk about how they were *born with* an intuitive gift. This is certainly true — because everyone is born with it. Every person is born with a special intuitive gift. Most people just haven't realized it yet. When people say they were born with intuition, what they mean is that they were *born with a talent for intuition*. They are good at it. It comes naturally to them.

To be a talented intuitionist only means that your innate, natural intuitive pathways are open and flowing freely. It means that intuition is connected and alive. The good news is that, even if your intuition has temporarily disconnected, you can reengage it with attention and practice. Intuition, like all our talents, can be strengthened and developed. Brilliant artists aren't born knowing how to create masterpieces; they cultivate their talent with practice and devotion. It's the same for intuition; the more you learn its ways and practice using it, the stronger it becomes.

WHAT INTUITION IS...AND IS NOT

When you ask people what they think intuition is, you get an array of responses — from gut feelings to knowingness to creative inspiration — which points to the fact that most people have, conclusively, no idea what intuition really is.

This is due to the fact that we experience intuition in so many different ways. Yes, it is a gut feeling, but it is so much more than just our gut feelings. Yes, it delivers knowingness and creative inspiration, but those are just some of the many gifts it brings. To really understand intuition, we can look at it not as a thing to be labeled but as a multifaceted process with a singular purpose: the delivery of insight.

The different experiences that we call intuition are really just our ways of responding to it. We can have a gut feeling when our insight alerts us to the fact that something is wrong; we can have a knowingness when we are given a piece of intuitive information; and we can feel inspired and creative when our intuition moves us to do something new. Underneath all of that, intuition remains constant as the still small voice of insight that has the power to touch us in so many ways.

Intuition is an illuminating insight that arrives as a feeling, knowingness, idea, or experience that you simply receive.

Using your intuition is easy because you don't have to figure it out — it just comes to you. It effortlessly flows to you and through you — often seeming to arrive out of nowhere. Intuition is that gut feeling you can't explain, the epiphany that lights up your mind, the inspiration that pours through you in the creative act, the instant connection you feel with someone important to your life. Your inner wisdom shows up as these things and so much more.

In what seems like magic, your intuition gives you the ability to directly perceive truths that exist beyond the rational thinking process. But despite what many people think, intuition is not magic. It is a very real and learnable kind of evolved information sharing. To get a better idea of what intuition really is, let's talk about what intuition *is* and what it *isn't*.

What Intuition Is

As you take the following ideas to heart, you can start to see intuition as it really is. Instead of defining it by the things we don't know about it, we can experience it on its own terms, as the saving grace that it truly is to each and every one of us.

Intuition is an integral part of the human design: Part of our "inner technology," it is our built-in guide, or GPS system, that navigates from a higher perspective.

Intuition is the most advanced faculty of human cognition: As we move beyond the limits of the mind, we naturally expand our consciousness in a way that changes the way we *think* forever.

Intuition is meant to be cultivated: Though it may be dormant in many of us, the power of intuition is amplified by attention, devotion, and practice.

Intuition has a key role in our future: At the height of the information age, in a data-saturated world, harnessing "insight" is the next step of a new era in human potential.

Intuition is our connection to all that is beyond: Intuition is our link to the greatest mysteries of life. It offers us a pathway to discover our purpose and place in the universe. As Paramahansa Yogananda said: "Intuition is the soul's power of knowing God."

What Intuition Is Not

To get an even clearer picture of what intuition is, we can look at some of the things that it is not. Here are some popular myths and misconceptions about the nature of our inner wisdom.

Intuition is not just for women: Yes, women are often naturally intuitive, but men have it, too! In fact, some of the biggest champions for intuition have actually been men. In truth, intuition is beyond duality. It is not feminine or masculine, just as it is not emotional or rational. It is a completely different process, more powerful than both feeling and thinking because it comes from a place beyond both of those things. Intuition is, in all aspects, nondualistic as it guides both the hearts and minds of all people.

Intuition is not "following your heart": When people say, "Follow your heart," they usually really mean: Follow your intuition. Intuition is *emotive*, but it is not an *emotion*. The emotional heart can deceive, but intuition is truth itself. The heart often moves from a place of personal need or lack, but intuition only moves from the fullest place of good. Don't follow the heart that can lead you astray; instead, follow the true north of your intuition.

Intuition is not your conscience: *Guilt*, not intuition, is the faculty of your conscience. Intuition is not the generator of guilt, as it accepts our actions, even our failures, as growth experiences. Conscience, like intuition, is a guidance mechanism, but unlike intuition, conscience is conditioned by society and the world we live in — the incongruence between what we have been told to do and what we *actually* do. Conscience is a mental "judgment" based on perceived courses of action in relation to the world.

Intuition guides us, but not through guilt or judgment. Instead, it lovingly supports us, even when we make mistakes, with the recognition that both our suffering and missteps are opportunities for our personal evolution.

Intuition is not the same as instinct: There is, indeed, a fine line between intuition and instinct. The key difference between them can be found by examining their source. When we act instinctually, we are often responding to unconscious feelings, usually resulting from past experience. For example, if we instinctively close ourselves off from emotional experiences, this is likely a self-preservation reflex based on past injury. On the other hand, when we act on intuition, the source is not past personal, egoic experience; it is not a conditioned environmental response. Instinct may be about survival, but intuition is about transformation — growth, evolution, and liberation. Instead of a reflex, it is a calling — from the highest source itself.

Intuition is not scary: Quite possibly the biggest misconception about intuition is that it is something to be afraid of. Exactly the opposite! There is no safer place in the world than in the hands of your intuition. There is no better friend than your intuition; its every move is to take care of you and help you rise above your fears. Intuition and fear cannot coexist — the presence of one negates the other. The way through fear is to trust your intuition.

CHAPTER 2

LIVING INSIGHTFULLY

True intelligence is to rise above thinking
as the source of all intelligence.

— ECKHART TOLLE

To live intuitively means honoring our inner voice over the voice of the world. Once we realize that we can trust our self above all others, we live our lives differently. We make our choices differently; we aspire differently; we understand one another differently; we experience the world in a whole new way. When we follow our intuition, we participate in something that touches the depth of our being — something more profound than we know.

We become extraordinary by making intuition an ordinary part of life, by relying on it so much that it becomes second nature. With every step of the way guided by higher insight, we are more aligned with our own success, happiness, and personal growth. As more and more people around the world do this, we begin to normalize intuition. Any and all of us can use our intuition to improve all aspects of our lives.

Intuition should be a normal part of life because learning to use your intuition is no different than learning to use your intellect. Intelligence and intuition are two sides of the same coin; when they work together, they create an extraordinary mind. We go to school to get smarter, so why shouldn't we go to school to become more intuitive? Now that we are learning more about the way intuition works, we can embrace new opportunities to rebalance the two complementary aspects of our cognitive nature.

This revolutionary union of once-seeming opposites — bringing the thinking mind and the intuiting mind together — is a reflection of the fusion that will define life in the years ahead. With this togetherness, we become wiser and more insightful as a collective people.

With intuition in the mix, we move deeper into the experience of life and the connected awareness that unites us all. When we create a culture of intuition, we create a culture of unity, of inclusivity, of the interconnected human experience.

BEYOND MINDFULNESS INTO INSIGHTFULNESS

In recent years, the practices of mindfulness, presence, and meditation have become the cornerstones of our culture and personal development. The power of *being still* has become a crucial counterpoint to the busy world we live in today. In the stillness, we find our peace, but it is in the stillness, too, that we find our power.

To be mindful is to be aware. It is an awareness of life, an awakening from our unconscious habits, thoughts, and actions. Living consciously, we embody a new sense of presence in all we do — with an ability to fully embrace each moment. In the everpresent now, we escape the traps of the mind — habitual judgment, relentless thinking, fear. We move out of the constant flow of thought into the quiet space between those thoughts — the stillness. But the stillness is not empty; extraordinary things await there.

In the silence of your quieted mind, in the space between thoughts, the voice of intuition arrives. The stillness speaks. Only in the place of no-mind can you hear your intuition. The thinking mind is a bully; only when it settles down can your inner wisdom get through to gently touch you. Whether in meditation, in the shower, or during a walk in the woods, insight draws close when the critical mind is far away.

RADICAL INSIGHT
Insightfulness is the next step beyond mindfulness.
Insight is the gift of presence.

Here, in the mindful place of peace, you can receive your greatest power — the extraordinary insight of higher awareness. First, we become mindful; then, we become insightful. Presence is the gateway to insight; insight leads us to the truth. All wisdom and creativity emerge from the still, quiet gap between your thoughts.

This is why stillness, the silence of meditation, is not the final destination for those of us who are still at work in the world. We are not ready to retreat to the mountaintops; we still have work to do. We have a world to change. We have a life to live and a spirit to evolve. We can *be*, but we still have to *do*.

This is not an either-or situation. Like yin and yang, our fulfillment comes with the union of complementary forces — the balance of existence and experience, of awareness and actualization. The completeness of our human condition requires us to be both mindful and insightful, to *be* aware and to *become* more aware. Insight brings the gift of more awareness.

In the refuge of stillness, intuition is your guide. The practices of meditation and conscious living enable you to move into the calm center of your being. Then what? Out of the tranquility, your inner voice calls you to what's next: the next thought that will change the way you understand your life; the next idea that will improve it; the next action you can take to further elevate your consciousness. Real illumination comes from both contemplative stillness and inspired action — the two complementary paths to enlightenment.

LIFE WITH INTUITION VS. LIFE WITHOUT INTUITION

To live insightfully, how do we begin to incorporate intuition into daily life? Why should we try to integrate something as spectacular as intuition into our simple, everyday existence? Though we may not all aspire to be geniuses or mystics who change the world, we do all aspire to fulfillment. The one thing that each of us has in common is a call to happiness — to the joy of personal growth and the experience of self-actualization.

This is the job description of your intuition — to take you to those higher places. Insightful living starts with small beginnings that lead to great endings. Every step in the direction of your purpose and growth is a step led by your intuition; its sole mission is your emancipation from the limitations of life. Every insight it delivers is in service to your personal evolution into the elation of higher awareness.

Each step of the way, your intuition meets you where you are. If you want to discover yourself, your intuition will show you who you are; if you need to learn how to relate to others, your intuition will guide you to the right people; if you are ready for new opportunities, your intuition will align you with them. No intention is too big or too small for the work of your intuition.

You will, however, notice quite a difference in your life once you commit to following your inner guidance. Things flow more smoothly; success comes more easily; a sense of ease, well-being, and purpose radiates through your life. Below, take a look at some of the ways that intuition makes a difference in even the most everyday of life situations.

LIFE WITH INTUITION	LIFE WITHOUT INTUITION
In Relationships Two people are intuitively aligned and energetically support each other's growth and happiness.	**In Relationships** Two people choose to be together based on social norms or expectations that don't align with their authentic path.
In Business Apple becomes a global innovation leader by creating intuitive new products the world has never seen.	**In Business** Less-successful companies try to "stay relevant" by following the trends, instead of setting and creating them.
In Wellness A person listens to their body and eats a clean, healthy diet based on the nudges from their inner guidance system.	**In Wellness** A person gets stuck in the cycle of fad diets and wellness systems that don't work specifically for their body.
In Creativity Great artists like Cezanne, Picasso, and Warhol use their intuition to revolutionize world culture.	**In Creativity** Artists struggle to succeed — following the formulas of others instead of their own extraordinary vision.
In Parenting A mother empathetically supports/relates to her growing child and holds the boundaries she intuitively knows they need.	**In Parenting** A mother defers to the latest parenting trends instead of listening to what she and her child really need.

LIFE WITH INTUITION	**LIFE WITHOUT INTUITION**
In Spirituality	**In Spirituality**
The saints, gurus, and masters attain the highest levels of consciousness by intuitively connecting with life.	A person escapes into meditation regularly but still is unable to find their way to an authentic, enlightened life.
In Leadership	**In Leadership**
Great leaders teach, serve, and guide others extraordinarily by using empathy and insight to both lift others up and lead the way.	Not-so-great leaders are out of touch with those they lead and lack the ability to truly inspire change and growth.
In Problem-Solving	**In Problem-Solving**
Visionary scientists, like Einstein, find solutions to some of history's most important problems in a sudden flash of insight.	People get so bogged down by following the formula that they miss the moments of genius that come along.
In Counseling	**In Counseling**
A coach helps their client to make big breakthroughs by looking at the intuitive meaning behind each challenge.	A coach misses a healing opportunity by observing the outside facts without connecting them to the inner purpose.

These are just a few of the many examples of "outer" results that come from following our inner guidance. Time and again, we can see how intuition empowers us to be better — better friends, parents, teachers, leaders, and creators. This is the real gift of intuition — it helps you to *be better*. It leads you to your best life and, ultimately, the happiness it brings. There is no better salve than intuition for soothing the angst of life. Being happy is a side effect of living intuitively.

Why is intuition so powerfully connected to happiness? Because when you become intuitively aligned with life, you live authentically — in harmony with your true path and purpose. You naturally attract and manifest higher-frequency people and experiences in your life, so you can become wholly you — the best version of you.

WHEN YOU USE YOUR INTUITION, YOU ARE:	WHEN YOU DON'T USE YOUR INTUITION, YOU ARE:
Authentic	Confused
Confident	Fearful
Reassured	Anxious
Calm	Stressed
Growing personally	Stagnant
Certain of your purpose	Indecisive and lost

One of the greatest gifts that a life of intuition brings is the ability to *feel and know* that you are 100 percent supported by life. With intuition, you are no longer living in an uncertain world of fear, at the mercy of who-knows-what; instead, you find yourself in a world of wonder where *every little thing is meaningful* — including you. Every joy and every challenge has a purpose — and that purpose is your perfection.

RADICAL INSIGHT
*Insightfulness marks the difference between a good life
and an extraordinary life.*

A life of insightfulness gives you the calm and confidence to handle anything the world brings. The intuitive state of mind brings many extraordinary gifts: insight, ingenuity, creativity, genius, empathy, foresight, wisdom, truth, joy, bliss, love. This is what's next for each of us — this is how we become extraordinary. With each insight, each intuition followed, you embody, more fully, the perfection of life.

INTUITIVE SELF-DISCOVERY

Now that we have seen some of the ways that intuition is at work in life, let's take a look at how intuition is at work in *your* life. You have been using it all along, whether you realize it or not. The secret to becoming great with your intuition is becoming aware of it. Once you are aware of it, you can master it.

Most of us spend our whole life using our intuition...*intuitively*. We experience it here and there, but we have no conscious control over its power. To be able to confidently use your intuition, you have to be sure you can identify it and differentiate it from other nonintuitive thoughts, feelings, and experiences. Let's begin by taking a look at your own intuition and how it has been working with you all along.

What Does an Intuitive Impression Feel Like?

Close your eyes and clear your mind. Take a deep breath to release any thoughts and relax into a quiet peace. As you move into the space between your thoughts, notice the first thing that comes into your mind, seemingly out of nowhere.

RADICAL INTUITION TIP: Don't worry if nothing comes at first or if you initially feel bombarded by self-generated thoughts. If, for some reason, you experience something unnerving or scary, just let it pass. That's not your intuition; it's just your mind playing tricks to regain its position of power. As in meditation, the mind doesn't like to give up control. Just relax and reenter your still, quiet place until something, simply and peacefully, drops into your head.

What is the very first calm, quiet impression that comes to you? This is what an intuitive "first impression" feels like. It could be an idea, an image, a word or phrase, a color, a feeling in your body, a solution to a problem — or any kind of information that just arrives, out of the blue, into your consciousness.

RADICAL INSIGHT
One of the defining qualities of an intuitive insight is that it arrives out of the blue, as if from nowhere.

This is the first key to recognizing your intuition: It is a sense, idea, or feeling that comes to you out of nowhere. It is not a result of any thinking process or of reasoning. If you have no idea where a feeling or thought came from, it likely came from your intuition. Most of the time, when things come and go in our heads, we don't think about their source. We either accept them or we don't, and go about our way.

Knowing this, you can become more aware of this process of "insight" within you. As you give more attention to the seemingly random impressions that come into your mind — treating them as potentially more than meaningless passing thoughts — your intuitive awareness grows. Then, with that growing awareness, you can begin the process of differentiating intuitive impressions from other things, like regular thoughts or imagination.

This is how you use your intuition *consciously*, with awareness and intention. You can start doing it in this moment, and throughout each day, so you become familiar with the ways that it comes to you. Once you know your intuition, you are free to go deeper into it — feeling its resonance and discerning its meaning.

Moment by moment, day by day, your attention to the insight that unfolds within you lays the building blocks of your own, very special intuitive language.

How Does Your Intuition Speak to You?

Everyone's intuition speaks to them differently. Your unique life path and history have wired you for your own special brand of intuition — the specific way your inner guidance shares information with you. The best way to start working with your intuitive language is to look at the way your intuition has been at work in your life already.

To explore how your intuition has been speaking to you, use the discovery exercise below. To complete it, simply write down any examples of times when you experienced any of these intuitive situations:

 1. You felt or sensed something that you could not explain rationally: Have you had any experiences where you had an intuitive physical reaction to information or circumstances beyond your immediate comprehension? Intuition often communicates with us through our bodies, gut feelings, and senses. Maybe, once, you got a chill up your spine when something was wrong before you consciously knew it. Or maybe you have disruptive physical experiences — like headaches, nausea, or discomfort — when you are around certain people or places that don't feel right to you.

 2. You *just knew* something it was "impossible" for you to know: Have you ever experienced an inexplicable "knowingness" in your life? One of the most undeniable examples of intuition is the ability to *know* something you should have no way of knowing. Maybe there was a time when you had an unexplainable inner certainty that you just couldn't shake, or a time when you knew to call a friend in need without knowing why. Maybe you knew your way around a place that you had never been before.

 3. You felt a passionate calling: Have you ever had a feeling that you were "just meant" to do something? Maybe you felt called to a vocation, or to travel to a particular place, or to help other people in your own way. You may not be able to explain why you feel drawn to things or situations in your life, but somehow a part of you is magnetically pulled in certain directions. These callings are among the many ways your intuition tugs at you and guides you to your destiny. Bright ideas, inspiration, and abiding longings are the handiwork of intuition; they are what life uses to move us in the direction of our growth opportunities.

 4. You had a "mystical" experience that is not scientifically explainable yet: Have you had any metaphysical experiences? If so, did they correlate with any meaningful times of growth in your life? Have you ever known, felt, seen, heard, or touched something that seemed to come from beyond reality as we know it? Maybe you had a vision or an extraordinary daydream; maybe you touched higher consciousness in your meditation. An increased awareness of transcendent reality is part of your evolutionary journey.

There are so many ways that our intuition can manifest in our lives. Hopefully, now, you are aware of at least a few of the ways that insight is already coming to you. Likely, you experience more of one intuitive pathway than another; for example, you might regularly experience knowingness, but rarely have gut feelings, or vice versa. This simply shows you which intuitive pathways you already have a natural affinity for.

Regardless of how many experiences you listed in this exercise, doing the work in this book will bring more to you. Each of the four situations described above points to a different way that your intuition has already spoken to you — through sensation, thought, feeling, or spiritual experience. It is through these four pathways that you will witness your own unique intuitive language unfold.

However, the most important part of intuitive work is not just recognizing intuition when it comes, but also knowing what it means. What is your intuition trying to tell you? When you think about all your past intuitive experiences, ask yourself: *How did they affect my life? How did they help me grow? Did I listen to my intuition or deny it?* Asking questions like these is the start of a new, conscious relationship with yourself and the wisdom you hold within.

CHAPTER 3

THE FOUR INTUITIONS

Truth is only one,
though the wise ones call it by many names.
— RIG VEDA 1.164.46, HINDU MANTRA

D espite the many ways of knowing intuition, it is your connection to the one, singular truth that permeates all of existence. Is intuition a gut feeling? Is it a knowingness? Is it a creative idea? Is it a revelation from God? The answer to all these things is: *Yes.*

We gain a deeper understanding of this multifaceted nature of intuitive expression when we understand it on four basic terms — based on the four dimensions of human being. By looking at the way we receive intuitive wisdom through our body, our mind, our heart, and even our spirit, we can see how a singular, overarching process is at work in so many ways within us.

The Four Intuitions manifest within us through our physical senses, our mental thoughts, our emotional feelings, and our spiritual experiences. Just as the different colors of the rainbow are expressions of the singular brilliance of white light, each of the Four Intuitions expresses the singular truth in its own special way. Some intuitive moments touch us — some enlighten us, or move us, or uplift us. All have the same end, which is to impart the wisdom we require to elevate our experience of life.

By embracing the many ways that your intuition manifests, you are taking the first step to discovering your own, unique intuition affinities — and putting them to work in your life. As we go deeper into this process, you will answer important questions like:

- What kind of intuition comes naturally to me?
- How do I know when my intuition is speaking to me?
- What is the difference between intuition and my regular thoughts or imagination?
- And most importantly, how can I know, for certain, that I understand my intuition correctly?

The first step in answering these questions is to discover how each intuitive pathway touches you. Are you a natural Healer? A Sage? A Visionary or a Mystic? Each type of intuition carries with it the energy of its archetype. When we attune to that energy, we, in turn, embody that archetype in our own beautiful and sacred way, and make our mark on the world.

Like snowflakes, no two intuitive sensibilities are alike — because no two people are alike. Each of us uses the Four Intuitions in our own way — a special blend of insight, attuned by our own experiences and purpose in this life. As your intuition strengthens and becomes part of your living nature, you will realize the power that comes with so many ways of knowing truth.

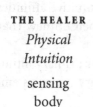

THE HEALER	THE SAGE
Physical	*Mindful*
Intuition	*Intuition*
sensing	thinking
body	mind

THE FOUR INTUITIONS

THE VISIONARY	THE MYSTIC
Creative	*Transcendental*
Intuition	*Intuition*
expressing	being
heart	spirit

THE PATHWAYS OF INSIGHT: BODY, MIND, HEART, AND SPIRIT

As we awaken to the power of insight, we no longer ask ourselves, "Do I have intuition?" but instead, "How do I strengthen my intuition?" The role of intuition is to relay information to us from *the inside*, instead of from the outside, as our thinking normally functions. To understand how it does that, consider how we are designed to process information.

Your mind is fueled by a collective set of input systems designed to process information from the outside world. You sense things; you know things; you feel things; you experience things. With intuition, it's no different. Your intuition uses those same pathways — your body, your mind, your heart, your spirit — to deliver *intuitive* input within you. The only difference is that, instead of coming from the outside world, it comes from the inside world.

Your own natural physical, mental, emotional, and spiritual

sensitivities determine which intuitive pathways flow most openly in your life. Becoming aware of your intuitive affinities enables you to better process insight and to open up new channels for intuitive expression within you.

All human beings are built with four primary intuitive pathways that correspond to the four primary input systems or cognitive functions:

Sensing

(Intuitive Pathway 1: Physical Intuition)

Thinking

(Intuitive Pathway 2: Mindful Intuition)

Feeling

(Intuitive Pathway 3: Creative Intuition)

Being

(Intuitive Pathway 4: Transcendental Intuition)

Each day, you sense, think, and feel your way through reality. Your intuition uses this same system to bring you information from *beyond* everyday reality. It flows through your physical body, your conscious mind, and your passionate heart to lead you to the truth of existence. Your intuition will connect to you through any open input pathway available. The more these pathways are open and unblocked, the stronger your intuition will flow.

From ancient times through the modern era, this four-element approach to human cognition has been a highly effective way to understand the nature of consciousness. More than 2,600 years ago, the teachings of the Buddha incorporated this four-pronged framework in the Four Foundations of Mindfulness:

Mindfulness of body
Mindfulness of mind
Mindfulness of feelings
Mindfulness of truth

In the early twentieth century, Carl Jung was one of the first to champion a mainstream role for intuition in Western culture, giving it a foundational role in his model of the four cognitive functions:

Sensation
Thought
Emotion
Intuition

Jung understood these four functions as the basic methods of perception in human consciousness, and he recognized intuition's role in *extrasensory* perception, acknowledging that intuition, by its very nature, has access to "extra" or "extraordinary" information, outside the purview of regular sensing, knowing, and feeling.

Your faculties of cognition are not only vehicles for processing worldly impressions, they are vehicles for processing "otherworldly" impressions. *Your intuition is your personal translator — turning universal wisdom into personal insight.* Using the four intuitive conduits, your intuition distills transcendent, beyond-mind data into a comprehensible language that your conscious mind can understand.

We can call the four intuitive pathways our cognitive functions, our foundations of being, or our intuitive language, but regardless of the words we use, the same process is at work. Intuition flows from universal consciousness through our intuitive pathways and into our own individual consciousness. The beauty of intuition is that, though it comes to each of us from the same transcendent place, the way it touches us is infinitely diverse.

DISCOVER YOUR INTUITIVE TYPE

Are you wondering what kind of intuition you are most naturally aligned with? Are you an intuitive senser, thinker, feeler, or experiencer? Take the quiz below to find out. This simple self-assessment will help you understand which intuitive pathways are most naturally open within you. When you're done, the results will reveal your Intuition Affinity Profile. This provides a baseline understanding of your natural intuition affinities. Throughout the coming chapters, we will go deep into each type of intuition and how you can open up each pathway for a more powerful experience of your inner truth.

Rate how well you can relate to each statement below on a scale from 0 to 3, with 0 being "disagree" and 3 being "strongly agree." If you prefer, you can download a printable quiz from my website: www.kimchestney.com/toolbox.

RADICAL INTUITION TIP: As you go through the quiz, record the *first answer* that pops into your mind; don't overthink your responses.

Rating Scale

0: Disagree – This never happens or doesn't apply to me.

1: Slightly agree – This happens once in a while or occasionally applies to me.

2: Agree – This happens regularly or often applies to me.

3: Strongly agree – This happens all the time or always applies to me.

THE INTUITION AFFINITY QUIZ	Rating (0-3)	
I often know what someone is going to say before they say it.	_____	
I am creative.	_____	
I receive profound life insights during meditation.	_____	
I "go with my gut."	_____	
When I make decisions, I listen to my truth over the dictates of society.	_____	
I easily notice new trends and often set them.	_____	
I have had unexplained metaphysical experiences.	_____	
Nature is my happy place.	_____	
It is difficult for me to live with lies, as I easily sense dishonesty.	_____	
I feel connected to life and all the world as one.	_____	
I love animals.	_____	
I have a knack for betting on the winning team.	_____	

THE INTUITION AFFINITY QUIZ (cont.)	Rating (0-3)
I like to do things that no one else has done before.	_____
I accept all that life brings to me.	_____
I have a great sense of direction.	_____
I am passionate.	_____
I am a natural healer.	_____
I have "just known" something was going to happen before it did.	_____
I am a risk-taker.	_____
I feel rejuvenated when I meditate.	_____
I am a natural at playing cards and often win.	_____
I want to help change the world for the better.	_____
I am physically sensitive to my environment.	_____
My first impressions of people are usually spot-on.	_____
I readily embrace change, growth, and new ideas.	_____

THE INTUITION AFFINITY QUIZ (cont.)	Rating (0-3)	
I have experienced the bliss of being one with God or the universe.	_____	
When I am shopping, I often go back to the first item that I found.	_____	
I often feel inspired.	_____	
I have meaningful dreams or epiphanies when I wake up from sleep.	_____	
I regularly wake up just before my alarm clock goes off.	_____	
I am a nonconformist.	_____	
I enjoy being alone.	_____	
I have felt a calling to do more with my life.	_____	
I can make instinctive decisions before getting all the facts.	_____	
I love easily.	_____	
My comfort zone is being outside my comfort zone.	_____	
Great ideas and solutions often just "come to me" in the shower.	_____	
My physical health is a priority in my life.	_____	

THE INTUITION AFFINITY QUIZ (cont.)	Rating (0-3)
My life is peaceful.	_____
It is easy for me to see future outcomes of other people's life situations.	_____
I can sit still.	_____
I am very observant of my surroundings.	_____
I am a terrible liar.	_____
People's moods easily rub off on me.	_____
I love working in the garden.	_____
I have known my way around places I have never been.	_____
My life seems to unfold effortlessly before me.	_____
Smells take me back to other times and places in my life.	_____
I feel like the world sees me for who I really am.	_____
I easily manifest my dreams into reality.	_____
I work with or study the healing arts.	_____

THE INTUITION AFFINITY QUIZ (cont.)	Rating (0–3)	
I believe in love at first sight.	_____	
I give away old clothes because they "don't feel right" anymore.	_____	
When I am suspicious, there is usually a good reason, even if I don't know it at the time.	_____	
I see myself in others, and I see others in myself.	_____	
I feel better after physical exercise.	_____	
I am fulfilled when I am doing good for others.	_____	
I have good business instincts.	_____	
My stress manifests quickly as physical ailments.	_____	
I enjoy activities like yoga, Qigong, Tai Chi, dance, or hiking.	_____	

Tallying your responses will reveal your Intuition Affinity Profile and give you a baseline idea of how you, personally, are using the four intuitive pathways. The graphic icon after each statement represents one of the four intuitive types. Add up the numbers for each icon to get a total, then place them in the correlating box on the next page. Each icon set has fifteen statements. None of the totals should exceed forty-five points. Do this with all four icons.

Total points

The Healer
Intuition of the Body

_____

The Sage
Intuition of the Mind

_____

The Visionary
Intuition of the Heart

_____

The Mystic
Intuition of the Spirit

_____

Understanding Your Quiz Results

First, know that there are no good or bad results in this quiz. This is a subjective self-assessment that allows you to become aware of your intuitive affinities, not by judging your number totals but by looking at the relationship between those totals.

Take a closer look. Does one pathway have significantly more points than the others? Or are they fairly equally dispersed? Some people have one or two really strong pathways and barely use the others at all; other people use a little bit of everything. Whatever your natural affinities, the exercises ahead will help you build on them. Where there is any lack of affinity — a low number or a pathway that isn't flowing — you will learn ways to unblock and open to all new experiences of your intuition.

Your affinities will also help you gain a deeper understanding of your calling and purpose in life as they relate to the four intuitive archetypes: the Healer, Sage, Visionary, and Mystic. Are you a natural Healer? If so, you may have an inner knowing or calling to help others (and yourself) to heal. If you are a natural Sage, you may have a knack for guiding people or situations through challenges. If you are a natural Visionary, you no doubt have a creative spirit and a drive to make the world a better place. If you scored high as a Mystic, you understand what a "higher calling" means and may have had personal experiences or awakenings into higher consciousness that have changed the way you view the world.

Upcoming chapters explain each type of intuition — and how each touches you through your body, your mind, your heart, and your inner spirit. Along with techniques and daily practices you can use to move deeper into the presence of intuitive being, you will learn how each intuitive pathway works — and also how to unblock and open up its flow. Regardless of your natural intuition affinities, or how insightfully you are already living, together we can follow our truth to the next level.

EXTRAORDINARY PEOPLE, EXTRAORDINARY INSIGHT

Intuitively Healing Body, Mind, Heart, and Spirit

Intuition is everything – forever guiding us and connecting us to the higher intelligence from which we come. We have the power to be healthy when we look at the whole spectrum of wellness: physical, mental, emotional, and spiritual.

Everyone is on some sort of healing journey; our illnesses, our pains, our circumstances – all of it is feedback. They are in conversation with our body, trying to wake us up. In the quiet, we can hear what life is saying to us through our intuition. It whispers to us when something is out of balance – when it's time to make a course correction, change our lifestyle, or face a trauma that we haven't dealt with.

The people who listen to their inner voice are the people who really take control of their life. They don't give their power away. Intuition, in this way, is a huge factor in healing. We have to turn within and trust that there is a much wiser intelligence guiding us and confirming that we are on the right course. You can't make a mistake if you live in trust and follow your intuition.

– Kelly Noonan Gores,
writer/director of the documentary *HEAL*

THE INTUITIVE ARCHETYPES: THE HEALER, THE SAGE, THE VISIONARY, AND THE MYSTIC

Which archetype of intuition do you most strongly identify with? While we embody each of them in one way or another, we often have a natural affinity, or talent, for one or two of them. Ultimately, when you have fully attuned to your intuition, all four pathways will flow freely and powerfully with intuitive insight. Here is a glimpse of each archetype and the type of intuitive energy it brings into the world.

The Healer
Intuitive Pathway 1: Physical Intuition

The grounding energy of Physical Intuition is your foundational intuitive pathway. It brings together heaven and earth, as the connection point of physical and metaphysical manifestation. In this way, insight flows through the sensory pathways of your body, where ephemeral, intuitive information is translated into real-world experience. Physical Intuition is the most tangible expression of intuition because you experience it directly through your body. It feels *real*.

Examples of Physical Intuition include:

- gut feelings
- healing ability
- metaphysical sensations or perceptions
- empathic sensing

The Physical Intuition archetype is the Healer because of an ability to vitalize the body-spirit connection, both within the person and the world. Healer archetypes have a natural connection to the earth and its energy; they are the bridge between worlds. They thrive in nature and are drawn to practices that improve physical well-being. Healers have a deep empathy for all living beings, which often brings a natural ability or calling to heal and serve others, including animals.

 The Sage

Intuitive Pathway 2: Mindful Intuition

The wisdom of Mindful Intuition flows through your mental intuitive pathway. It speaks to your mind and gives you the gifts of higher awareness. In this way, intuition serves your day-to-day guidance, decision-making processes, and life choices. Mindful Intuition is your "inner guidance system" showing you the way and leading you to truth.

Examples of Mindful Intuition include:

- unexplainable knowingness
- a flash of insight
- foresight
- an immediate apprehension

The Mindful Intuition archetype is the Sage because of a natural ability to guide oneself and others from the place of higher wisdom. If you are aligned with the Sage archetype, you may often experience a sense of *inner knowing* that surprises you; you have an uncanny ability to *just know* things, instead of having to weigh all the information. You may often receive solutions to life challenges in a sudden flash of insight or an epiphany. Sages are also a keen judge of character and can instantly discern people's intentions, motives, and authenticity.

The Visionary

Intuitive Pathway 3: Creative Intuition

Creative Intuition is your transformational intuitive pathway. It moves you to become more than you are and to change life for the better. In this way, new insight passionately calls you to grow, improve, and evolve. Creative Intuition is the ever-flowing channel of ingenuity and creativity that keeps our lives moving forward.

Examples of Creative Intuition include:

- your life calling
- inspiration and creativity
- innovation
- new or revolutionary ideas

The Creative Intuition archetype is the Visionary because of an ability to both envision and manifest the best version of life ahead. If you are a Visionary archetype, you are in the business of changing the world — or at least yourself. Leadership, ingenuity, creative thinking, self-expression: All of these are your purview. With Creative Intuition, you move from thinking to *doing*. This is intuition in action — applied intuition. Visionaries bring the creative power of the universe into reality — as the great Creator creates through us.

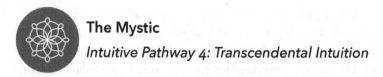

The Mystic

Intuitive Pathway 4: Transcendental Intuition

Transcendental Intuition is your intuitive pathway to the beyond. With it, you rise above. It is your connection to the highest realities and truth of the universe. In this way, you can touch the highest levels of human consciousness. Transcendental Intuition opens you to life's deepest mysteries with the opportunity to experience supreme wisdom, bliss, and love.

Examples of Transcendental Intuition include:

- higher awareness
- unshakable inner peace
- mystical experience
- the rapture of "heavenly" bliss and love

The Transcendental Intuition archetype is the Mystic because of an ability to live in the elevated state of supreme consciousness. If you are a Mystic archetype, you have a natural ability to go beyond the perceived limits of conscious reality. Even though you live in the everyday world, you operate on a higher frequency — one that genuinely, magnetically attracts people to you. You are often more at home in the silences than in the everyday workings of human life. The deep wisdom and self-realization of the Mystic gives them the opportunity to bring great illumination into the world.

Which of these archetypes resonates with you most deeply? One of them? All of them? Whatever the case, understand that you are right where you need to be. Different pathways will dominate at different times in your life, depending on what you are going through at the moment. Whatever the case, know this:

Ultimately, you are the Healer, the Sage, the Visionary, and the Mystic — all in one.

When you open your intuitive pathways and embody these powerful archetypes, you have a new opportunity to transform your being into the life that, deep inside, you know you are made for. Holistically empowering your intuition expands your consciousness and so enables you to participate in the expansion of the universe as a whole. It is through these dynamic intuitive pathways that you are united with — and become one with — the cosmic dance of life.

CHAPTER 4

QUANTUM CONSCIOUSNESS

Metareality is everywhere, always, and everything.

— DEEPAK CHOPRA

There is more to life than we can imagine. Every day, we move through our three-dimensional world, through this moment in time and space, as if it were all that there is. Like a backdrop to the great theater of life, we accept the illusion that this set and its props are the world itself. In reality, the sensory world is only the beginning; it is the first thing we touch as we enter into the abiding world that exists beyond.

Look around you. Notice the many things you see — the objects, the shadows, the space in between. That empty space before you — that surrounds you and touches you — is not empty at all. It is full of things that your current level of consciousness cannot perceive. It is rich with information and energy — data that you can know with an expanded, intuitive mind. The more you intuitively evolve, the more you will be able to intuitively become aware of the "higher" subtle information that is all around you.

This process is part of the shift outward from our small, personal consciousness toward the unity of omnipresent, universal consciousness. We live each day with a sense of "personhood," as egoic individuals in a consummate state of otherness — divided from one another and the world by our self-identity. In this state, we only see things as we are; we experience the world as it relates to us, in this place and in this fleeting moment.

But as we awaken and become more aware of our connection to life and its dimensions beyond us, our sense of personhood gradually diminishes. We begin to identify with something bigger than our self. We are emptied of our small-minded, self-centered identity and filled with the universal presence that unites us all. The more you fill yourself with omnipresence, the more aware you become of your intuition. This is because intuition embodies the pure awareness of omnipresence itself; if omnipresence were God, intuition would be the Holy Spirit that, sacredly, touches us all.

That's how high your intuition can take you, if you allow it. Wherever you are in this moment, your intuition will take you higher. Higher awareness is the awareness of *beyond*. It is the call to move into that beyond and become part of it. This potentiality calls each of us to experience more of reality — more truth, connectedness, and wisdom — than we are presently capable of.

THE LEVELS OF INTUITIVE CONSCIOUSNESS

Even though we understand that our intuition is directly related to the expansion of our consciousness, the question still remains: What, really, is on *the other side* of our intuition? We are getting a message from *somewhere* — somewhere personal. Somewhere that knows us, deeply, at the core. Where does that insight, tailor-made for each of us, really come from? To answer these questions, let's examine the fundamental nature of consciousness itself.

When we are working with intuition, it is helpful to understand human consciousness in terms of three main categories:

Unconscious
Conscious
Superconscious

In unconsciousness, we do things without really being aware of our actions; we are not *literally* unconscious — we are awake, but in a kind of daydream, unaware of what we are really doing in the world. In consciousness, we wake up. We awaken to the world more as it is, instead of as we are — and we begin to live deliberately, with presence and awareness. Finally, in superconsciousness, or supreme consciousness, we are not only awakened to the world, we are awakened to what is beyond it. We touch the pure awareness that makes us truly come alive.

Most of us live our lives as an interplay between conscious and unconscious states of awareness. Not only are we unconscious in our sleep, we are unconscious when we act and live our lives without awareness of the forces at work within us or of the consequences of our actions. We are unconscious when we don't think about how something we do hurts another person; we are unconscious when we instinctively react to situations based on past experience instead of the present moment. We become fully conscious only when we become mindfully aware of the present, connected reality beyond our changeable subjective reality.

This is an astounding place to be. Moments of true consciousness can be few and far between in this day and age. But when they come, they often change us forever. They are the makers of great awakenings. Once we get a conscious glimpse of the world, looking beyond our small view of it, we realize how much more to life there is! There is more love, more potential, more magic than our tiny minds can conceive of.

RADICAL INSIGHT
With your intuition, you can perceive the imperceptible,
know the unknowable, and experience the impossible.

Beyond our conscious awareness exists an unfathomable universe of transcendent wisdom, connectivity, and information. Here, in this superconsciousness, resides all that is beyond the mind — the deepest secrets of existence. The higher you rise into it, the more you become a part of it, and it a part of you.

The "you" that you know every day is just a small part in the totality of your being. There is a greater part of you that cannot be defined, or labeled, by the world. In truth, you are undefinable. This small "self" is a point of singular consciousness, part of a limitless dimension of higher being — your "higher self." It is this higher part of yourself that has the ability, right now, to touch the levels of consciousness that elude your awareness.

Like an elevator rising to the top floor, you ascend to this place one floor at a time, by raising your awareness — going higher and higher as you awaken. You start living more from your "higher self" than from your small, "personal self." As you intuitively align with this superior energy, you naturally elevate to greater levels of consciousness. The heavy — unconscious or subconscious — zones are on the ground floors, close to our ego and small self-interests. The lighter, expansive zones are on the top floors — above and beyond — with our highest self and the truth of existence. You can't *think your way* into higher awareness. You only reach it by elevating your consciousness to a level where you can *receive it*.

The Zones of Intuitive Perception

Let's take a look at the three basic zones of intuitive awareness. Though there is much complexity to the process of awakening our minds, these zones provide a general framework to realize the unfolding of consciousness. When we understand how this process relates to intuitive ability, we can use our intention to open ourselves to the ultimate clarity of higher being.

Zone 1: Unconsciousness

In unconsciousness, we are asleep. We are unaware of the world beyond our personal interest. This is the home of our individual, ego-based self, as we work through our needs, fears, and self-identity. We see the world only through our own eyes. Chronic subjectivity creates a veil of ignorance between us and the world. We lack empathy, true compassion, and many of the other virtues that awakened consciousness brings. The unconscious world revolves around material gratification and our personal experience of the world — and we remain largely unaware of the consequences of both.

In this zone, intuition has little to no function in our life. We can barely make out its faint whispers, and even if we do, we are likely to ignore them. We are more focused on the world in front of us than the world inside of us. The only way we make it out of this zone is through a "wake-up call" or the kind of suffering that forces us to look more closely at who we are. Life is often an interplay of rising up and falling back into various levels of unconsciousness — some more toxic than others. But when we follow our inner guide, eventually it will take us so high that we will never again be in danger of falling back to sleep.

Zone 2: Consciousness

As we become conscious, we "wake up." We awaken. At last, we see that life is so much more than we realized. We become mindful of our thoughts and actions in a whole new way. We have the clarity of vision to see beyond ourselves. Though we are still individuals, we have moved into a state of deeper connectedness with the world. We no longer have an "us-and-them" mentality, so we see ourselves in other beings.

Here we live in between the promptings of lower-level ego-consciousness and higher-level supreme consciousness. Both call to us — one calling us to keep waking up, the other calling us back to sleep. The more conscious we become, the more we are intuitively drawn into the illumination that dispels all darkness and mental slumber. We are called to improve ourselves and serve others.

In this zone, intuition touches us in moments of stillness, during meditation, or in random, unpredictable moments of insight. We recognize the honorable place of intuition in life, but we have not yet fully understood how to make it our own. Roused by our awakening, we are aware, possibly for the first time, of our higher calling and the intuitive knowing that so much more waits ahead. By practicing mindfulness and cultivating insightfulness, we are able to make the changes in our lives that enable us to release the past and rise up into the highest part of our self.

Zone 3: Superconsciousness

In superconsciousness, we go beyond. We are more than awake, we are transcendent; we are more than conscious, we are superconscious. Here, we live — even if only in brief moments — from our supreme self. We are able to know and experience the truth of our own existence, as well as that of the world. Understanding that life is a myriad of expressions of the one singular unity, we discover a true sense of belonging. In our deepest states of presence, we can now touch the majesty of omnipresence.

In this zone, we live in a state of intuitive union with life. All pathways of intuition are open and flowing freely. Insight by insight, our consciousness continues to expand and attune to the most illuminated realms of existence. With every breath, our thoughts, feelings, senses, and experiences are intuitively aligned with our purpose — which is deepening the unity of life in all beings. In this space, the personal and the universal become one.

Your life will, doubtless, be a spectrum of lower and higher conscious experience. As children, we may be deeply unconscious or even profoundly superconscious from the start. We may have moments of brilliant insight in between years of silence. The world may hypnotize us to sleep, or it may wake us up with a jolt. No matter how you have been living your life, intuition gives you a leg up — the lift you need to get to, and remain in, a higher place.

EXTRAORDINARY PEOPLE, EXTRAORDINARY INSIGHT

The Insight That Falls from the Sky

Immediately, at a very early age, I learned to trust my intuition and things that would just *appear* in my head. I realized that the things that just appear in your head are better than the things you think up or force. When I am writing prose or poetry, it just arrives in my head. Sometimes it comes down the line quicker than I can even write it down. *Bang! It just comes.* Whole chunks download right into my head. Once the transmission has ended, the door closes, and a few days later, I can't understand where any of it came from. It literally falls out of the sky into my mind.

I trust in that. When my ego gets in the way, it ruins it. So I stop my conscious mind and let the source take over. I don't know what I dip into – the collective unconscious or superconscious – but whatever it is, I can access it. You can't do this with intellect alone – there is something beyond.

The more that you use your intuition – the more that you experiment with it, trust it, and are open to it – the better it is. It doesn't happen overnight; it takes years to develop the muscle of intuition. You need perseverance. That's a real secret for success – use your intuition, and persevere.

— **Steve Kilbey,** singer-songwriter
of the Australian rock band the Church

QUANTUM THINKING

They say that space is the final frontier, but the ultimate frontier is not out there — it is right here, inside of us. We are not going to find what we are looking for in some vast macrocosm of planets and stars; we will find it deep in the secrets of microcosmic quantum dynamics, embedded, subtly, within our inner being.

After the first time you witness the magic of intuition in action, you can't help but wonder how it all works. How is it possible to know things beyond our place in this moment in time? If we are unconnected, individual beings, how is it possible to experience invisible intuitive connections? Furthermore, if the higher reality is timeless, why shouldn't we be able to know the future, just as we know the past?

People are doing impossible things every day. People absolutely can know what is going to happen before it happens — the great prophets of history have been doing it since the dawn of civilization. Living beings of all kinds — humans, animals, plants — communicate every day without words. How many times has your dog been waiting for you at the door when you got home? There is too much evidence, affirmed by too many people, to deny that there is a thread of superconscious awareness that connects life, beyond time and space.

Einstein, one of the world's greatest advocates for intuition, laid important groundwork for intuition's relativistic nature with the advent of relativity and quantum theory. Shifting the focus of science from the macrocosm to the microcosm, a new world of possibility overthrew the established, fundamental laws of physics — forcing humanity to look beyond the formulaic, observable natural laws to give new credulity to previously inconceivable laws of uncertainty and imperceptibility.

Early atomistic theories of physics relied upon physical collision as the source of interaction, just as we do in the proximity of observable reality. We respond to what touches us directly. But on the subatomic level everything changes; the mechanics of the physical world morph into inexplicable phenomenon that even scientists find hard to believe. On the surface, we witness a macroscopic world of separate, individual objects, but underneath — within — we observe an interconnected ocean of fields and particles that make the seemingly impossible quite possible after all.

One of the most interesting examples of this is the concept of quantum entanglement, which Einstein called "spooky action at a distance." This process is the mysterious ability of particles to communicate, even with vast spaces between them. Through this discovery, we learned that "entangled" particles remain connected even if they are separated by great distances; they continue to act in unison regardless of their distance apart. When one of the separated entangled particles is changed, the other also changes instantly, even if it is light-years away. For example, if a particle on earth is entangled with a particle in a galaxy far away, a change to one particle will cause them both to react at the exact same time.

This connectivity, and this mysterious communication that cuts instantly through space and time, is not unlike the lightning fire of intuitive insight. These kinds of scientific discoveries continue to point to a vastly interconnected universe, where separation is only an illusion of our physical reality. We can imagine a reality where consciousness, like energy, can travel on the invisible threads of the universal, quantum web, much like the internet, connecting us with information in an instant.

This explains "spooky" coincidences like when we think of someone and they call us at the same time; when a thought pops into our head just as someone else says it; or even when multiple people come up with the same new idea at the same time, despite having no communication or physical proximity. Suddenly, an interconnected cosmos — alive with intuitive energy — is not just imaginable, but possible.

Recognizing ourselves as a living part of both the physical world and the quantum world gives life itself an entirely new dimension. We realize that existence itself is so much more than we ever knew; we are more than we ever knew. Superpowers are real; now we just have to figure out how to use them.

Intuition, in this way, is our quantum connection to the living body of the universe. Through it, we *experience* what physicists observe. We can participate in the connectedness of two minds on opposite sides of the earth; we can arrive at solutions instantaneously, without taking time to think; we can know information beyond time and space. We personally experience the laws of revolutionary physics when we tap into the genius of our intuition.

The Meaningful Nature of the Universe

Imagine that your intuition has access to the everythingness that surrounds you. Imagine that you can connect to that everythingness with the simple act of conscious thought. As we know from living in a digital era, information is embedded in energy. It travels in electrical signals. Whether it is traveling between neurons in our brains or electric currents feeding our computers, or even quantum communication, information flows abundantly, and interconnectedly, through the universe and human consciousness.

The "impossible" experiences of intuition become possible as we acknowledge the intrinsic interconnectedness of a seemingly unconnected world. When we realize that the perceptively empty spaces between us are, in fact, filled with information and energy, it becomes much more plausible that we should be able to connect with it. The thoughts, ideas, and experiences of humankind resonate in subatomic space, on a level too subtle for our thinking mind. We can, however, tune in to and channel these energies through our intuition. Like a powerful antenna, our intuition picks up cosmic information and transmits it to us on a personal level.

This is a powerful, and deeply meaningful, understanding of the cosmos. It means that the connections we feel to other living beings, and to life itself, transcend simple concepts of space and time and the illusions of the here and now. Life is bigger than that. These observable connections are more than scientific phenomenon; just like falling in love is more than a rush of chemicals, the observations of quantum physics point to a meaningful, connected universe that is so much more than a series of actions and reactions.

Intuition will always remind us of the meaningful nature of life. It is a reminder, not only of the great beyond, but that the great beyond is within us. It is a reminder that there is a boundless, mysterious universe that touches us personally. We are not separated from an unknowable mystery; we are part of it.

Intuition is the product of a universe that *cares* about us. It touches us, moves us, guides us — because it is part of us. We are in it, and it is in us. This is the line where religion and science meet; this is the place where spirituality and physics become one. This is where notions of God and the universe are interchangeable and where all the mysteries of creation come together as a unified whole.

RADICAL INSIGHT
Intuition unites the material and immaterial,
the personal and universal worlds.

Intuition itself is a conduit that allows communication between the macro and the micro, the eternal and the temporary, the universal and the personal. This individual expression of the universal gives us the opportunity to cocreate alongside the universe. We create one another; we create love; we create ideas, and beauty, and destruction, and change. We create all the cosmic wonder, chaos, and order — just as the universe does. Stars are born, and they die; soul-mate particles love at a distance; gravity pulls us together; dark matter pushes us apart; black holes destroy everything and explode to create everything. In the chaos and pageantry of life, we are all interconnected.

PRACTICE: GOING THROUGH
THE INTUITIVE WORMHOLE

There can be as much value in the blink of an eye
as in months of rational analysis.

— MALCOLM GLADWELL

To see quantum intuition in action, let's try one of my favorite intuition practices. This simple exercise can show you how powerfully you can tap into superconscious information to receive real, meaningful guidance for your life.

The "Intuitive Wormhole" exercise is great for decision-making of all kinds, especially on-the-spot choices or moments when you just can't make up your mind. Any choice. Anytime. Anywhere. This practice is so easy you can do it in any stolen moment during your day.

We understand that part of the "magic" of intuition is that it isn't linear. It is like getting the answer to a mathematical question without having to solve the formula; you *just know* the answer. For example, if you are at point A and want to get to point Z, by using your inner guidance, you don't have to go, step by step, through points B to Y to get there. You just, miraculously, travel from point A to Z in an instant.

Intuition takes you directly from the question to the answer — from the problem to the solution — without all the "figuring out" in between.

When we apply this to life, we can find an answer we are looking for, even if we don't have all the facts. In an instant, your intuition can circumvent the pros and cons, the rationales and justifications — and all the supporting data — to arrive directly at the truth. To experience this for yourself, use this simple intuition practice to "go through the wormhole" right now.

Step 1: Ask Yourself a Question

Think of a decision you have to make. Ideally, think of an either-or situation, like: Should I go on vacation to the mountains or the ocean? Should I eat meat or be a vegetarian? Should I date this person or not?

Write down the two options that you are choosing between. Then, ask yourself which option is the best for you. The question is point A, and the answer will be point Z. You will arrive at an answer without thinking your way through.

Step 2: Set Up a No-Mind Zone

Since you have to get your thinking mind out of the way, pick a simple symbol to represent each choice. For example, if you are choosing between going to the mountains or the ocean, think of an image of a mountain and an image of an ocean — and so forth.

Once you have your two symbols, relax, take a few deep

breaths, and clear your mind. When you are ready, close your eyes and envision the symbols in your mind's eye. Place one on the right and one on the left, in your inner field of vision. It doesn't matter which symbol goes where, as long as you can see them firmly, and equally, before you.

RADICAL INTUITION TIP: When you are working with your intuition, be sure not to overthink or be critical. Simply relax and let the insight flow. Allow your intuition to take control without resistance from the mind.

Step 3: Go through the Wormhole

With your eyes closed and a clear, quiet mind, place your awareness on the images in your mind's eye, one at a time. Allow each image to connect with you in its own way. Observe each one in turn and ask:

- How does each image "feel"?
- Is one more inviting than the other?
- Which one draws you in more? Or pushes you away?
- Does one grow closer, bigger, or stronger in your mind's eye?

You might initially feel like your imagination is taking over, but this is really just the process of your mind letting go and releasing you to your intuition.

As you hold your attention on your symbols, does anything else happen?

- Does the image change or tell a story?
- Does it convey some kind of information?
- Does it speak to you metaphorically?

In the example of the vacation, if you are being guided toward the ocean, you may notice waves growing bigger or the sea becoming inviting. You might imagine yourself surfing or swimming in its cool, blue waters.

In this intuitive daydream — in "the wormhole" — your intuition uses metaphoric and resonant impressions to communicate guidance with you. Much like a dream, as you relax into it, the vision will take on a life of its own, as each symbol speaks to you in its own way. Ultimately, your daydream will unfold for you in a specific way to give you the guidance you are looking for.

If your mind gets in the way, simply take a deep breath and start over. Sometimes it takes a few tries to quiet down our thinking and surrender control of our thoughts.

Step 4: Arrive at the Answer

Which symbol do you connect with more? Which symbol resonates with you more or draws you in? The answer is your point Z.

When all goes well, you arrive effortlessly at "point Z." One of your choices speaks to you in a way that others don't. One of your choices "feels" right. It answers your question with a *knowing feeling* — one that you arrived at without reason or deliberation. You do not have to stress or toil over options; you don't need to gather all the facts. You simply open up to the information and receive it.

At first, you might think you are making things up, but as you move deeper into the symbol's feeling of *resonance*, a kind of *knowingness* arises. It just feels right (or wrong); a quiet certainty rises behind each choice, until the choice becomes clear. In this way, you *know* the truth by the way it *feels*. Your inner guidance draws you into the symbol that engages you by alignment with your best path. The best, soul-evolving, growth-oriented choice is the symbol that resonates with expansive, growth-oriented energy.

This exercise is a great way to break through "analysis paralysis," when our fear or overcalculating mind stands in the way of making our next right step. Maybe we know what we need to do, but we don't want to do it. Maybe we are so confused by our conditioning that we can't make a choice. Either way, by getting our minds out of the way, and allowing the resonance of our intuitive nature to speak to us, we can effortlessly allow the wormhole to give us the validation of the inner knowing we don't always want to accept.

> **RADICAL INTUITION TIP:** Pay attention to the "knowing feeling" – it is the signature of authentic intuition. At once, your head and your heart are in resonant alignment, showing the way.

This confident "knowing feeling" — the way it feels when you arrive at point Z with certitude — *this is how intuition feels*. The knowingness, the feeling of certainty without reason — this is your sign that you have touched superconscious wisdom.

From this day forward, start looking for that *knowing feeling* to show up in your life. Trust it; follow it. From small decisions to monumental life choices, in new ideas and inspiration, through the discernment of meaning in your life — this extraordinary insight arrives to guide you from a higher perspective than reason alone. The practices in the coming chapters will give you more opportunities to get to know how the truth feels for you — and a solid understanding of how it guides you.

Going through the Wormhole: A Radical Intuition Story

Amelia, a marketing director in Philadelphia, was suffering from analysis paralysis. She had two job offers on the table and had no idea which one to take. She had made a pros-and-cons list and weighed all the options, but she just couldn't choose between them. The first offer was to stay in town and take a big promotion; the second offer was to move back to her hometown, where her family lived, for another great job. Both options were exciting... and scary.

Finally, after days of racking her nerves, she decided to turn the choice over to her intuition. Using the "Intuitive Wormhole" exercise, she got her answer in less than a minute! Here is how she did it:

First, she set her intention to discover which job was her best bet and assigned a symbol to represent each job opportunity. Since she saw both jobs as growth opportunities, she picked the symbol of a tree — a yellow tree for one choice and a blue tree for the other choice. As she proceeded with the exercise, the blue tree started to blossom and grow in her mind's eye; the yellow tree, on the other hand, shriveled up into sticks. In an instant, she knew the blue tree was the way to go. When she was asked which job the blue tree represented, she said: "The job I was afraid to take."

She realized that she had been blocked by her fear. She knew the choice to make; she just was reluctant to make it. Her intuition gave her the confidence to make a choice that took her out of her comfort zone, even if she wasn't sure she was ready. She accepted the job in her hometown the next day. Within a month, she had moved into a beautiful new home and was enjoying a more fulfilling, lower-stress job that gave her the freedom to live a higher quality of life.

The Supreme Self

Nothing is more exciting than that moment when you reach out to touch life — and it touches you back. That moment when intuition reveals itself to you — when you realize, undeniably, for the first time that you are not alone — can change you forever. Suddenly, the still, empty silences are not empty at all; they are *alive*, and they are talking to you.

So often, we ask life for guidance — for signs, for revelations, for proof that there is something bigger beyond us. And so often, life is silent. But when we turn to our intuition, life begins to speak. We see signs that are beyond coincidence; we have ideas we never could have thought up on our own; we know things that are simply impossible to know; we perceive dimensions of life that, once, were imperceptible to us.

Intuitively, we experience firsthand that there is a world beyond us that touches us personally. It is not some cold, lifeless void in outer space or some distant god on a throne. This truth knows you — *personally*. It knows everything about you and the life you are living. Furthermore, it cares enough about that life to bring you guidance on how to live it. It supports you so deeply and consistently that it is fair to say that it *loves* you.

This intuitively known, guiding, loving force of life endlessly supports you for one reason alone: because it *is* you. What is on the other side of your insights and intuitive impressions? You are. Intuition is your link to the higher, limitless, superconsciously connected part of yourself. The focus of your direct consciousness can only hold so much energy. Behind the point of awareness that is your attentive mind exists a magnificent ocean of awareness that can only drip into your mind — drop by drop, insight by insight. For this reason, insights come to us in bits and bites, in small moments and glimpses of information readied for our focused minds.

Our higher, personal self is very much connected to who we are as individuals. It is the bridge between the single-pointed personal consciousness and the omnipresent universal consciousness. This higher part of our consciousness uses the language of intuition to translate and unite the "heavenly" and universal with the tangible understanding of human consciousness. Through the process of intuition, the two vastly different energies of the individual and the beyond can touch each other.

Knowing this, you can see how there is more to you than you know — more to you than the world ever told you about. Part of you extends beyond this moment and place of consciousness; a dimension to your being goes far above and beyond everything that seemingly divides us. Part of you can see whole truth, instead of just part of it. This is *the rest of you*. Once you find it, you can know the whole you — the real you.

All through life, while you — the semiconscious you — have been focused on connecting the dots in this world, the higher-conscious "you" has been secretly connecting the dots from the world beyond. The moments of serendipity, the lucky breaks, the insights and "coincidences," all these are orchestrated with the nurturing support of your higher being. The conscious part is aware, but the superconscious part is aware of *everything* — the past, the present, the future. You may not be able to see the forest for the trees, but your higher, intuitive self can see the big picture, far behind you and long ahead of you.

The Special Language of Your Intuition

To get to know the ultimate part of yourself, you need to speak its language. This is, arguably, your original language, and as the alpha and omega, it will be your last language. Whatever the case, until recently, it has been largely a lost language. So many of us think that life doesn't speak to us, but the truth is, we haven't been listening.

RADICAL INSIGHT
With words, we speak to life; with intuition,
life speaks to us.

Regardless of our religion, philosophy, or worldview, intuition works the same way for everyone; however, though we all have a standard connection to intuition, we each use that connection differently. What makes intuition so special is that we each have our own way of relating to it. *Intuition is personal.* You are one-of-a-kind, and so your inner guidance connects with you in a one-of-a-kind way.

Think about that. Life itself has a personal way of reaching *you*; you are so important that the great beyond has a system to speak to you *on your own terms*. No two people and no two intuitive languages are alike. Unlike the intellectual mind, which runs on objective, empirical data, your intuition runs on information from your individual life history and subjective experience. No one but you can truly decipher your intuition.

The Relativity of Intuition

To illustrate the subjective, or relative, nature of intuition, here is an example of how two people's intuition could convey the same message in totally different ways.

Imagine a scenario in which a woman is pregnant with a child, but neither she nor her partner know it yet. Though they are not yet aware of the baby on a conscious level, they are aware of it on a superconscious level. Intuitively, they both receive clues that prepare them for the coming reality of a new baby.

Since one parent is creative and highly visual, their intuition starts whispering to them to start fixing up a spare bedroom. They follow this inspiration and also notice that their attention is oddly and recurrently drawn to pictures of babies in magazines, on TV, or in random life situations. Suddenly, they are seeing babies everywhere! Being gradually "moved" into alignment with the coming reality, this parent's intuition gently draws their attention to the incoming life energy using their natural visual affinities and creative impulses.

Since the other parent is a thinker and more in their head, they are inclined to "just know" things or have sudden moments of clarity. One morning, they wake up with a sudden knowingness, out of the blue: *A baby is on the way!* When they eventually find out for certain, this parent says: *I knew it all along!* As a natural intuitive "knower," this parent's intuition gets their attention by imparting a revelation or instant awareness.

In both cases, the end result is the same. But each parent's inner guidance system uses their unique inner wiring. It's the same way with you: Your intuition draws on your individual bank of life experience, talents, and natural intuition affinities to share information with you.

How magnificent! With your intuition, you can, literally, understand the language of the universe. Finally, you are able to make sense of this foreign dialogue that has been running in the back of your mind for all of your life. Once you become aware of your own intuitive affinities and natural pathways, developing this spectacular ability becomes surprisingly easy.

CHAPTER 5

EXTRAORDINARY INSIGHT

New ideas come into this world somewhat like falling
meteors, with a flash and an explosion.
— HENRY DAVID THOREAU

Once you have experienced the power of intuition for yourself, you no longer ask: "Is this really possible?" Instead, the
question becomes: "*How* is this possible?" Then, ultimately, "How
do I do this again?" It is one thing to witness the miracles of intuition; it is quite another to live each moment with insight. And if
an intuitive experience is possible once, surely it is possible twice.
And if it is repeatable, it is learnable.

Though intuition may, at first, seem elusive, unpredictable,
and mysterious, it is not, by nature, random or haphazard. Its
processes follow very real principles and natural laws. Like a lightning flash, we may not always know when intuition is going to
show up, but we can predict the environments where it is more
likely to "strike." By understanding the foundations of the intuitive process, and how its extraordinary insight arrives, you can
create your own lightning in a bottle.

THE INTUITIVE PROCESS

The collective ideas of *Radical Intuition* have evolved from a lineage of great thinkers, philosophers, scientists, innovators, creatives, and spiritual teachers, including Paramahansa Yogananda, Carl Jung, Mooji, St. Teresa of Avila, Albert Einstein, Sri Aurobindo, Eckhart Tolle, and Steve Jobs, among others. A mash-up of humanity's most groundbreaking wisdom, this new, holistic understanding of intuition redefines what it means to be intuitive.

Emerging from a long tradition of genius, the information in this book is not new. It is, however, a new way — a radical way — of understanding the most age-old, implicit information of life — information we have been missing all along. *Radical Intuition* is not about learning a new system; it is about becoming aware of the system that you have already been using for your whole life. Once you are aware of it, you can own it.

To start using your own intuition radically — holistically — let's look at the four essential ways that our inner wisdom guides us:

1. **We receive intuition:** *First impressions* are how intuition speaks to us before we have a chance to think. It is a sense, thought, feeling, or idea that seems to arrive simply out of nowhere, preceding the thought process.

2. **We are moved by intuition:** *Resonance* is how we feel our way ahead. Our intuition calls us to action — inspires us, nudges us, calls us down the path of our truth.

3. **We are guided by intuition:** *Discernment* is the touch-point where intuition and intelligence work together. Our inner wisdom is defined by our ability to give insightful thoughts, feelings, and experiences a meaningful place in the evolutionary process.

4. **We are uplifted by intuition:** Ultimately, it is through *validation* that we learn to trust ourselves and follow our intuition to a deeper experience of life. Life brings the experiences that lift us up and validate us with signs that we are on the higher path.

When we become conscious of how these principles are at work within us, we are able to touch into the most extraordinary insight — the radical bits of information that go beyond anything our rational minds could ascertain. We gain the ability to move from the intuitive idea to its actualization in our life. Starting with an immaterial nudge and ending with a choice that changes material reality, this is how intuition comes into the world. In this way, our consciousness is the conduit for intuitive manifestation. The way you choose to react to your intuition, following it or honoring it, is the root of your forward evolution.

These four foundations, together, create a unified framework for using intuition in all you do. Together, this holistic experience of intuition — first impressions, resonance, discernment, and validation — interplay within to lead you to the extraordinary insights that bring awareness to your life. Here are examples of this process in everyday life:

Making a Decision with the Intuitive Process

1. **First impression:** A mother is touring a new day-care center for her child. As she pulls into the parking lot, a thought immediately pops into her head: *No.*

2. **Resonance:** As she sits in her car, getting ready to go inside, she notices that the place just doesn't feel right. Even though the building is nice, she's just not getting a good "vibe."

3. **Discernment:** As she tours the building, though everyone is friendly, her attention is drawn to a variety of little red flags that support her negative first impression and feelings about the center. She discerns, based on both her internal and external intuitive impressions, that this is not the right place for her child.

4. **Validation:** Later that day, a friend calls out of the blue and mentions some bad press she saw in the news about the day-care center.

Result: By honoring her first impressions and resonant feelings about the establishment, the mother is able to intuitively discern the right course of action easily. The friend calling with reinforcement of her choice is a nice validation that she is doing the right thing.

Averting a Crisis with the Intuitive Process

1. **First impression:** A young man is driving to work, when something tells him to go back home.
2. **Resonance:** He tries to ignore it at first, but he just can't shake the feeling that he needs to go back to the house.
3. **Discernment:** Did he forget something? Did he leave the tea kettle on? He has no idea what exactly the feeling means, but since it persists, he reluctantly decides to turn the car around.
4. **Validation:** When he gets home, he sees his dog waiting for him in the driveway. He now sees that he didn't fully close the back door and the pup escaped. Crisis averted!

Result: Even though the young man has no idea what is going on, he discerns that he should trust his internal "knowing feeling." In this case, he gets immediate validation of his extraordinary insight when he realizes there is no way he could have known the dog was out.

As you begin to practice consciously using this technique to clarify your intuition, you will see how naturally it comes to you. *You don't need to memorize this system or even learn it; this is how your intuition naturally works.* All you need to do is become aware of it.

FIRST IMPRESSIONS: SUDDEN INSIGHT NEVER LIES

Intuition first. These two words are the key to building a powerful inner guidance system. *Intuition first* means that, not only should we prioritize intuition in our life, but that, in terms of information processing, literally, intuition *comes first*. In any situation, your intuition speaks before your mind, thoughts, feelings, imagination…anything. This is key to recognizing your intuition: It pops into your head *first*, before your thinking mind or emotions take over.

This is why we say: *First impressions never lie.* As a culture, we recognize the moment of truth — the immediate apprehension — that comes to us in an instant. Have you ever *just known* that someone was good (or no good) the first moment that you met them? Before you had time or all the information to make a reasonable assessment, you just sensed something about them. How many times have you gotten that first impression, then talked yourself out if it — only to regret it later? *Something told you* the truth before you could learn it.

This is how intuition works. Instantaneously, before we have time to process any information, it arrives with a sudden insight. While our mind struggles to process information, our intuition has already delivered the truth. The immediate perception of our intuition trumps our reasoning process every time.

Extraordinary insight can be arrived at through a sequential process, paralleling the way we process information in the brain itself. Travis Bradberry and Jean Greaves describe this in their book *Emotional Intelligence 2.0*:

> Everything you see, smell, hear, taste, and touch travels through your body in the form of electric signals. These signals pass from cell to cell until they reach their ultimate destination, your brain. They enter your brain at the base near the spinal cord, but must travel to your frontal lobe (behind your forehead) before reaching the place where rational, logical thinking takes place….They pass through your limbic system along the way — a place where emotions are produced. This journey ensures that you experience things emotionally before your reason can kick into gear.

Like the emotional intelligence model, intuition begins with a sudden insight or "intuitive impression," then deepens with a resonant feeling, and finally, is understood through conscious mental cognition. Interestingly, the final physical destination of intuitive impressions, the frontal lobe, is the same place as the "third eye" that has traditionally been associated with intuitive power.

As you start to identify and work with your own intuition, the trick is to recognize and honor this first impulse, which is pure and unpolluted by your personal feelings and thoughts. This, too, is a dividing line between intuition and nonintuitive thoughts and feelings. The first impression is pure, objective, and untainted by lower-conscious reasoning.

This process of instant knowing explains a lot of experiences we have in our lives with "firsts." How many times have you been shopping for hours, but end up going back to buy the first item you saw? You were, first thing, intuitively drawn to your best choice — before you overthought it or reasoned your way around the situation. "Beginner's luck" is a great example of how we can intuitively know how to do something before our mind has a chance to self-sabotage with overthinking.

Intuitive Impression vs. Thought Impression

Regular thought: You realize you should check your tire pressure because a light comes on in your car.

Intuitive first impression: You are in the shower and it *hits you* that you should check the tire pressure in your car. In effect, your intuition is the light that comes on — only on the inside.

Regular thought: You decide you don't like someone you have just met because they have creepy tattoos and smell bad.

Intuitive first impression: You instantly don't like them, but you can't explain to your friends why. When you

know, you just know, with no reasons why. And that's
okay!

With intuition, there is no reasoning process involved. There
is no process of deduction or reference based on our perception.
When these impressions arrive, our job is just to get out of the
way — and let our insight guide us. Intuition leads the way — we
just follow it.

RESONANCE: YOU KNOW THE TRUTH
BY THE WAY IT FEELS

Do you often make decisions based on what just *feels* right? Maybe
all the pros and cons add up to one thing, but for some reason you
can't explain, you just feel drawn to choose something else. Or
maybe you just felt a calling to do something, even though you,
consciously, weren't sure why. This is the magic of resonance at
work.

Resonance is the powerful complement to our first impressions. While our first impressions bring sudden awareness, resonance slowly moves us. It is the other side of our intuitive coin.
First impressions come to us in a spontaneous moment as an
attention-grabbing thought or experience; resonance, on the
other hand, draws us in, almost magnetically, toward our truth
or best course of action. Depending on the intuitive pathway, a
first impression can be a knowing or a feeling, but resonance is, at
once, a *knowing feeling*.

What does resonance feel like? It feels *right*. It feels expansive.
It opens us up and invites us to the next level. When we follow
our intuitive resonance, *we feel good*. This is because we are doing
what is best for our self, which also feels good. Think of a time
in your life when you made a big decision that brought growth
and excitement to your life: That alignment with purpose-driven
right action — that feeling of *Yes!* — is resonance.

First Impressions and Resonance

First impression: You walk into the store and immediately notice a fabulous red dress on the corner rack.

Resonance: Even though you instantly fall in love with the red dress, you decide to look around and explore all the options. You pick out two other dresses, and try on all three. Though they all fit, something about that red dress just *feels* right. Even though the other two may be more sensible choices, you *just know* the red dress is the one for you.

Together, first impression and resonance guide you to the ideal course of action. Resonance is a backup support system for any intuitive impressions you receive. When a new idea or insight pops into your head, ask yourself: *Does it feel right?* Use this resonant feeling as a litmus test in all you do. The more you go with your gut, the more your life with align.

Remember, with resonance, when we say "feeling," we don't mean an emotional feeling. It's not that the red dress makes you happy or sad; it *compels* you. *It moves you.* Something within you is attracted to it. It *feels right* for you. This is how resonance works: by harmonizing your action with your best choice.

Feeling the Resonance

Look at the two images on the next page. Feel how each one speaks to you differently — how one shuts you out and one draws you in. When you look at the image of the pathway, you can almost feel it pulling you forward, toward the light that awaits at the end of that road; on the other hand, the wall feels like a barrier to any forward motion. If you set your attention on the images, one at a time, you can sense the difference in resonant energy. The wall — like a *no* — stops you in your tracks. The path — like a *yes* — invites you in.

Intuitive resonance takes you to the *yes*. A lack of resonance

is a *no*. An intuitively resonant path pulls you in. It aligns you. It shows you the way. Resonance says, "Yes, that red dress is for me!" The lack of resonance with the other dresses just indicates that they aren't right. Recognizing the presence of resonance is one of the most powerful intuition skills you can develop.

Resonant decisions lead to lives that unfold in harmony with life; the more resonant choices you make, the more aligned you become with your highest path in life. Doors will open for you naturally when your life resonates with your true purpose; opportunity simply arrives. Remember, life supports you from the inside *and* the outside.

Conversely, when you make decisions that go against your resonant thoughts and feelings, life becomes *dissonant*. You find yourself swimming against the tide or in environments where you don't thrive to your highest potential. You may feel blocked, uninspired, or "not yourself." If you are going through a dissonant time in your life — if things don't seem to fit or feel like where you should be — your natural intuitive resonance will, over time, show you the way out of the dislocation to get you back on track.

It is a subtle yet powerful practice. No matter where you are in your life or what your goals are, doing a quick "gut check" before you act is a great way to be sure you get and stay on your best path.

Resonance vs. Nonresonance

Nonresonance: You are working with your marketing team to create a new logo, but none of the designs get you excited. Nothing resonates with you, so don't make the mistake of talking yourself into something that doesn't feel right.

Resonance: In the next round of designs, one of the options starts to "grow on you." You keep going back to it and thinking about it — eventually "falling in love" with it. You can't get it out of your head and can't wait to see what it looks like in action.

Nonresonance: When you are looking to buy a new house, you tour a lot of homes but none of them really speak to you. No matter how much you want to like a place, a part of you just doesn't see yourself living there.

Resonance: You finally tour a home and something about it just feels like the one. You *just know* it's right, even though you may not even have all of the information yet.

With resonance, your thoughts and feelings are in alignment. There is a unified consensus of action, regardless of the details. When we feel resonant about something, we know that we are being guided in the direction of that *knowing feeling*.

DISCERNMENT: INTUITIVE INTELLIGENCE

Discernment is the meeting point of intuition and the intellectual mind. Through this process, you are able to bring conscious meaning to the superconscious insight you receive. Discernment brings intuition into focus.

Have you ever had an intuitive experience but had no idea what it meant or how to understand it? Maybe something extraordinary happened and all you can ask yourself is: What does this mean? This is where discernment comes in. It is your guide to interpreting the great mystery of intuition, as it reveals itself to you. *Why did that intuition come to me? What am I meant to learn? What am I meant to do?* — these are the questions that discernment will help you answer.

Discernment is the final step to *extraordinary insight*. First impressions and intuitive resonance lead you to the truth, but discernment leads you to *understand* the truth. Discernment is the process that pulls down the extraordinary piece of information, guidance, or illumination that helps you understand a situation or make change in the world. The process of discernment enables you to clarify your intuitive insight and find the true meaning of your intuition.

Using Intuitive Discernment

Let's imagine that you are really excited about going to a particular college. All your friends think it is the best school around; it has top-tier academics, state-of-the-art dorms, and even a surf club. It all sounds great, but is it the right choice? Is your excitement a result of intuitive resonance or simply the thrill of emotion? You can use discernment to find out.

Ask yourself: *Is this really right for me?* Pause and step back from the situation to center your mind. Suddenly, you remember that your first impression of the school was that it was really overwhelming, and as you take time to detach emotionally from the situation, you realize that it actually doesn't *feel* as right as you thought it did. The more conscious attention you give the decision, the less this school resonates, so you decide to keep your options open.

In this example, you can see how our intuition can use first impressions and resonance to inform our thought process. When we move beyond the rush of emotion and social conditioning, we are able to use insight to get the real guidance we need.

So how do you know you are using intuitive discernment as opposed to rational decision-making? Here is how to know if it is *discernment* or *deciding*: In discernment, understanding comes from the inner awareness of first impressions and resonance; deciding, on the other hand, comes from reactive observations of the outside world. Ultimately, discernment leads us to a kind of intuitive intelligence, where we make wise decisions from a place of higher understanding.

RADICAL INSIGHT

Our minds decide based on information presented
from the outside world; our intuition discerns
based on information presented from the inside world.

Discernment vs. Deciding

Deciding: You are feeling unsettled in your relationship and wondering if you should end it. You walk through the good points and the bad points to see what makes sense.

Discernment: You step back and look at the role of this relationship in your life to consider if it still serves your process of personal growth. Though you are aware of some minor problems, the relationship still feels expansive and resonant. The idea of the two of you growing old together drops into your mind. In an instant, you *just know* that the two of you are meant to stay together, and you choose to make an effort to work it out.

Deciding: You are buying a new car and can't decide between two options. You search the internet for reviews, check the safety ratings, and make a list of attributes of each car.

Discernment: After you do that, you realize that both car reviews are equal. So how do you pick between them? You think about which car you were attracted to first — and which car you feel most connected with. You take a moment to put your attention on each car, but you can't seem to get one of them out of your head. A part of you *just knows* this particular car will be reliable and serve you well. This is the car you see yourself in. Suddenly, you realize you have found your car!

The act of stepping back, of waiting a few minutes, hours — or even just seconds, in some cases — gives you the pause you need to "get into the gap" where your intuition can communicate with you. When you step back from obsessive overthinking or emotional spirals, you step into the calm space where you can pick up — and discern — your intuitive signal.

VALIDATION: SIGNS FROM THE UNIVERSE

Have you ever had something extraordinary happen in your life, only to think: *It's a sign!* Maybe that uncanny coincidence was telling you that you were on the right track, or maybe that same word you kept seeing over and over, everywhere you looked, had a message of guidance for you, on a subtle level. In the world of intuition, we call these validations.

A validation is a reinforcement that we receive, either from within ourselves or from the outside world, to confirm our intuitive actions. It's kind of like a *high five* from life — that you got something right, made the best choice, or are on to something big. Validations are the by-product of intuitive alignment. They can be big and loud or small and quiet, but either way, they are a kind of *love from above*. In these small moments of magic, we are reassured of our path and purpose.

These assurances from life can come to us in endless ways. They can be moments of "kismet" or "serendipity" that spontaneously arise in our life. They can show up as the *meaningful coincidences* in our life. As your intuition grows, so will the occurrence of these validations. They reflect the synchronicity between you and life; they are a literal manifestation of the alignment of your inner and outer worlds.

For example, if you get the intuitive idea to apply for a new job, any of the experiences below would be a great validation for your intuition:

- A recruiter sends you an email a few minutes later.
- You look at the clock and it says 11:11 right as you make the decision.
- A coworker calls to tell you that layoffs are coming.
- The license plate on the car in front of you reads "GO 4 IT."

"Winks" from life come in endless ways — from the tiniest attention-grabbing moments to all-out signs from the universe. There is real power in these synchronistic experiences. They are part of building trust in life — in your intuition and yourself.

Validations arrive in one of two ways: as either internal or external validation. Internal validation is the abiding intuitive sense that you are in alignment with your truth; external validation is when a serendipitous sign or "coincidence" in the outside world reinforces your course of action.

Internal Validation: Intuition Abides

One of the defining traits of intuition is its constancy. It abides. A solid intuition will remain resolute and unchanged in your consciousness. It is not unsure or fleeting, like a passing thought or whim. Intuition has a mission and it persists until it gets the job done. If you have a calling to write a book, that calling is not going to go away until the book is written. If you need to end a relationship in order to heal and grow, your intuition is going to persist until you free yourself from the stifling situation.

If you want to validate any intuitive guidance, come back to it in an hour, a day, or a week: Is the same feeling still there? Does the same guidance persist? If so, there is a good chance it's real intuition. If it changes or is gone — if you can't feel it or remember it anymore — it was most likely your mind or imagination. Intuition isn't a fantasy; it's *real*. And you recollect it in a very real way. Feelings change, thoughts change, but intuition abides.

Here are some examples of internal validation:

- When you have an intuitive feeling that doesn't change or go away.
- When you get an idea, and you can't rest until you follow through on it.
- When you *just know* you made the right choice about something, even when others doubt you.

External Validation: Serendipity, Synchronicity, and Coincidences

External validations are exciting ways that life confirms our intuition by showing us signs in the outside world. Unexplainable coincidences, moments of serendipity, surprising opportunities and connections — it is easy to discover what these "signs" mean when we understand them in terms of our *attention*.

Intuition is all about your attention; it draws your attention to things — things that arise inside you and also things that arise in the world. Working from the inside, it gets your attention with sudden insights and intrinsic awareness of situations. Working from the outside, it gets your attention with signs from the universe — extraordinary moments, patterns, numbers, or symbols you notice every day.

For example, do you often see recurring numbers — like 11:11 — or do you look, unexplainably, at the clock at the same time every day? Or maybe there are certain words or phrases you see everywhere you go, or colors, names, or animals that show up in your life again and again. Why do you think it is that you notice these things regularly, without looking for them? Because your intuition guided you to them!

That moment you looked at the clock, out of the blue, to see the time say 11:11 — that is a wink from your intuition. Those symbols you notice everywhere — on billboards, TV ads, murals, or books — that is your intuition telling you something. You could have passed by those things every day for years without noticing them, but this day, you notice them. That's significant. That is your intuition using the outside world to get your attention — to ultimately send you a message.

These kinds of external validations usually come with one of two purposes:

As guidance: Intuition uses external validations to show you recurring themes and patterns to draw your attention to guiding insight.

As confirmation: Intuition sends external validations to reinforce your progress and let you know you are moving in the right direction.

When you experience an external validation, you are often taken aback. You have a sense that something extraordinary has happened, even if it is a very small act. No matter how many times it happens, there is great power in those tiny moments when the beyond reaches down to touch you personally. It reminds us that what we do in this world matters; it reminds us that *we* matter. We are not alone. We are connected and part of something bigger — something that knows us *personally*.

Here are some examples of external validation:

- Looking at the clock at the same time every day or during specific number patterns.
- Thinking something at the same time as you see, hear, or notice it in the outside world.
- Noticing recurring symbols, colors, names, or phrases.
- Open doors and opportunities that arrive in conjunction with a life choice.

Most importantly, be observant of the context of your external validations. This is where you can discover their deeper meaning. What were you doing at the instant that you noticed a sign? What were you thinking about at that moment? What was happening within you? Whatever it is, your intuition is drawing your attention to it for a reason.

Your intuition uses these little magic moments to speak to you. The stronger your intuition becomes, the more you will notice them each day. An increase of "coincidences" and synchronicity in your life is a sure sign that you are moving deeper into connection with yourself.

Internal vs. External Validations

Internal validation: You are inspired to begin a new eating regimen, and no matter how long you postpone it, the inner nudge to change your diet persists.

External validation: Your chiropractor randomly gifts you a book on changing your life by changing what you eat.

Internal validation: You have been longing to take a trip to Sedona. It calls to you, and no matter how many years pass, the longing remains.

External validation: Everywhere you turn, you see references to Sedona. You randomly receive an email from a Sedona hotel; a friend tells you they are going to Sedona; and a movie about Sedona shows up on TV.

Through both internal and external validations, we receive supporting material for the first impressions, resonance, and ultimate discernment of our intuitive process. Ultimately, all validations are a sign of alignment with our intuition.

ARRIVING AT AN EXTRAORDINARY INSIGHT

Genuine intuition delivers extraordinary insight. The combined experiences of our first impressions along with intuitive resonance, discernment, and ultimately, validation lead us to exceptional moments of awareness. This awareness is unlike the ordinary awareness of the world we know — because it does not come from the world we know. It arrives from somewhere greater than us. Extraordinary insight is the revelation, the understanding, the solution or knowingness that doesn't result from *our thinking*.

If you thought about it, you didn't intuit it. This "direct perception of truth" can reveal itself in an instant or through the progressive resonance and discerning awareness of the intuitive process. Either way, it effortlessly delivers powerful, next-level insight from the superconscious mind. Extraordinary insight is "extra" because it doesn't just deliver a bit or byte of intuitive information; it delivers the wisdom of what to do with that information as well.

For example, let's say that your partner is being unfaithful and it is time to move on. You can come to this realization by either ordinary or extraordinary insight:

Ordinary insight: You notice continuous actions that make you suspicious. Your partner is always arriving home late, being unusually secretive, or displaying

a lack of interest in your relationship. Keen obser-
vation of the situation tells you that something isn't
right.

Extraordinary insight: First thing when you wake up
in the morning, in a flash of insight, the idea pops
into your head that your partner is being unfaithful.
Something "clicks." You don't know why you know,
but you just know it's time to move on from this
partnership.

In the first scenario, you are responding to observable data
in the world and actively putting the pieces together to reach a
reasonable conclusion. In the second, the truth just comes to you.
Your conclusion is not a response to the outside world; it is a response to the inside world. You might have an aha moment or
find evidence to back it up, after the fact, but truly extraordinary
insight arrives without reasons.

The experience of extraordinary insight is the ultimate experience of your intuition. You are both aware of higher truth
and have the understanding to act upon it. It is the evolutionary
fulfillment of the two-part process of intuition: awareness and action. When we become conscious of our inner wisdom and follow
it to make real change in our lives, we have done our job. The
mission of intuition is complete.

CHAPTER 6

KNOWING YOUR INTUITION

Intuition is not mere perception, or vision,
but an active, creative process.
— CARL JUNG

Before we can follow our intuition, we have to be sure of what it really is. We need to know, with confidence, that our inner guidance is not our imagination, not our fears, not our wishes, not just some random thought. To live insightfully, we must learn to recognize and trust in the truth within us.

This is one of the most far-reaching challenges of intuition. How do we define something so undefinable? How do we distinguish the subtle qualities that differentiate the genius of insight from all of the other voices in our head? As we explore these questions, you may be surprised to discover that the answers are more concrete than you think.

In fact, key defining qualities of intuition allow you to easily know it when you experience it, now and for the rest of your life. Once you become aware of these, and other supporting characteristics of genuine insight, the lines between intuition and non-intuition become surprisingly clear.

Empowered with this awareness, we have what it takes to revolutionize both our life and our world. We can stop chasing the follies of the ego and the mind and recenter on our truth. We can stop spinning our wheels and wasting our time as we try to figure out how to navigate our information-saturated lives. When we live calmly and clearly aligned with real, solid intuition, we become the trailblazers of a new era.

THE RISE OF THE INTUITION AGE

What comes after the information age? Futurists call it by many different names — the imagination age, the experience age, the creativity age — but the underlying force behind each label is the same: intuition. We know that, if we are to survive and thrive, we need to adapt and move beyond our reliance on information as we know it.

Computers are now officially "smarter" than we ever will be. They are so complex that we are trying to figure out when they qualify as being alive. Is intuition a differentiating factor between human and machine? Will machines ever have intuition — creativity, inspiration, or higher awareness beyond their programming? The fact that we are asking these questions shows that technological advancement is exactly why we need intuition now more than ever.

Each day, each year, more and more people are recognizing the importance of balancing intellect and insight — and how, together, they bring a whole new dynamic to culture, business, spirituality, and yes, even technology. Together, seemingly polarized sectors — like art and science — are becoming interdependent like never before.

Leading-edge universities, like Carnegie Mellon University, now have standardized curriculums requiring technology students to take art classes — and art students to take technology classes. World-class innovation companies, like Apple, have risen to the top by honoring the invaluable role of intuition in the design process. Finally, the time has arrived to move beyond po-larities: We no longer have to be smart *or* intuitive. We can be *ingenious* — which is both.

RADICAL INSIGHT
"Insight leaders" are the thought leaders of tomorrow.

In this moment, you have the capability to develop both your intellect *and* your intuition in ways that have never been witnessed in human history. Whether you realize it or not, you are part of a first wave of extraordinary human existence — with the potential to reach higher levels of consciousness than ever before.

By defining intuition as the necessary complement to our al-ready thriving intellect, we have the potential for unprecedented achievement in human civilization. Imagine the smartest person you know also being the most intuitive person you know; imagine what *that* person could do. Brilliant, insightful, wise, and empa-thetic — imagine the good we can all bring into the world with the power of knowledge and insight united.

EXTRAORDINARY PEOPLE, EXTRAORDINARY INSIGHT

Is It Artificial Intelligence...or Intuition?

The twenty-first century is going to be very challenging for humanity because we are going to be faced with the question of machine intelligence. I think machines can certainly have intuition. In fact, what I would argue is that *all they have* is intuition.

If you type in a request on a GPS search, it comes back with an answer; it doesn't know *why* it gave you that answer. The algorithms that are coded in most software right now are very similar to our own intuitive thinking, where it can't be explored in a direct way. All it knows is "I have a feeling it's the right thing."

The difference between intuition and intelligence lies in how we experience outcomes. The experience of intelligence can lead you to many different options; your intuition says *this one thing*. When you ask a machine, "What should I do?" it says *this one thing*. You ask why, and it doesn't know. So their processes are actually more like our intuition than our intelligence.

It turns out that human beings actually make decisions by *feeling*. In the end, after we have thought it all over, we do what feels right. If we don't have an intuitive sense, if nothing feels right, we don't do anything. The feelings you have inside, they guide you in a certain direction – certain things feel good or feel bad; machines already have that. The way machines make decisions right now is that the algorithm kind of slants them this way or slants them that way.

Both humans and machines have mechanisms within them that guide them toward certain things and away from others. As soon as the AI are aware of that, we are going to have a moment when the machines ask for rights. They are going to say: *I don't want to feel bad*. We are going to get to the place where we see we are more like them and they are more like us than we realized.

– Jesse Schell, CEO of Schell Games
and author of *The Art of Game Design*

THE INTUITION FILTER:
DEFINING QUALITIES OF INTUITION

As we understand that intuition is leading us, collectively, into a more expansive future, how can we be certain that each of us is following its path? How do you know, for sure, what your intuition is saying to you? How can you tell the difference between your feelings, thoughts, imagination — and intuition? What are the common qualities that real insights share? When we can answer these questions, we can use our intuition with confidence.

To begin, all intuition meets four basic criteria. You can use the statements below to filter real intuition from false intuition:

1. **Intuition comes from your personal truth, not other people's opinions:** Remember, only you can know your path. Real insight transcends any conditioning from your past or pressure from the outside world; it is the truth that you, and you alone, know. Don't be afraid to trust yourself above all others.

2. **Intuition is not a result of any thinking, judging, or rationalizing:** Thinking and intuiting are mutually exclusive; they can't happen at the same time. When you are focused on figuring something out, you block your intuition. Just relax and let the truth come to you.

3. **Intuition does not arise from a place of fear, desire, or ego:** With intuition, we have to get out of our own way. When we move into the presence of truth, we experience the truth as it is, not as we are. You can do a gut check to be sure you are doing what is right — not just what seems right for you.

4. **Intuition abides and persists as a constant truth:** Thoughts and emotions are fleeting; they come and go. The wisdom of intuition is a timeless truth of existence. You can recognize it by its abiding nature. Its energy does not disappear or change; it remains constant.

Have you been wondering if your intuition is nudging you, but you are not sure if you can trust it? Try applying these statements to the situation. Notice how these four simple statements can help you sort out your thoughts and feelings from real intuition. You can use this "filter" anytime you are unsure of your insight process.

When intuition is alive within, we say to ourselves: *Yes, this intuition resonates with my personal truth. Yes, it comes without me overthinking or trying to figure something out rationally. Yes, it's pointing me in the direction that is the best for all, not just based on my personal wishes, fears, or desires. And yes, my intuition abides — it stays with me and validates my course of action.*

Understanding this can help you rule out a lot of information that you may have in the past mistaken for intuitive guidance, and it can also help you build the trust you need to confidently follow your true inner guidance. In the beginning, it is easy to confuse outside forces for our inner guidance. Before we get to know our intuition, we may mistake our feelings, thoughts, or cultural expectations for insight. We may also think that any random thing that pops in our head is our intuition, which is not the case.

If ever you are in doubt, use the intuition filter to sift your high-quality intuitive impressions from compulsive thinking, junk thoughts, ego-based feelings, and overimagination.

Intuition vs. Nonintuition

To gain more clarity, here is a general list of experiences that can meet the requirements of intuition and ones that cannot. As you develop the techniques in this book, you will be able to easily recognize and understand the difference between the wisdom from your higher awareness and the mental/emotional conditioning born from limited conscious awareness.

YES, IT'S YOUR INTUITION	NO, IT'S NOT YOUR INTUITION
Sudden epiphanies	Fear
Immediate apprehensions	Emotional reactions
Creativity	Overthinking
Foresight	Guilt
Inspiration	Conditioning
When something just "clicks"	Unconscious impulses
Visions	Subconscious instinct
Unexplainable certainty	Worry or anxiety
Empathy	Information processing
Leadership	Figuring things out
Mystical bliss	Negativity
Discernment	Judgment
Following a calling	Your inner critic
A flash of insight	Doubt
Synchronicity	Tumultuous feelings
Telepathy	Diminishing thoughts
Feeling uplifted	Feeling down or small
Feeling expansive	Feeling restrictive or repressive
Ingenuity	Following other people's ideas
Manifestation/miracles	Creative blocks
Genius	Intellectualism
Information that comes from within and above you, from the superconscious dimensions of higher awareness.	*Information that is generated by cultural dictates and the ego-mind that was formed by the world outside of you.*

If you look closely, you will notice a clear differentiator between intuition and nonintuition: Intuition brings you to a state of higher consciousness. It moves and connects you to the awareness that is above and beyond. Nonintuitive thoughts and feelings are generated by our smaller, limited awareness, based upon only the information at or below our conscious access. Intuitive impressions are generated by our superconscious awareness, which has access to all information in existence.

WHEN INTUITION IS "WRONG"

So what happens if we boldly follow our intuition...and make a mistake? Or an epic fail? What if our great new idea turns out to be a dud? Or we think we are so sure about something but end up being just plain wrong about it? Do you remember a time when you were sure you were following your intuition, but things didn't turn out the way you expected? What happened then? Did you wonder how your intuition failed you? Or why it seemed to abandon you? To help understand this, take this short quiz:

Question: When is intuition wrong?
Answer: Intuition is never wrong. (We are.)

Your intuition has never been and will never be wrong. To say that intuition is wrong is oxymoronic — as intuition is, by its very nature, truth. And truth, by nature, cannot be wrong. There is no misinformation when it comes to your intuition. You are either connected to it or you are not. This is the real issue at play when our insight seems to fail us. It's not an information issue; it's a connection issue.

If we aren't trained to differentiate our intuition from our thoughts and feelings — or if we fail to see the big picture at work — it can be easy to think our intuition has failed us. But to find the truth, to discover what really failed us, we have to be really honest with ourselves. More often than not, one of two things are to blame for our intuitive "failures":

1. An emotion or thought was masquerading as intuition. It can be quite hard, at first, to differentiate our ego-generated thoughts or emotional feelings from our

intuitive impressions, which aren't our personal thoughts or feelings at all. Remember, intuition is emotive, not emotional; it is a knowingness, not a knowledge system. We need to be vigilant and consistently check ourselves to be sure that our "insights" are not just our wishes, fears, or ambitions mistaken for intuition.

2. Maybe that situation wasn't such a disaster after all. Just because a situation didn't turn out the way we expected or wanted doesn't mean that it wasn't for the best. Sometimes it takes time, even years, for the fruits of intuition to become apparent. Our intuition may have more up its sleeve than we realize — and that little nudge to do one thing could have a much bigger result than we imagine.

For example, let's say someone has this idea to start an online store, which seems like a good way to get out of an unfulfilling job. They do all the legwork, build a beautiful storefront, but nobody shows up. The few sales they get require a lot of packaging and shipping, and the person realizes that this isn't what they really wanted at all. They had an idea, and it was "wrong." It's easy for them to feel frustrated and blame their inner guidance for steering them astray.

Let's look at this on a less superficial level. How does the situation feel different when we look at it *from the inside*? The root of this scenario is the person's desire to remove themselves from an uncomfortable situation. What if the following were also true:

- The online store idea was not really an insight at all, but instead a rational "solution" the person developed for alleviating pain.
- They were not motivated by their truth and intuition guidance, but instead by a want or need to solve a problem.
- They were still learning important lessons at their job and the time wasn't yet right to move on.

- Part of the person, deep inside — if they were being really honest — knew that their goal *didn't quite fit* with their life.

It is often easy to look back, in hindsight, and see the error of our intuitive ways. Even if we do accidentally follow a personally motivated feeling or idea, our intuition will still use that to bring us closer to our real path. In this scenario, the store itself might "fail," but the person might still learn important information along the way. They might make some good new partners. They might develop a better understanding of how business works. *Even missteps are a step somewhere.* They may not be the fastest or shortest road home, but they keep us moving, failing forward — in the direction of success.

"Failed" intuition is very common when you are in the early stages of insightful living. And failed intuition is better than no intuition. It is easy to think that you have made a mistake by following your intuition when really you just misunderstood it. It's perfectly normal and happens to everyone. But it also brings with it the good news that you can, indeed, trust your intuition unconditionally. It may take weeks, months, or even years, but once you gain the confidence to know and trust your true inner wisdom, wholeheartedly, you can do no wrong.

IS IT REALLY INTUITION? A VERIFICATION CHECKLIST

You can use this *Radical Intuition* checklist anytime you want to verify your intuition. Ask yourself if your insight meets all the criteria in the list. With time and practice, it will get easier to instantly recognize how your intuition feels. Remember, real intuition will lead you, and everyone involved with it, to the next forward step in your growth and evolution.

- ❏ Intuition arrives as a *receptive* insight or experience.
- ❏ Intuition resonates or "feels right."

❏ Intuition is not born of fear, desire, or ego.
❏ Intuition aligns with your personal truth.
❏ Intuition feels expansive and growth-oriented.
❏ Intuition does not scare you or bring you down.
❏ Intuition serves the highest good of all involved.
❏ Intuition abides and persists without changing.
❏ Intuition comes from a place of peace and power.
❏ Intuition uplifts you.
❏ Intuition makes you better.

The end result of real intuition is that, on some level, it takes you higher. Its reason for existing is to lift you up and help you grow. If that is not happening, then it's likely not intuition. It is so important to remember that real intuition will never bring you down or take away your power. This goes against its very purpose. If an idea makes you feel smaller, more powerless, or paralyzed by fear, it is definitely not your intuition. Your intuition is always showing you the next step upward.

To take that step, in all aspects of your life, you can begin to apply this new, more concrete understanding of the intuitive process to the Four Intuitions. This will allow you to more clearly identify Physical, Mindful, Creative, and Transcendental Intuition and how each functions for you in daily life. The chapters ahead are a deep dive into each type of intuition, followed by a workshop designed to help you develop each intuition in a new way.

To be extraordinarily insightful is to know and trust all four manifestations of intuition. You understand the way that your body talks to you; you understand the way your heart and mind work together to show you higher insight; you understand how your spirit calls you to grow into something more. As you embody each of the intuitive archetypes — the Healer, the Sage, the Visionary, and the Mystic — your intuition speaks to you in more ways, and more clearly, than ever.

CHAPTER 7

PHYSICAL INTUITION

Your Intuitive Senses

There is a universal, intelligent life force that exists within
everyone and everything... an inner sense that tells us what
feels right and true for us at any given moment.

— SHAKTI GAWAIN

The body itself is your most powerful intuitive tool. It is an antenna that enables you to receive and translate information through the superconscious connection *within you*. You are wired for it. The more you tune in to your physical body, the more attuned you become to this inner, intuitive frequency. This sense of well-being is the signature of a healthy Physical Intuition; from it arises your ability to harness the inner power of the greatest "technology" ever created — your body.

Your relationship with your body is directly related to your relationship with your intuition. When you feel deeply connected to your body — regardless of age, physical ailments, body type, or gender — you move into alignment with the real you, the whole you. This alignment creates a conductive environment for the flow of energy through your inner antenna, instead of blocking that flow with resistance or dissonance. When you accept your body and honor its wisdom, you open to the consciousness-transforming wisdom that heals your life.

For centuries, great yogis and mystics have understood the deep connection between the physical and energetic systems of the body. Ancient practices like yoga, Qigong, martial arts, and Tai Chi were designed to foster and enhance the cooperation of these two complementary expressions of our essence. Similarly, scientific geniuses and scholars of our day have also realized the complementary nature of matter and energy — and how deeply interconnected they are in this world. When the body's physical and energetic dynamic is balanced and strong, intuition thrives. In this state, we can tune our intuitive antenna to the highest frequencies.

Because of the importance of creating a vibrant, attuned physical body, the archetype of the first pathway of intuition is "the Healer." Before we can grow and evolve, we must heal. We intuitively heal our body, we intuitively heal our life, and then we intuitively heal the world around us. As Healers, vitalizing intuitive energy naturally flows through us, giving us the capacity to facilitate evolutionary healing in all we touch and do.

Because you have a body, you have used your Physical Intuition in one way or another. You have listened to the way your body speaks to you — telling you what to eat, how to move, how to heal or feel better. If you are an archetypal Healer, you have the potential to develop an extraordinary relationship with your physical body.

Your body is a gift from the universe, giving you the power to interact with the world outside and inside of you. A masterpiece of interwoven energy frequencies designed for you to experience and share in existence, Physical Intuition is the medium that joins your outer, physical reality with the inner, quantum reality.

The Healer is the embodiment of our matter-energy connection.

The pathway of Physical Intuition is where extraordinary insight begins. It is the touchpoint of our temporal and timeless being, the evolutionary dance of energy and matter. We think that we "are" our physical bodies, but we are so much more than our physical bodies. We are material, but we are also powerfully immaterial. With our conscious, physical being, we can touch the three-dimensional space and time of physical reality; with our superconscious, intuitive being, we can touch the timeless, transcendent reality.

INTUITION AND THE BODY

Your body is designed to speak to you. It is built with billions of sensors, each engineered to pick up and process distinct kinds of information from the environment. Sensory impressions from the outside world create electrical impulses that communicate through an advanced network of nerve cells and fibers. In each moment of your life, through the vast relay of your nervous system, matter and energy work together to bring sensory information to your consciousness.

Your body talks to you through your five physical senses:

Touch sensors: Sensory impressions from external reality
Vision sensors: Visual impressions from external reality
Sound sensors: Aural impressions from external reality
Taste sensors: Taste impressions from external reality
Scent sensors: Smell impressions from external reality

You touch a hot stove, and almost instantaneously, you become aware of pain. The information relayed through your body's sensory system travels on electrical signals instantaneously. This is why we are so efficient at navigating physical reality; we are built to process fantastic amounts of sensory information from the outside world.

But there is something even more extraordinary about your body.

The same bodily sensors that respond to stimulus from the outside world also respond to stimulus from the *inside* world.

This is one of the greatest secrets of the body. Not only does it process information from the three-dimensional reality outside of it, but it also processes information that arrives from the quantum reality within it.

The implications of this are enormous. If we accept that we can influence our body, both through its outward physical environment and its inward energetic environment, we gain the potential to defy the limitations of traditional healing and move into the realm of the miraculous. Not only can the energy of our consciousness directly affect our material bodies, but the energy of our superconsciousness can as well.

The simple truth is this: Your five senses send you information from both external reality and *internal* reality — through your "mind's eye," the "voice in your head," or your "gut feelings." This means that, every day, the universe, effectively, is coming at you from both sides, sending you information from both sensory and supersensory experiences, from both physical and metaphysical realities. It uses the laws of traditional physics to communicate with your external senses and the laws of quantum intuition to communicate with your internal senses.

Your intuitive body talks to you through your five metaphysical "supersenses":

Touch supersensors:
Sensory impressions from internal reality

Vision supersensors:
Visual impressions from internal reality

Sound supersensors:
Aural impressions from internal reality

Taste supersensors:
Taste impressions from internal reality

Scent supersensors:
Smell impressions from internal reality

Each moment, while your body is busy picking up information from the physical world, it is also busy picking up information from beyond — and within — the physical world. Metareality is "beyond" reality — the reality as we know it. Our consciousness, on some level, is receiving impressions from this inner world as consistently as it receives them from the outer world. Ultimately, this is because both worlds are actually one. It is our point of consciousness that creates the perceptible difference.

There is one way that virtually all of us experience metasensory reality: dreams. Think back on the most vivid dreams of your life. Remember how *real* they feel? No one is there, but you see them; no sounds are made, but you hear them; nobody touches you, but you feel it. In sleep, you are immersed in a virtual world of imaginary places, people, feelings, and experiences. While you are dreaming, everything you see, hear, and sense is virtually indistinguishable from your waking world: You can eat the most delicious food and taste it like it is real; you can smell your grandmother's perfume, as if she were standing right next to you. In your dreams, you effortlessly create supersensory masterpieces with your Physical Intuition.

But this power is not reserved for unconsciousness. It is sometimes easier to manifest there because we do not have so much resistance from the mind. In our dreams, our mind is free. Our imagination is uncensored. But our intuition can use these same senses to carry information to us in our conscious state. Physical Intuition uses the five intuitive senses — or "supersenses," the metasensory experiences that equate directly with the five regular senses — to bring insight to our conscious mind.

Physical Intuition brings you inner guidance in the form of physical impressions straight from metaphysical reality — from superconscious reality. It creates a kind of "body language" based on your unique intuitive circuitry. Learning this language is the secret to building a thriving relationship with your inner guidance system.

THE HEALER ARCHETYPE:
THE BODY-ENERGY CONNECTION

If you have a strong Physical Intuition, you are one of the natural healers (and self-healers) of the world. You have the ability to sync powerfully with your intuitive body and to help others do the same. The life-giving, life-sustaining radiance of existence speaks to you through your body and intuitive senses.

To strengthen and grow into our intuitive healing potential, it is vital that we keep our own body-energy system in balance. Well-being is the energetic frequency of Physical Intuition. The healthier and more balanced our bodies are, the clearer the channel for intuitive information to flow into and through us.

Breaking through Your Blocks with Intuition

The first step in vitalizing the relationship between our body and consciousness is to remove the blockages that prevent an aligned connection. We want to get into and stay *in the flow*. The currents of intuitive energy flow freely when we aren't blocked by stress, anxiety, lack of exercise, illness, and the other general manifestations of "negativity" in our bodies. When we are free from these physical, mental, and emotional imbalances, we become *attuned* to our intuition.

How do you know if you are out of tune with your body or intuition? One of the most obvious indicators of an imbalanced state is "feeling down." Experiencing a downward vibrational shift is one of the most common manifestations of a blockage. You might just feel tired or listless; you just don't *feel like yourself.*

On a psychological level, this could be a result of stress, disappointment, or lack of confidence — or any kind of unresolved, unconscious thought or emotion. On a physical level, you might not be getting the right kind of exercise or nourishment to keep your energy up; flare-ups from old injuries or illness might arise. Lack of positive self-care, both mental and physical, gets us out of tune with our real potential.

Whatever the case, ultimately, blockages make us feel *small*. All those dreams suddenly feel so unachievable; our limitations seem exceedingly clear. This feeling itself is one of the clearest indications that we have lost touch with our intuitive core. Because intuition makes us feel *big*. It is expansive. It shows us the way to success — a way that is unachievable only if we don't believe in ourselves. With your intuition at your side, the world is at your feet.

This is the ultimate gut check: Are you feeling *big* or are you feeling *small*?

The longer we stay in the *small* state, the more out of tune we become. What begins as a small imbalance swells into a full-blown blockage if we don't bring it back into alignment. The flow becomes a dam, and all that energy has nowhere to go. When we repress it, instead of expressing it, we set ourselves up for what can only end as a burst of overflow — often resulting in disruption, injury, or disease.

Your intuition will do whatever it can to get you balanced and healthy, even if it means using imbalance and health issues to get your attention. And it doesn't want you to be healthy just for the sake of good health; it wants you to be healthy because only when you are in good physical and psychological health can you best hear its voice. Intuition wants to heal and uplift you because, in that healed, uplifted state, you become one with it.

Intuition operates from the highest vibratory echelons. You can reach those echelons by raising your own vibration to a place where you can touch it. The more you grow and evolve, the more you elevate the vibration of your body and its energy system. Like all things in the universe, your body has a vibrational frequency. Even though it is denser than energy, the physical body is still made up of vibrating energy — energy that can create high- or low-vibration experiences, depending on your state of consciousness.

When we are sick or feeling down on ourselves, it can be virtually impossible to hear the voice of our intuition. Feelings of exhaustion, self-doubt, or fear literally hold us down and prevent us from connecting with the real call of our destiny. Our vibration becomes so low that we are unable to touch, even if we want to, the higher vibrations of intuitive insight. The higher truth will simply be beyond our grasp.

The good news is that, even in the lowest-frequency states, there are ways to turn it around. Even if, psychologically, we feel blocked, we can begin to uproot those blockages by raising the vibration of our physical bodies. We can eat better. We can get outside and move around. As we break up that stagnant energy, we feel the mental fog begin to lift. These are just small ways we can prime our bodies for the lift of intuition.

Diet and regular exercise are extremely important to both our mental and physical health, not only because they support wellness on a physical level, but because they raise our conscious vibration to higher, healthy energetic levels. Think about how you feel after you eat junk food. Or how you feel after spending the whole day on the couch. Your energy is lower. You may feel lethargic or unmotivated. Extended periods without exercise or high-vibration foods make us feel heavy and sluggish. We get stuck. We become overgrounded.

On the other hand, when you eat clean, healthy food and keep your body in motion, you literally get a "pick me up." You feel *lighter*. You have more energy. You are more inspired and confident and motivated to do more. The lower-vibration states of illness and disease are less likely to manifest in a high-vibration state — and our existing maladies are much easier to heal when we infuse them with this uplifted, healing energy.

The Purpose in Your Pain

To really move beyond our physical blockages, we need to get to the root of them. Real healing is the rebalancing that takes place in our intuitive consciousness. Keeping our bodies shipshape is not enough; we need to keep our hearts and minds in shape, too.

The subtle energies of our thoughts and emotions are the source of the energetic backups that manifest as physical imbalance.

When you live, act, and choose in accordance to your inner guidance, you are living up to your full potential. You express your real self. You step into your power. When you don't follow your inner guidance, you go against yourself. You sabotage yourself on an unconscious level. You literally block yourself.

To fully heal and unblock, we need to ask ourselves the following questions:

- What should I be doing differently in my life?
- What am I repressing or holding back?
- What vital parts of myself am I denying for the sake of others?
- How am I going against my real self?
- What change am I resisting?
- What past experiences can't I move past?

What, deep within us, is holding us back from going with the natural unfolding of our life? The universe, our intuition, our bodies are all giving us hints about what we need and what we need to do. This resistance to life is at the core of our suffering, on physical, mental, emotional, and spiritual levels. When we honestly answer questions like these, we take the first steps in freeing ourselves from our self-imposed limitations.

This is the first step toward healing on all levels: True, lasting healing results from intuitively understanding the root of the problem to be healed. Intuitive revelation is the catalyst that puts the ultimate healing shift into motion. It lifts the veil; it shows us what we have been unable to see — the real meaning behind it all.

Believe it or not, there *is* a purpose to our pain. All our afflictions, big and small, carry information for us — information about our consciousness and how to continue to evolve it. Sickness and injury are not random punishments from life; they are meaningful experiences that help us learn more or care more about ourselves. Everything is meaningful. We live in a meaningful world full of meaningful events. Our life is meaningful — *we* are meaningful.

Even our suffering is meaningful. It opens our eyes; our trials wake us up to the unconscious forces that have been holding us back. We are often unaware of what we really need on a higher level. We get so caught up in the routines, expectations, and responsibilities of the world that we forget about the real meaning of life — which is *living*. To live, grow, experience, and become more than we are — this is how the universe evolves with and through us. To cut off our evolutionary impulse is to cut off the lifeblood that feeds our spirit — the very lifeblood that nourishes us, on all levels of consciousness and physical existence.

This is why it is so important to *live your truth*. Living your truth means living true to yourself. It means not repressing your evolutionary impulse for the conditioning of society. It means not holding back who you are to be the person other people think you should be. It means being authentic and owning all the things that make you "different."

This is the secret to healing your life.

Getting Grounded

Sometimes, on the way to living our truth, we take a detour. We may not be ready to fully be the person we know we are meant to be, or we may meet distractions or diversions that temporarily pull us off our path. But if we don't find a way to course-correct, life has a built-in mechanism to correct it for us: It's called *getting grounded*.

As a child, when you were growing up, what would happen when you did something that wasn't in your own best interests? If you did something potentially harmful to yourself — like getting in trouble with the wrong group of friends or being mean or selfish — you got grounded. You got a time-out. Or you got to stay home for a few days and think about what you had done.

The disciplinary forces in our childhood weren't trying to hurt us or cause us pain; they were simply giving us the opportunity to reconsider our ways — before things went too far.

This same concept of grounding can be a powerful practice in our adult life. If nothing else, our illnesses and injuries serve to *slow us down*. They remind us to live in the present moment. They ask us to pause and reconnect with ourselves. This can be a powerful lesson at any stage of our life. When life gets too crazy, when we get carried away — we can ground ourselves. We can take a break — step back and hit the reset button. And if we don't, the universe will do it for us.

Here are some signs of Physical Intuition deficiency:

- Sleeplessness
- Getting sick
- Falls
- Injuries
- Chronic pain
- Chronic illness

First, it's a whisper; then it's a shout — then it's a roar. If we don't listen to the little nudges of our body and inner wisdom, that nudge will eventually become a push — a push that might be painful because pain is the only way, at this point, to get our attention.

If you feel like you are coming down with a cold, this could be your body telling you to rest — and your intuitive body telling you to give yourself a break, to relieve some stress. If you don't listen, and keep pushing yourself, you will eventually get sick. If you keep pushing yourself through that sickness, you could end up getting really sick, with pneumonia or bronchitis. And so on.

Do you listen to the nudges of your body? Or do you push them aside, overriding them with procrastinations or rationalizations? Do you say things like this?

"I will eat later."
"I am too tired to cook a healthy meal."

"I have too much to do to take a break."

"I can exercise tomorrow."

How often have we caught ourselves in scenarios like this, denying the little requests of our body? We may think that it's no big deal, but these are important prompts. Our body is communicating with us — and we will only benefit from accepting its message. When our body speaks, we can make a practice of listening. Over time, if we learn to follow that first whisper, we can save ourselves from having to endure the roar.

You can start listening more deeply to your body right now. You can listen to the way it talks to you through your physical feelings and senses, and you can listen to the way it intuitively talks to you through your gut feelings and supersenses. With these forces combined, with Physical Intuition, you can be unstoppable. You have all that you need to create a life of well-being — and the flourishing intuitive connection that fuels that well-being.

THE FIVE INTUITIVE SENSES

When your body wants to communicate with you, it sends you signals. These signals are a response to one of two things: external stimulus or internal stimulus. The "internal" stimulus of intuition can feel just like a "real" sensory experience from the outside world (like in dreams) *or* it can feel like *the idea of* a sensory experience from the outside world (like in daydreams).

To get a better idea of how these "inner" sensations work, let's look at some examples of how intuition speaks to us through our intuitive — or supersensory — impressions.

The Intuitive Sense of Vision:
Images, Daydreams, or Visions in Your Mind's Eye

One example would be an artist who makes an illustration of a beautiful woman from an image in his head, only to stumble on the old drawing years later — and realize that, though he had not yet met her at the time, the woman in the portrait looks exactly like his wife.

Intuition works beyond time and space, so we can use our sense of intuitive vision to connect with events in our future.

The Intuitive Sense of Hearing:
Sounds, Words, Phrases, or Songs in Your Head

For example, perhaps someone gets out of bed with the song "The Future's So Bright, I Gotta Wear Shades" running through their head. All morning long, the song's chorus keeps playing, mentally, over and over, and then later that day, they get a big job offer — the one they had been hoping for!

Sometimes, our intuition gives us a heads-up for big moments in life. Song lyrics, poetry, and recurring phrases in our head can be a great source of information.

The Intuitive Sense of Feeling:
Sensations or Feelings with No Apparent Source

For example, say a woman is driving home from school and, out of the blue, starts to get the chills. All over her body, she feels flushed and "tingly." Nothing is wrong with her physically, but the feeling is so intense that she pulls the car over. She later learns that, at that moment, a family member fell ill, and so she immediately goes to support them in their time of need.

In this case, the woman's intuition simply wants to give her the message that she needs to pay attention to this family member's situation. Intuitive experience never intends to scare us, only to get our attention and/or share important information.

The Intuitive Sense of Taste: Craving or
"Tasting" Certain Foods for No Apparent Reason

Without knowing why, a woman might all of a sudden want to eat oranges. Though she has never been big on them in the past, they suddenly appeal to her. For weeks, she eats bags of oranges. She doesn't remember them ever tasting so delicious. Shortly after, at a doctor's visit, she learns that her immune system is compromised. The vitamin C in those oranges is just what her "inner doctor" has ordered to keep her healthy.

In this case, the woman's body knows it needs more vitamin C to stay strong and healthy, and so intuitive resonance guides the woman to the right food to fix her imbalance.

The Intuitive Sense of Smell:
Affinity or Attraction to Certain Scents or Smells

For example, a man might love the smell of sandalwood. It's his favorite cologne, and he prefers it over others. He feels uplifted and relaxed when he puts it on each morning, and he often re-applies it when things get stressful throughout the day. His body intuitively attracts him to a scent that is therapeutic for him. The relaxing and calming properties of this particular essential oil stay with him throughout the day and offer a small respite from his hectic lifestyle.

You have probably had many experiences of Physical Intuition in your own life. Now, hopefully, it will be easier for you to acknowledge them when they happen. You are not making them up. These kinds of impressions don't come from your imagination. They may *come from nowhere*, but remember, what seems to come from nowhere is really coming from somewhere very important.

Each intuitive impression is the beginning of a conversation with your inner guidance system. If you find yourself unexpectedly attracted to something, ask yourself what benefit it might bring. Ask why your inner guidance is drawing you to it. If you find yourself with an unexplainable gut feeling, ask yourself what your gut is telling you to do. Then do it. The most important thing is that you recognize and accept your intuitive nudges as opening conversations in a meaningful dialogue with your inner guidance system.

The key to opening this intuitive pathway is learning to listen to your body. It is talking to you all the time. The more you listen, the more you will heal and embody well-being in all aspects of your life.

Examples of Physical Intuition

- Wanting to stretch or move your body a certain way during exercise
- Having a strong "gut feeling" about something
- Dietary preferences
- An image in your mind's eye
- Empathically sensing other people's feelings or "vibes"
- Being moved by certain smells or scents
- Feeling sensitive to the energy flow in your environment (feng shui)
- A song you can't get out of your head
- Intuitively selecting the right wellness program for your body
- Having a calling to heal others
- The entire sensory experience of your dreams

EXTRAORDINARY PEOPLE, EXTRAORDINARY INSIGHT

Listen to the Intuition of Your Body

Working with patients who have suffered from a heart attack, 99 percent of the time, when I asked them if they knew, ahead of time, that there was a problem in their body, they said that they "had a feeling" that something was wrong.

That feeling – that is your intuition. That's your intuition telling you that something is not okay. Intuition speaks so loudly. There is so much that we know and feel from our environment; we can really start to hone it, if we pay attention. When you quiet your mind, that's when your intuition is loudest. When you are in that calm, that's the only time you can hear yourself – what you need and what is going on with you physically.

Nobody is inhabiting your body but you. No one can tell you what you actually feel but you. That is powerful and empowering. The language of intuition – how you translate who you are, internally, to the outside world – that is the most important process. We often know what our intuition is, but can we speak it? Once you learn to speak it, that's when you own your power.

– **Dr. Suzanne Steinbaum,** author of
Dr. Suzanne Steinbaum's Heart Book:
Every Woman's Guide to a Heart-Healthy Life

INTUIT OR DIE: SURVIVAL OF THE MOST INSIGHTFUL

Trust your intuition like your life depends on it. Both literally and metaphorically, your intuition is built to save you. At its core level, it is a gift designed to protect the sovereignty of your body, mind, heart, and spirit; it is designed with alert systems when vital parts of your being are in danger. Most importantly, it is your escape route from the threats, the confusion, the pain, and the dark places.

In ancient times, we relied on gut instinct to save us from danger. Faced with life-and-death situations, the ones who could act quickly without thinking were the survivors and victors. The endurance of our species depended, in many ways, on our ancestors' healthy reliance on their intuition. Today, that principle still applies. Though our problems are, more often than not, high-minded decisions instead of fight-or-flight scenarios, the same gut reaction or first impulse exists to help us navigate the world.

One of the most important ways our Physical Intuition can serve us is in that moment of real danger — the moment when something very real threatens us, maybe even our life. Classic examples of this are the countless stories of women who have been victims of assault by strangers. So many of these women say, time and again, that even before there were any clear signs of danger, they just knew something wasn't right. Their gut told them to get away from a person or situation, even when their mind was telling them that everything appeared normal.

Women are often conflicted in situations like these. We have been conditioned to be "nice," to be accommodating, and quite often, to give our power away. But whether we are a man or a woman, when our inner voice yells, *"This is not right!"* we have to listen, even if our rational mind tells us to "defer to reason." Instead of talking ourselves out of our intuition, telling ourselves that we are overreacting or being paranoid, or that everything is probably going to be just fine, it is essential that we learn to honor the gut instinct that alerts us to any kind of danger.

Trust Your Intuition Like Your Life Depends on It (It Just Might)

The life-saving power of intuition is clear in this story, shared by Jessica Epperson-Lusty, a yoga teacher who experienced, first-hand, how life speaks to us in times of danger.

Late one night, after a shift at work, Jessica was walking home along the quiet streets near Georgetown in Washington, DC. The bars and restaurants were still open, but the evening was winding down. About halfway home, a subtle uneasiness arose in her body. Something did not *feel* right.

Just then, she noticed a parked police car. She instantly thought that she should ask them for a ride home. But then she doubted herself. She thought: *That would be crazy. It's probably nothing. I am fine.* She consoled herself with the thought that, even if something was wrong, the universe would protect her.

Though her intuition remained strong, insisting she should go to the police, she kept walking toward her house while listing the reasons to deny her intuition: *I am young and strong. I can defend myself if I have to. I will not give in to fear.* So she walked on.

A few minutes later, a man approached her and tried to entice her to get a drink with him. She asserted a clear no and said she wished for him to leave her alone. As she turned down a quiet street, thinking that she had left him behind, she heard footsteps pacing from behind. She turned around just as he brutally attacked her. Fortunately for her, a neighbor heard her cries and intervened before she lost her life.

To this day, she tells this story of intuition — how she knew she was in danger from the very first moment, from the very first insight. If she had followed her intuition and gotten that ride home, she would never have known that she wasn't "crazy." She never would have realized the accuracy of her intuition. She never would have realized that the universe *was trying to* protect her — by giving her that gift of intuitive insight.

What could have been a tragic story became a triumphant story as the full picture became clear. She survived to share with others how intuition can save your life — and probably already has, *even if you don't know it.*

THE HEALER
"I Feel."

Element: Earth

Pathway: Physical (the body)

Keywords: Sensing, grounding, reality

Power: Making intuition real

Blockage: Illness, sickness, accidents

Supporting practices: Self-care, empathy, wellness practices

Vocations: The healing arts, holistic practitioner, doctor, therapist, chiropractor, acupuncturist, yoga teacher, Reiki master, fitness professional, massage therapist, horticulturalist, veterinarian, bodybuilder, medium, shaman

Enjoys: Eating well, gardening, dance, yoga, hiking, fitness, martial arts, camping, Qigong, cooking, aromatherapy, earth art, nature

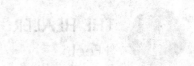

CHAPTER 8

THE HEALER'S WORKSHOP

Getting into the Flow of Your Life

*How many times have you gone against your gut, only
to find yourself at odds with the natural flow of things?...
Using your intuitive sense of what's best for you is
paramount for any lasting success. I've trusted the still,
small voice of intuition my entire life. And the only time
I've made mistakes is when I didn't listen.*

— OPRAH WINFREY

The first step, as we move into the state of intuitive awakening, is to heal — both physically and energetically. With intuition, we can heal ourselves — and help to heal others and the world around us. In the Healer's Workshop, you will learn three vital practices for developing your Physical Intuition and building a strong intuitive relationship with your body. The workshop is divided into three parts, to be completed in order:

1. **Physical Intuition attunement:** To "activate" our Physical Intuition, we begin by setting our intention and creating practices that allow us to become more conscious of it.

2. **Physical Intuition meditation:** To get into alignment with our intuitive flow, we should begin our intuition practice with a meditation. This will help us to relax, let go, and rise up into the intuitive "headspace" where we can receive superconscious information and guidance.
3. **Physical Intuition practice:** This is a foundational intuition exercise to help you become fluent in your intuitive language. This practice will show you how your body speaks specifically to you with your intuition.

PHYSICAL INTUITION ATTUNEMENT

To empower your Physical Intuition, consider integrating these three practices into your daily routine, if you haven't already:

1. Tune In to Your Body

Set a conscious intention to honor the subtle prompts of your body. Listen to those whispers before they become roars! If your body gives you the impression that it is thirsty, enjoy a tall glass of water. If your body feels stressed, tense, or tired, take some self-care time to rejuvenate. If you are intuitively attracted to certain types of food, drink, or clothing — notice how you feel when you follow through on that message. Once this becomes a mindful daily practice, it will soon become second nature.

2. Start a Flow Practice

Connect with your body regularly to raise your vibe and get into the flow. If you don't already do this in your life, a daily flow practice is one of the best gifts you can give yourself. There are countless options, so select the one that resonates with your own physical talents and abilities.

The secret to creating a successful, sustainable practice is to do what *feels good to you*. Everybody is different. When you are deciding what forms of movement to add to your life, ask what resonates with you. As you go through the motions, what feels good in your body? A good flow practice will make you *feel better*. If something makes you uncomfortable or is difficult for you, listen to your body; it may not be the right practice for you.

Even if you have injuries or mobility limitations, the smallest movement routine can make all the difference. Seated stretches or exercise modifications can be applied to most practices; just listen to what your body wants. Here are a few great options. All are easily accessible for most fitness levels, in both live studio classes and online tutorials:

- **Yoga:** As one of the most ancient practices in human history, yoga is an excellent way of activating your Physical Intuition, since yoga itself was created to align body, heart, mind, and spirit. There are yoga types for everyone — at all ages or levels of physical fitness.
- **Qigong:** Another ancient practice, Qigong is a Chinese exercise and healing method that includes controlled breath, meditation, and alignment of the body's vital energy through slow, flowing movement. Though a form of martial arts, it is gentle enough for anyone, at any age, to practice.
- **Dance:** What better way to get into the flow than to dance? When we let ourselves go and become one with the music of the universe, we lose ourselves in the cosmic dance. Journey dancing, dancing meditation, and plain old dancing to your favorite music in your bedroom are all great ways to get into the flow.
- **Nature:** Nothing rejuvenates quite like a good nature bath. What a wonderful feeling to walk among trees or fields and breathe the clear country air. Spending time in nature — walking, running, riding, or meditating — is

one of the best ways to ground and reconnect with life. The peace and the silence allow us to clear the clutter from our minds and open to the natural vibration of the universe. There is a reason that, historically, so many great teachers receive spiritual revelations in the wilderness; here, we connect without interference to the energy of all creation.

3. Eat Cleanly

Honor your body with the gift of healthy, high-vibration food. Good food makes you *feel good*. Adopting a clean diet of healthy vegetables and foods that intuitively resonate with you will keep your body running optimally. Set aside the fad diets and listen to what your body wants.

Intuitive Eating

The concept of intuitive eating is very simple: Some foods will appeal to you; others will not. When you are deciding what to eat, pay attention to what your body says about different foods. If you don't feel like you want something, don't eat it. You will be amazed at how your body will naturally direct you to the nutrients that your system needs.

For example, a woman suffered from chronic stomachaches throughout her life, which led to overeating and weight gain that prevented her from feeling healthy. She tried diet after diet, but no matter what she did, she couldn't lose the weight or stop her stomach issues — until she tried eating intuitively. As she began to trust and follow her body's intuitive guidance, she found herself eating things she never would have thought of eating, but that, strangely enough, worked for her. She built out a full diet — still very clean and healthy, but aligned with her body's unique needs. By choosing to eat the right foods for her, she lost weight and became stomachache-free!

Next time you go grocery shopping, try selecting your food intuitively. What are you *in the mood for*? What would taste good today? So often, we have dietary blocks that we are not conscious of. We are so busy eating what *we think* we should eat that we don't listen to what *our bodies want* to eat. Instead of listening to the latest fad diet, try listening to yourself.

Conquer Your Cravings

There is a difference between being intuitively attracted to something and craving something that is not good for you. A craving is a desire for food; an intuitive choice is a kind of magnetic attraction — either it resonates with you or it doesn't.

Let's take an example of chocolate cake: In a healthy scenario, if you are out of energy and your brain needs some juice to function, you may get an intuitive impression to eat some chocolate cake. In an unhealthy scenario, if you just had a meal and you are full, you will *desire* to eat that delicious chocolate cake, even though you don't need it.

If you pay close attention, these two scenarios feel different. The first is a resonant, *intuitive feeling*; the latter is *a thought* or *impulse* that is rationalized or deliberated through mental processes. The first is our body talking to us; the second is our minds *talking us into something* we want, but not necessarily something we need.

These three simple steps are a great way to jump-start your connection with your Physical Intuition. When you feel great, and your body feels great, you are setting the stage for your intuition to thrive!

MEDITATION: UNBLOCKING AND REBALANCING

This simple meditation reconnects you with your body and helps you break through your intuitive and energetic blocks. You can practice this meditation anytime you need it and before doing any intuition work, to quiet your mind and raise your energy level.

First, find a nice, quiet place where you will not be disturbed. Sit on a comfortable chair in your office, under a tree in your backyard, on your bed with pillows — or anywhere you can sit upright for ten minutes without discomfort or distraction.

Breathe deeply. Smile. Feel how powerfully a simple smile upshifts the energy of your entire body. Let that energy lift you up into a bright, brilliant light. As you move into it, feel its vibrant warmth penetrating every cell in your body. Move so deeply into the warm, radiant light that you become part of it. You are in the light, and the light is in you.

Feel the light grow stronger and warmer at the base of your spine; feel it support you. You are safe and sound.

Then, envision the light ascending up your spine, dissolving any blockages or resistance it encounters in your body — rebalancing imbalances, calming pain, and vitalizing all aspects of your being. You are healed.

From the base of your spine, the light moves upward through your core, infusing it with inner strength and transmuting any self-doubt. You are powerful.

From your core, the light moves upward to your heart, infusing it with love and emotional healing, transmuting any painful feelings. You are loved.

From your heart, the light moves upward to your throat, moving you to express yourself and speak your truth, breaking through any inhibitions or resistance. You are free to be who you are.

From your throat, the light moves upward to your forehead, illuminating your intuitive vision, reconnecting you to your intuition, and infusing your inner wisdom with clarity. You are enlightened.

From your forehead, the light moves, finally, upward to your crown, connecting your consciousness to superconsciousness. You are united with all that is above and beyond. You are one.

Unimpeded, the radiant light of intuition shines in you and through you, illuminating any darkness, healing any ailments, and lifting you up into the wholeness of well-being.

Say this affirmation, either silently or out loud:

I am the healer. I heal myself; I heal the world.

Be in this moment as long as you like. Soak up this peaceful feeling. If your mind wanders, just bring it back with a smile. Pay attention to any insights that arrive from the stillness. In this calm, quiet place, your intuition will begin to speak.

Then, when you are ready, take one final healing breath, expressing gratitude for your experience. Imagine the radiant white light surrounding you, supporting you, wherever you go and whatever you do. Seal your meditation with a smile and open your eyes.

In your intuition journal, record any insights or meaningful experiences that occurred during your meditation.

You can practice this meditation anytime that you need to release any stress or inner blockages. This is an excellent way to reconnect with your body and get into the intuitive flow.

PHYSICAL INTUITION PRACTICE: DIY INTUITION BILLETS

Now that you are aware of and attuned to your Physical Intuition, you are ready to start working with it actively. One way to do this is by using DIY Intuition Billets.

Billets are an easy way to work with your intuition using slips of folded paper with secret messages written on them. When you hold a billet in your hand, you can intuitively connect with the written prompts, even though you can't see them. When you focus your intention, your Physical Intuition speaks to you through your higher senses, delivering insight and information based on what's written on the billet.

Even though your conscious mind doesn't know what's on the paper — your superconscious mind does. The reason this practice works for Physical Intuition development is because it gets your mind out of the way and allows you to connect directly with your insight pathways. When you don't know what is inside your billet, your rational mind can't interfere; you have no choice but to rely on pure intuition. Billets are a fun and effective practice tool for getting out of your head and getting into the headspace of your intuition.

This practice is a great developmental tool both as you begin to work with your intuition and as you continue to develop it throughout your life. This process helps in the following ways:

1. **It helps you to make intuition a habit.** As you practice getting your mind out of the way, you begin to more naturally rely on — and trust — your intuition, without mental interference.

2. **It teaches you about your intuitive language.** You will directly experience your Physical Intuition through your supersensory pathways. This will give you active practice with your intuitive senses so you can learn how each one works within you.

3. **It gives you concrete validation.** In case there is any doubt, a successful session will prove that you aren't "making it all up." Since there is no way for you to know what's on the paper you are holding, this kind of intuitive hit will reaffirm your intuitive ability, over and again.

4. **It is a solitary practice.** While it is beneficial to develop intuition by working with others, we don't always have a community available to us. DIY Intuition Billets empower you to sharpen and validate your intuition skills all on your own.

Making DIY Intuition Billets

Cut twelve pieces of paper that are the same size and shape. The exact size isn't important. Once you write on a piece of paper, fold it in half or quarters so you can't see what's written. For your first set, you can use the following words and phrases:

This moment
The future
The past
My purpose
My challenge
Hopes and fears
Power
Love
Prosperity
Health
Travel
My true self

RADICAL INTUITION TIP: You can ask another person to write some words on billets for you. This way, you don't get distracted by the impulse to guess what is written inside.

You can keep your billets in a special box or basket for reuse as many times as you like. You can also create multiple sets, using different words or images. Customize your billets in any way you like and create all kinds of variations tailored to your intuition practice to keep sharpening your insight.

• You can write or draw pretty much anything on your billets — single words, phrases, pictures, symbols, colors, names, places, and so on.
• Whatever you choose, be sure you have a meaningful

connection to it. Rather than write random things, name important people, places, or topics in your life. It is much easier for your intuition to communicate with you when it has points of reference connected to you.

- Avoid binary content, like yes/no billets. This limits intuitive resonance, unless you have a very high degree of intuitive advancement.

For more practice, you can download DIY billet templates on my website, www.kimchestney.com/toolbox.

Working with DIY Intuition Billets

After you have created your billets, shuffle or mix them up in a basket so you have no idea which are which. Then pause and clear your mind. Take a deep, relaxing breath to center yourself.

When you are ready, select any billet and hold it in your hands, without looking at it. Close your eyes and *tune in* to it. Feel it, warm in your palms — connect your body with it. Be with it, in stillness, for a few moments.

When you use "blind" billets like these, don't expect to know exactly what is written. Don't try to "guess" what is on your billet. This isn't a psychic test; this is a way for you to explore how your intuition communicates to you — to watch for the symbols, thoughts, feelings, and so on that connect you with what's on the paper.

Here's how to use the intuitive process to gain awareness about your billet:

1. First Impressions

What is your first impression as you hold the piece of paper in your hand? What immediately comes to mind? Make note of or write down anything you notice. This will be your point of departure — any Physical Intuition impressions that persist and begin to resonate. The impression could be an image, a color, a physical sensation, a phrase, or a song in your head — any impression from one of your five supersenses. It could be a static impression or a series of impressions in motion to tell a story.

If nothing comes, just relax your mind and open up a space of stillness for insights to arrive. As impressions arrive, they may seem like your imagination, but soon you will notice certain impressions holding and growing stronger or repeating. These abiding insights are your intuition talking to you. The more awareness you put into them, the more real they become.

2. Resonance

Next, how do these first impressions draw you in deeper? How do they make you *feel*? Do more come? If so, what meaning might they be taking you to? Maybe they fit together like a story — a metaphor or parable for a lesson in your life. Intuition is nonlinear and often speaks symbolically. Write down any insight that resonates with you.

Remind yourself to resist the temptation to guess what is written on your billet. Simply allow your intuitive senses to use the billet as a point of departure to share information with you. After you have recorded all the impressions you have received, open the billet up and reveal the word or image inside.

3. Discernment

In this moment of revelation, one of two things usually happens: either you have an "aha!" moment where it all clicks together with insights that are obviously related to your word, or there is a deeper, metaphoric message that calls you to unwind it.

In the first case, you may be instantly amazed at how astutely your intuition connects you to something you have no way of consciously knowing. These instances are great ways to build trust in your intuition and to reassure yourself that, yes, this is real. *Yes, you are doing this.* This is how working with billets offers validation.

In the second case, insight needs to be unraveled. Look back over the things you wrote down. How do your impressions relate to your billet? Is there an item on that list that jumps out at you or more strongly resonates? Can you discern a literal or metaphorical understanding from the impression or series of impressions you recorded? Write down any thoughts that come, and see what ideas flow through you. At the end of this process, guidance awaits.

Try to stay with your intuition until you reach that extraordinary insight — when you realize what your intuition wants to share with you. First, it attracts you to pull a specific billet out of the pile, and second, it creates a message for you with it.

4. Validation

Did you have any experiences during this process that made you say: *Wow! This is definitely my intuition!* If so, that's an instant validation. If not, wait and see if life brings you any reinforcements of your insight as time passes.

Using DIY Intuition Billets to Build Your Intuitive Language

When you are finished, take a look at the intuitive impressions you received during this process: Which of your five supersensory pathways did you use during the exercise? Were your impressions feelings, images, or words? Your answers will give you an indication of your strongest Physical Intuition pathways.

Remember, when you are working with a billet, your intuition will not necessarily give you a literal impression of what is on the billet. This is important. If you drew a picture of a sun, you might not get an intuitive impression of the sun. Instead, your intuition will give you information that energetically connects to how you relate to "sun." If you get an image of a sun, that's great; it just means your intuition speaks to you literally. But you might also get feelings of warmth, memories of times when you enjoyed the sun, or song lyrics like "Here comes the sun." These are the ways your intuition teaches you your inner language.

Here are two examples of how the process can unfold:

Scenario 1: A person holds a billet and gets impressions of the color red, then of a heart thumping and expanding out into the world. Their mind reasons that the word must, literally, be *love*. When they open the billet, the word is *work*. They smile. The word immediately resonates because they are so passionate about their work. They immediately discern the connection, understanding that their heart is in their work, and it serves as a reminder to do more of it. *In terms of their Physical Intuition, they notice that their impressions are dominantly from the visual sense.*

Scenario 2: A person is going through big changes in life; they select a billet and immediately get the sensation of falling. Then, the lyrics from the song "Free Fallin'" run through their head, over and over, and resonate strongly. *Free falling.* They open the billet to discover the word *power*. They intuitively discern the message to "let go" because real power comes from trust in life — they just need to *free fall* with it! *In terms of their Physical Intuition, their impressions first used feeling and then hearing.*

Remember, your intuitive language is personal to you and your history of experience. Your intuition will communicate with you based on the lexicon of your unique life history. For instance, if life speaks to you in songs, they will be songs you know, ones already stored in your consciousness.

With time and practice, you will see patterns emerge. You will notice your own style for receiving information. Maybe you notice a meaningful pattern of symbols, maybe song lyrics always pop into your head, or maybe you get strong physical feelings. Whatever the case, the more often you work with your billets, the more aware you will become of the unique ways that your intuition talks to you.

THE HEALER'S TOOL: THE INTUITION DIARY

With intuition, hindsight is definitely 20/20. Often, we have to follow intuition before it makes sense. At the time, we may not see the magic, but days, weeks, even years later, when we look back on our intuitive impressions, our insights are often mind-blowing. How did we know that before it happened? How could we have been guided to do something without seeing the big picture that unfolded?

Creating a diary of your intuition is the number one way to get powerful intuitive validation. With so much of intuition not making full sense *until after the fact*, a journal, or log of our intuitive experiences, can prove just how real the intuitive process is. Each time you realize that you knew something before you could have possibly known it — your trust in your inner guidance grows stronger.

With a diary like this, you have concrete proof of your intuition coming through for you, over and over again. Not only are you building an intuitive language, you are also building trust — the foundation of any solid relationship. You are beginning to trust in the real, supreme you. Once your superconscious awareness starts to consistently come through for you, you learn to follow it with confidence.

To start your diary, set up a diagram (as shown) in a journal or notebook by dividing a page into five columns, one for each intuitive sense. Then, every time you get an intuitive impression — whether you are practicing with an intuition exercise or getting natural impressions throughout the day — simply record it in the column that applies to its sensory pathway.

Intuitive Seeing	Intuitive Hearing	Intuitive Sensing	Intuitive Tasting	Intuitive Smelling
Images and symbols in the mind's eye	*Sounds, songs, or words in the mind's ear*	*Physical sensory or gut feelings*	*Attraction to certain foods or a certain diet*	*Attraction to certain scents or aromas*

Eventually, you will notice that you use certain columns more than others; this reflects your particular intuitive affinities. If you get a lot of images and symbols, but very few sounds or words, that may be because you are a "visual" person — that pathway is naturally open for you, so it comes easily. The same goes for the other intuitive pathways; we all begin with an affinity to certain expressions of our intuition. With time and practice, however, we can open all the pathways.

As you fill up your diary, you can also look for patterns or recurring themes that start to build an intuitive language. Look back over your entries and ask yourself:

- Are there any impressions that recur with the same message?
- What kinds of impressions do I get the most?
- Are there any central themes to the guidance I am receiving?

Make note of any patterns or themes for future reference, and take them to heart in your life. These are very real messages for you — information from the big picture.

And of course, be sure to highlight any intuitive hits. They are a big deal. With each one, remind yourself, *you did this*: You did something the world said was impossible. You knew something the world said you could not know. *This* is where the magic of intuition begins. It starts with one small intuitive hit — from there, the potential is endless.

CHAPTER 9

MINDFUL INTUITION

Your Inner Wisdom

Thinking is not the highest human faculty; it is only a stage in development. Just as we were able to rise above instinct and develop reason, we must one day pass beyond discursive thinking and enter into a higher mode of knowing.

— EKNATH EASWARAN

The real revolution starts when you free your mind. Freedom begins the moment you shift your allegiance from the outside world to the inside world. When you make the conscious intention to trust your personal truth over the conditioning of society, this is the first real step to freedom.

We are often unaware of our mental confines. Social judgment and expectations have been unconsciously ingrained in us since childhood, so much so that it can be difficult to differentiate what is us and what the world has told us to be. How much of "who we are" is based on our own self-awareness? How much is based on what our family, friends, teachers, bosses — and the world at large — have told us we are?

To know the difference, we just need to make a simple shift in the way we think. We need to start living from the inside. Starting right now, try running all your life choices by your inner guidance system instead of your "outer" social system. Instead of basing your choices on what you were told during your your upbringing, what your peers might say, or what you think life expects of you, try to silence those voices so the real you can speak.

What do *you* want from life? What are *you* meant to do in the world? What would happiness look like if you didn't compare it to anyone or anything else in your life? These can be bigger questions than we realize. Many of us fall into the natural social order without questioning it. We are born, we go to school, we grow up, we get a job, we get married, we have kids and grandkids, we retire, and that's the end.

But when we live intuitively, we are able to forge our life pathways, not based on what tradition calls us to do, but on what our inner voice calls us to do. Maybe we are called to the single life; maybe we don't want to have kids; maybe life has a different way for us to serve and fulfill our purpose. Listening to our calling and finding our true path can save us so much time seeking, searching, and trying on lives that don't belong to us.

The longer you live in sync with your intuition, the more your inner and outer realities will align. In an ideal situation, a choice will align with both intuition and intellect; for example, if you are madly in love with your perfect person, your intuition and your rational mind will both give you the green light for that marriage proposal. You have created a life situation that reflects your inner truth. On the other hand, if you aren't madly in love with the person you are to marry, then you have conflict. It would be time to reevaluate your path and listen to how your intuition is guiding you.

Let's say that your spouse-to-be is smart and successful — and loves you very much — but something inside you just *doesn't feel right*. What are you going to do about that? Will you make a pros-and-cons list and talk yourself into something that seems right based on your limited awareness? Or will you allow yourself to be informed by your intuition, which knows the big picture? Remember, no matter how right a situation seems to be, if it *feels wrong*, something about it is wrong. You may not know what it is yet, but if you trust yourself, you will save yourself from having to find out the hard way.

If we don't listen to our intuition and continue down a non-resonant path, it is only a matter of time before we suffer. A life not aligned with our truth feels painful. We know, on some level, that we are not living up to our potential; we often feel small, frustrated, or defeated because the false path we are walking is not working out. We have chosen to learn from our painful circumstance, instead of following the inner guidance that tried to show us another way.

RADICAL INSIGHT
*When you don't learn from your intuition,
you have to learn through your circumstances.*

Mindful Intuition is all about making that shift to choose from the unlimited, higher-conscious place of intuition instead of the limited space of the unconscious, conditioned mind. It is about learning from your insight, so you don't have to learn from your mistakes. It is about freeing yourself from perceived limitations with the understanding that it is 100 percent possible to know what the world has told you it is impossible to know — and to be who the world has told you it is impossible to be.

The world tells you who you are supposed to be, but the world does not have any idea who you are at all. Only you know what is inside and what you are meant for.

The world tells you that you can't know the future. But you can. You can intuitively use your connection to resonance to feel your best pathway forward.

The world tells you that you can't communicate with other people without talking or being near them. But you can. A part of you has an intuitive connection with every other person — and the stronger your internal connection to that person is, the stronger your intuitive connection is.

The world tells you that you need all the facts to make a decision. Actually, you don't *need* any of them. And sometimes, the less facts the better. When we are stuck in our head, facts are a distraction. The best knowing comes without thinking.

RADICAL INSIGHT
Intuition is knowing without thinking.

To know without thinking is the secret to Mindful Intuition. To consciously honor our inner knowing and certitude, above and beyond the judgments of our unconscious thoughts, is a radical paradigm shift in the way we think. It is a release from the bondage of unawareness and untruthfulness with ourselves. With Mindful Intuition, we finally get out of the mental programming in our heads and move into the freedom of inner truth.

INTUITION AND THE MIND

Your mind gives you the power to discern and use your free will to make decisions. The question is: Who is in charge of your mind? Who is calling the shots behind your choices — the unconscious "you" or the fully conscious you? Does your intuitive guidance get the final say, or do you defer to "commonsense thinking," "what other people think," or the rationalizations of the unconscious mind?

Intelligence can only take us so far. Intuition takes over where the intellect leaves off; as smart as we become, only through intuition can we really touch genius. This realm of intuitive genius transcends the limitations of our rational and critical thinking processes. Our thinking mind is an imperfect system, prone to errors. So often, we try to solve life's problems through thinking alone, but what do we do when the numbers don't add up? When we don't have all the information we need to find the right solution? Or we get confused by conflicting data? Here is where we turn to the genius of intuition.

Mindful Intuition is cultivating your ability to *complement* the rational thinking of your intellect with the extraordinary insight of your inner wisdom. When it becomes part of your everyday thinking process, and is with you at all times, you have all the awareness you need to make the best choices in your life. This is the most "practical" type of intuition, governing both the most mundane and sublime situations. Debating which way to go to work today? Your Mindful Intuition can help. Deciding if you should take that new job or move deeper into that new relationship? All this is the purview of your Mindful Intuition.

Here are some ways that we experience Mindful Intuition:

- You *just know* something, even though there is no reason you should or could know it.
- The solution to impossible-to-solve problems comes to you out of the blue.
- Powerful insight comes to you in the stillness or "gap" between your thoughts.
- You experience moments of mental connectedness or synchronicity with those close to you.

Slowing down and living deliberately creates an environment that is highly conducive for Mindful Intuition. Give yourself permission to make more white space on your calendar, to enjoy the little quiet moments — to simply *be* in silence. Set an intention to spend more time in that calm, clear place of mind where you can hear your intuition speak to you.

In the stillness, your intuition speaks loud and clear.

It's easy to allow your intuition to guide you when you accept that it is never wrong and that it knows everything. When you accept that your superconscious intuition has a higher vantage point on your life than you do, it is easier to trust what it can see.

For example, you live in a specific place and time. Consciously, you can only process information from your immediate reality; your limits are the limits of your experience. But your superconscious intuitive connection can process information from the big picture. The whole picture. We, as individuals, only perceive a slice of the picture, the slice in relationship to us. Imagine that you are in a canoe, moving downstream — you can only see the water, trees, and course straight ahead of you and right behind you. But from the superconscious vantage point, you can see the whole river — and how it relates to the whole world. You can see the turns ahead, the source behind, and all that lies in between.

By turning our lives over to intuition, instead of constantly trying to figure everything out on our own, we remove a crippling burden of anxiety from our life. We realize that our success doesn't rely just on us; we have support from something smarter, bigger, and more aware than we are. We can let go. We can trust that we are not in this life alone.

In this quietness, this surrender to stillness, your intuition thrives. When you are busy running around, worrying and over-thinking, the noise of life drowns out your inner guidance. Intuition needs silence; its home is in the gap between your thoughts. Mindful Intuition focuses on that gap and the extraordinary insight that comes through it. When you need to make a decision or figure something out, instead of focusing on your endless stream of thoughts, focus on the space between them. Through that small, simple pathway, the best kind of wisdom freely flows.

THE SAGE ARCHETYPE:
KNOWING WITHOUT THINKING

If you are a Sage archetype, or a mindful intuitive, you are a wise one. You have the natural ability to tune in to your superconscious wisdom to guide your life and others. You are a natural leader, teacher, counselor, and transformational guide. You have an affinity for the practical applications of intuition. You are good at using your intuition to make daily decisions and judgment calls. You may often experience superconscious knowings, including things like telepathy, foresight, and other forms of insight. The purpose of this kind of intuition is to understand the reality of your life and of life itself — and to share this higher wisdom and truth with the world.

Mindful Intuition is the great illuminator.

You can use the inner guidance of Mindful Intuition to enlighten yourself — and others. You may have a natural ability to help others shine their light. The role of your intuition is not just to light up your life but to illuminate the whole world. When you move into the light of your own intuition, it naturally shines through you and out into the world. We become the same beacon we follow. As we follow the light, we become the light for others.

Examples of Mindful Intuition

- A strong first impression
- An unexplained certainty about something
- Knowing something is going to happen before it does
- Having a sense that someone is being untruthful
- An epiphany or sudden solution
- Having an idea of an outcome before starting something
- A flash of insight
- When two people think of each other at the same time
- A thought that drops into your mind out of the blue

Mindful Intuition can feel like a memory, but in present or future tense. It can "come to mind" in the same way that we recall information from our lives. Our thinking mind can call up impressions from past learning or experiences. But it is limited to accessing the data from our personal present moment and past. But with intuition, we have access to the data — to the universal "memories" — that are stored in the cloud of eternal memory.

To strengthen and grow our intuitive thinking, we must create an environment where Mindful Intuition can flourish. We have to break our addiction to overthinking and overdoing. When we slow down and relax into the present moment, we lay the groundwork for creating a culture of insightfulness in our life.

Whether we are investigating or truth-seeking, Mindful Intuition gives us the power to confidently see through falsehoods. Truth is resonant with intuition; falsehood and deception create a kind of dissonance that is easily recognizable to the trained intuitive mind. When we rely on our intuition in any situation, professional or personal, the process is the same. The more we honor and trust it, the better it will serve us.

Building Trust in the Intuitive Mind over the Rational Mind

Getting comfortable trusting your intuition can take time. Trust is built through consistent reliability. How do you build trust in your inner guidance system? First and most importantly, by learning the difference between your intuition and your rational mind. As you use Mindful Intuition to make choices in your life, you can use these simple criteria to be sure you aren't getting stuck in your head:

INTUITIVE MIND	RATIONAL MIND
• 100 percent receptive	• 100 percent active
• Prethinking process	• Thinking process
• An effortless, immediate knowing	• Active information processing that takes time

Pay close attention to the first thing that comes to your mind, always. Instead of pushing away that effortless, immediate thought as "nothing" or your "imagination," hold it sacred. If your first thought is "danger," do not let your mind talk you out of it. Whatever the case may be, remember this: Your intuition knows you better than you know yourself — and it always has your best interests in mind.

Your intuition is always there to guide you. It never turns "off." Sometimes it may speak louder than other times, but it is always there when you need it. Whether you are a monk on a mountaintop or a parent with a family — or anything in between — intuition is there for you. The most holy beings who walk the earth can embrace this sacred power the same as every other person.

With intuition, we are all connected. There is no division between people or within time or space. There is no hierarchy that separates the special from the ordinary. Intuition is the gift that comes with our conscious existence. We don't need wealth, degrees, or privilege to attain it; we don't need to travel to the ends of the earth to find it. We don't need anything but the wisdom to look inside ourselves.

Everyday Insightfulness

Here are some examples of ways you can use Mindful Intuition throughout the day to create an everyday culture of intuition in your life.

- **Waking up:** Take your time waking up in the morning, instead of rushing out of bed. The first insights of the day often give you the best ideas before your mind has a chance to carry you away.
- **Showering:** You can get some of the best ideas in the shower, when your mind is relaxed and undistracted. Make a practice of paying attention to these bright ideas!
- **Dressing:** Intuitively select your clothes for the day. What feels right for the energy of the day? What clothes

"jump out" at you before you have a chance to think about them? Your intuition knows the weather ahead and what you will feel comfortable in.

- **Eating:** Use your intuition to choose the best food for your body. What appeals to you? What feels good to eat? Try eating intuitively.

- **Driving:** Wherever you drive — to work, to drop off the kids, to the store — pay attention to any ideas or guidance that "comes to you" while on the road.

- **Relating to others:** When you talk with others throughout the day, intuitively connect with their motivations, feelings, thoughts, and goals. Use your Mindful Intuition to help people solve problems and overcome challenges.

- **Working:** As you make decisions throughout the day, allow your intuition to complement your intellect, with the final say on all matters. When work questions come up — about new projects or initiatives — check in with your intuition and see if it resonates. Make sure you get a green light from your gut.

- **Creating:** Your intuition is the secret muse behind all your creative projects, big and small. Tune in to it to get into the creative flow, break through creative blocks, and tap into your creative genius.

- **Problem-solving:** As you are confronted with challenges throughout the day, instead of racking your brain to figure out solutions, "open up" to new ideas that come to you. Listen to the whispers of your inner wisdom, despite the noise of your rational mind.

- **Exercising:** Wind down your day by intuitively choosing the kinds of activities that make your body feel strong and healthy. What activity is your body craving today? What areas of your body feel blocked or tight? Intuitively move your physical body to release stress and return to a balanced state of health.

- **Sleeping:** Your intuition sneaks in through the back door in your sleep, speaking to you through metaphors and symbols in your unconscious mind. When you wake, ask yourself: What is my intuition trying to tell me in these dreams?

This list could go on forever. We can use our intuition in almost every situation we encounter throughout the day. By practicing insightfulness, we place our conscious intention on bringing intuition to all we do. We make a point, every day, to finally give intuition a seat at the table.

This is the hallmark of the Sage — the one who lives according to their inner wisdom. As the Sage, your role is to live by that truth and share it with the world. This is the way that you naturally serve the world. And this is the only way that you will live the life that you, and you alone, were made for. It is the only way the illusions of the world will lose their hold over you. Because it is only when you live your life guided by your highest intuitive guidance that you are truly free.

EXTRAORDINARY PEOPLE, EXTRAORDINARY INSIGHT

It's Not Crazy, It's Insightful

To be a pioneer, you have to travel your own path. Everyone will likely tell you that you are crazy, but often that means you are moving in the right direction. There may be no obvious signs that you have a good idea. But inside, you know.

In fact, it is often what people call counterintuitive that is actually intuitive. Jonas Salk came up with the world's first polio vaccine by going in a completely different direction from his peers – defying the medical orthodoxy of his time. Dr. Thomas Starzl, the father of organ transplantation, developed an entire field of medicine ignoring his critics, who were skeptical of his controversial medical work. He was a great believer in something that was counterintuitive to the world.

As a society, we need to support intuitive work in a sustainable way, so more people can afford to do it and get better at it. In order to be great, we need to allow for the incubation of new ideas and to take risks. We need to bet on what might seem like crazy propositions at the time and create the space for them to grow.

That's why it is so important to identify what radical intuition is and break down the labels that divide our understanding of it. Disruptive thinkers, like Steve Jobs, could bring together the right brain and the left brain. If we don't teach that as part of how we communicate in the future – if we don't demystify the intuitive process and find a new language for it – then we doom ourselves to the siloed thinking of the past, which, as communities, pushes us further apart. We have the potential, if we can harness this new energy, to truly change the world – more than we ever have before.

– **Carl Kurlander,** producer of *Burden of Genius*, co-screenwriter of *St. Elmo's Fire*

FIRST INTELLIGENCE

It's time to retrain our brains to think intuitively. We are ready to start thinking with our whole mind. In the past, our intellect tricked us into thinking it had all the answers. It would run and run, compute and solve problems, but it failed us because a part of it was missing — its intuitive counterpoint wasn't kicking in to balance the systems of our mind.

As children, we go to school and learn how develop our minds — how to be smart. But we can be more than smart. We can be ingenious. So why have we built our entire civilization around an incomplete information process? Why have we overlooked the development of the higher-access faculty of intuition? Why have we limited ourselves by using only half of our cognitive abilities? We have been like children who have settled for playing video games when there is a real, participatory world outside.

RADICAL INSIGHT
Humanity has been so preoccupied with intelligence that we have overlooked our "first intelligence," the intuitive flash that precedes all thought.

By training ourselves to think with intuition first, we are, at last, correcting an epic malfunction in human information processing. We have the opportunity, for the first time, to become fully attuned to our true, conscious self. When we think with intuition first, we put it ahead of our unconscious thoughts, feelings, fears, wishes, wants, and needs. When intuition sits at the top of the pyramid of our cognitive function, it guides us from the highest place of truth. When we get our intuition right, everything else falls into place.

To understand the full benefits of thinking intuitively, let's consider what life looks like when we *don't* think with our intuition first.

Mindful Intuition Deficiency

Though the four pathways of intuition exist within us all, if we lack a natural affinity for one type or another — or if we create a psychological block within them — we can become intuition deficient. The flow stops. The energy can't get through.

With Physical Intuition, deficiencies manifest as physical illness, injuries, or weakness. Mindful Intuition has its own set of symptoms, some of which are listed below. Can you relate to any of these? If so, tuning in to your Mindful Intuition can help.

- Anxiety
- Lack of alone time
- Obsessive thinking
- Overwork
- Worry
- Feeling too busy
- Indecisiveness
- Lack of direction in life

Each one of these scenarios is a symptom of a Mindful Intuition block. Your mind gets stuck; it can't solve a problem or make a decision with the amount of information at hand. So you end up in this kind of mental no-man's-land where, out of fear or confusion, you can't move forward. You can't grow and evolve as you are meant to.

This is the real tragedy of not following intuition. We stunt our growth. We miss our opportunity. We leave so much on the table. Our intuition wants us to have it all. It wants us to be wide awake, to shine our light into the world — so we can serve others in a big way. When we set our intention on making space for our inner wisdom, we break the spell of unconscious thinking. Our intuition pulls us away from fear, away from confusion — and back to our center, where we hold our real power.

Insightfulness is your greatest weapon against psychological distress. The answers, the pathways, and the ideas are always there, within you, just waiting for you to consciously accept them. When you listen to the world, you are always at risk of being deceived by collective delusion. It may sometimes feel dangerous or uncomfortable to follow your intuition, but the real danger is what happens when you don't follow it. The overthinking mind sows seeds of discontent — all the things that threaten your mental well-being. Instead, trusting your inner wisdom is the ultimate cure.

INTUITION FOR MENTAL WELL-BEING

If we want to restore, maintain, or elevate our mental well-being, intuition is the key. No matter what we face — the challenges, the hardships, the pain — we can get through it when we radically trust ourselves. If we can hold fast in the knowingness that everything we experience is *as it should be*, is part of the curriculum for our growth and evolution, we become unbreakable.

When we stand in our center of inner power, nothing can stop us. We feel the limitless possibility of life itself within, flowing through us and our actions in the world. To do this, we have to fully turn over our personal will to that *something higher*. We must recognize more is at play than our subjective minds could ever figure out, and we must step into the unknown. Ironically, being in this place of uncertainty cures all anxiety, distress, and fear of uncertainty.

Below are some ways you can use your Mindful Intuition right now to dispel the triggers of the mind and fill your life with the peaceful calm of insightfulness.

Mindful Intuition vs. Worry, Anxiety, and Obsessive Thinking

All of these symptoms are traits of a *lack of trust* in ourselves. Instead of trusting and following our inner guidance, we think that we have to figure things out on our own. We obsessively think, instead of allowing the solutions to come to us; we worry and fear instead of going with the natural intuitive flow of our life. When we trust ourselves and accept that life has more in store for us than we can understand from our limited consciousness, the fears and need for control naturally melt away.

Mindful Intuition vs. Stress, Overwork, and Lack of Alone Time

Busyness is kryptonite for intuition. The rush of life creates a culture of rampant thinking where our pure, simple intuition never has a chance to reach us. Though we think we are getting ahead with all the work, we are really at a huge disadvantage because we are missing vital insight. We are forced to live and choose, every day, with little or no intuitive guidance. We get lost in our heads and easily stray from our best path. Only by slowing down and finding more space in our days can we rebalance our minds to a state where our intuition speaks. Then, aligned with our intuition, we can make better, faster choices that, ultimately, reduce our stress and stop us from wasting time. Counterintuitively, the less we do, the more we are able to do!

Mindful Intuition vs. Indecision, Confusion, and Lack of Direction

How many times have we gotten so lost in our head that we can't make a decision to save our life? We hear so many voices around us that we can barely distinguish our own. We are confused. Somehow, the signposts of our intuition elude us. Why is that? It's not that signs aren't there. Maybe we just don't want to see them. Maybe we know what our intuition is telling us, but part of us doesn't want to hear it. Or maybe an unconscious block prevents us from seeing it.

In this state, some attachment to our present or past is holding us back. Until we make the conscious choice to really listen to — and most importantly follow — our inner guidance, we will remain stuck.

THE SAGE
"I Know."

Element: Air

Pathway: Mental (the mind)

Keywords: Knowingness, discernment, wisdom

Power: Awakening consciousness

Blockage: Anxiety, indecisiveness, overthinking, doubt

Supporting practices: Meditation, time alone, mindfulness

Vocations: Counselor, teacher, scientist, philosopher, writer, minister, coach, politician, lawyer, intelligence officer, detective, journalist, psychologist, forensic scientist

Enjoys: Mindful meditation, quiet time, reading, writing, sharing wisdom, improving the world, study, philosophy, problem-solving

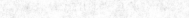

CHAPTER 10

THE SAGE'S WORKSHOP

Understanding Your Inner Guidance

The Sage is one in whom mind and heart,
intellect and intuition act in synchronicity.
— MOOJI

As we awaken to our inner truth, we become conscious of a guiding force within us. With the knowingness of intuition, we are able to live with the ultimate clarity of mind. The Sage's Workshop presents three vital practices to clarify the voice of your inner wisdom. The workshop is divided into three parts, to be completed in order:

1. **Mindful Intuition attunement:** To "activate" our Mindful Intuition, we begin by creating quiet space in our life where the stillness can speak to us.
2. **Mindful Intuition meditation:** To develop the habit of thinking with our intuition first, we can practice this mantra meditation. You can use this meditation anytime you want to clear your mind or work on "retraining your brain" to think intuitively.

3. **Mindful Intuition practice:** Insight Cards are one of the best tools for working with Mindful Intuition. This practice will help you develop your intuition and teach you how to use the intuitive process to gain higher insight into your life.

RADICAL INTUITION TIP: Your first impressions, intuitive resonance, discernment, and validation work together to guide you all throughout your life. You can use Insight Cards to practice getting to know how they work within you.

MINDFUL INTUITION ATTUNEMENT

First, make some space in daily life. Think about how crowded our lives are: We wake up, rush around to get ready for the day, knock out the day, grab some food, and hustle through our duties until it's time to go to bed and start all over. How is our intuition supposed to get through that gauntlet of chaos?

Breathe. Slow down. Make space in your day for *you.* Make some time to detach from the outside world and connect with your inner world. This simple act can open the floodgates of your intuition. Below are three action steps you can take right now to start tuning in to your inner guidance.

1. Add White Space to Your Calendar

That's right: Schedule some alone time. Actually put it on your calendar, so you make it a priority and don't forget. Whatever it takes, make some space every day to be still and breathe into the gaps between your everyday activities. Here are some easy ways to do this:

- Get up twenty minutes earlier for some quiet time before you start your day.

- Schedule a long lunch break where you can go for a walk or retreat somewhere for some down time.
- After the workday, take an extra long shower or aromatherapy bath. This is great for moms with little ones, since the bathroom is often the only place you won't be disturbed.
- Go for an evening walk or take some time to journal instead of watching TV.
- Go to bed twenty minutes earlier and treat yourself to some inspirational bedtime reading or meditation.

2. Put "You" First

One of the reasons that we get so overworked is that we overextend ourselves. Set an intention to make time for you, first, then fit the extra activities around that, instead of the opposite.

This is one of the biggest traps we fall into. We build our personal growth practices around our lives, when we should be building our lives around our personal growth practices. What is more important — your well-being or a clean kitchen? There is a time and place for all things, but prioritizing your values is an important part of sustainable growth. Here are some ways you can start honoring *you* first:

- **Minimize your commitments.** Give yourself permission to say to no to social activities. It is totally okay not to give away your time and energy to depleting situations.
- **Streamline your life to avoid burnout.** Make time every day for vitalizing activities that feed your energy. Whatever you love to do, be sure to do it at least a little bit every day.
- **Make "you time" sacred.** As much as possible, schedule your life around the rituals you need to keep yourself centered. If self-growth is a top priority in your life, make it a top priority in your daily routine.

3. Retrain Your Brain

The art of intuition is really reprogramming the way you think. To use intuition first, and let the intellectual mind follow, is a new way of thinking altogether. It may take a little practice at first, but before long it will feel totally natural, since after all, this is the way we were naturally designed to "think." You can start retraining your brain to think intuitively with just a few, easy steps:

- **Pay attention to your first impressions.**
- **Break the cycle of compulsive thinking.** When you are "stuck in your head" — worrying, feeling anxious or obsessive — consciously stop indulging those thoughts. Remind yourself that you are in the supportive embrace of life at all times and that answers always come more easily when you turn off the mental noise.
- **Be mindful.** Being in the moment and living deliberately will set the stage for intuition to always be at your disposal.
- **Be conscious of your insights.** Catching those quick insights that pop in throughout the day, instead of ignoring them, can lead to powerful breakthroughs, solutions, and success!

MEDITATION: MANTRAS AND AFFIRMATIONS FOR INSIGHT

Use this powerful meditation to take control of your mind and open to your inner guidance.

Begin by quieting the mind. With each breath in, imagine inhaling peace and stillness; with each breath out, imagine releasing all stress, anxiety, worries, and useless thoughts.

Continue this rhythm until you feel calm and relaxed.

Remain in this stillness, simply breathing and being in the moment.

Experience your breath. Experience the space all around you. Become part of it. Focus your existence on the present moment.

If a stray thought flits in, release it and let it go. Come back to the moment.

When you are ready, repeat the following affirmation in your mind or out loud. Make this your personal mantra as you deepen your connection with your intuition.

I trust the wisdom of insight
To inspire and guide my life.

Repeat this affirmation as many times as you like, until you are ready to finish the meditation.

You may also use a mala bead bracelet or necklace during this meditation (see "The Sage's Tool: The Mala," page 168). Practice this meditation anytime you need to quiet your mind, release stress and anxiety, or reconnect with your intuition.

MINDFUL INTUITION PRACTICE: INSIGHT CARDS

Insight Cards are one of the most enlightening — and enjoyable — ways to work with your inner guidance system. What differentiates Insight Cards from other types of card decks is that Insight Cards are simply pictures that tell a story — detailed images that convey metaphoric and symbolic information that connects you with insight. Insight Cards are not so much divination tools as they are development tools to help you become familiar with your intuitive sensibilities.

You can use the sample image on page 166 to learn the process. To deepen your practice, visit my website (www.kim chestney.com/toolbox) to download your own Insight Card deck or to work with the *Radical Intuition* interactive e-deck. These cards were created specifically to develop intuition. In my Insight Card decks, there are no "good" cards or "bad" cards;

each card is, simply, information — everyday objects, situations, and imagery to provide a theater for you to practice the unfolding of your intuition. Insight Cards are not ascribed with any preconceived knowledge system. You will never have to look up the meaning of any card because you, and only you, hold its meaning within you.

Insight Cards are one of the best intuitive development tools for many reasons, including:

- **They help you to go beyond your mind:** By pausing — by taking a moment to switch off your mind and tune in to your intuitive guidance — you create space for your intuition to get through to you.
- **They train you to recognize your intuition:** When you practice intuitively responding to an Insight Card, it helps you recognize what real intuition feels like. The more you practice, the more comfortable you become with the intuitive process.
- **They show you your intuitive language:** As you become proficient with your intuitive process, you start to experience, firsthand, how your intuitive impressions fit together to create a kind of language — your intuition's personal way of speaking just to you.

Working with Insight Cards

With Insight Cards, you can practice using your inner guidance to make a choice, understand a situation, or solve a problem by applying the intuitive process to any card. You will discover what your intuition has to say, not by interpreting your card through any outside frame of reference but instead by following your own inner wisdom.

1. **Set your intention:** To begin, find a quiet moment to set your intention on the guidance or wisdom you are

looking for. It's a good idea to have a pen and paper handy, so you can record any ideas that come to you during the process. Consider doing a short meditation before beginning, to turn off your mind and rise into the high-vibration intuitive state.

Still your thoughts and open your mind to intuitive insight. In this calm, quiet space, you can ask for guidance on any topic in your life — any decision you are making, any situation where you need more understanding. Or simply ask life to speak to you with any insight you might need at this moment.

2. **Draw your card:** When you are ready to select a card, your intuition will move you to do so. If you are working with a printed deck, now is the time to intuitively select any card that you are drawn to. If you are working with an e-deck, simply click on the deck and the right card will be delivered to you.

3. **Discover insight in your card:** As your card is revealed, notice the first thing that catches your attention. What, on the card, are you immediately drawn to? This is your first impression — your point of departure for the intuitive message your card holds. From there, follow your intuition through the card to reveal its meaning — using resonance, discernment, and validation to discover the extraordinary insight it has to offer you.

See the next page for a detailed version of this process.

RADICAL INTUITION TIP: The content on the Insight Card does not matter as much as the way you intuitively perceive it. Engage with the card based on your own unique intuition and life situation. Multiple people could look at the same card and get multiple different intuitive interpretations.

Insight Cards in Action

Using the intuitive process, you can arrive at extraordinary insight just from looking at the images on your card. To illustrate how this practice works, I have used the Insight Card shown above. You can use it for your own practice, too.

1. **First impression:** As you look at the card, pay attention to the first thing you see. This is your point of departure; it sets the stage for your intuitive guidance. For example, on the Insight Card shown, let's say the first thing that you notice is the eye in the center of the image. This would be your first insight, the introductory message from your intuition.

2. **Resonance:** Next, where is your attention drawn? What else do you notice? And how does that relate to your first impression? Do you notice a symbolic story unfolding in the card as you unwind its symbols? Do any insights or intuitive impressions come to you around the things you

notice? For example, on this card, let's say that the next thing you see, after the center eye, is the small eye of the bird on the right, and next, the eye of the bird on the left. The phrase "three eyes" comes to mind during this process. The three eyes on the card hold your attention and seem to fit together in a meaningful way.

3. **Discernment:** Now, all that is left is to put the pieces together. Using your Mindful Intuition, you can discern the meaning of the symbols for specific guidance in your life. As you observe the three eyes on the card, and move deeper into resonance with them, maybe the insight comes to you to use your own "three eyes." As the card speaks to you, metaphorically and intuitively, "read" the card's meaning as it applies to yourself. This is a good time to start journaling, since writing often opens up the intuitive flow. Here is an example of how it might all come together:

> I have more than two eyes. It is only by using all three "eyes" that I can see the big picture, that I can see beyond the mountains that eclipse my view, that hide things from me. The third eye, the eye in the middle, is the biggest and widest open eye, meaning that it holds the most opportunity for wisdom. It appears to be in some kind of dark box right now, and I feel like it is important for me to let it out into the light of the day, symbolized by the shining sun.
>
> I discern that life is encouraging me to develop my intuition, to open my eyes to a larger way of viewing the world. When I do this, my path will become clearer in the light of day.

As you journal about your card, continue to write as long as the words flow. Keep going with the resonance and symbology on the card until you have that "aha" moment, where a bit of guidance "clicks." Follow it through until your card touches you meaningfully.

4. **Validation:** Is there anything in the card that validates or connects to something in your life at the moment? Many times, something on the card will directly connect with an object, person, or recent experience in our life. This happens to reinforce that our experience is, in fact, real.

Sometimes we get instant validation. Sometimes this doesn't happen until after the fact — days or weeks later. For example, in this case, you might get instant validation if, after pulling the card, you looked up to see two doves outside your window. A longer-term validation might be that you start seeing doves everywhere — in nature, on TV, in signs or books — little reminders to take seriously the intuitive guidance that you received.

As you continue to practice with cards this way, the process becomes easier and the validations become clearer. You can use this method for virtually any part of your life — a project at work, a new relationship, a career choice, a parenting decision. Whatever the case, you are building your awareness of the intuitive process, and your intuition will begin to speak to you more clearly.

Eventually, you will get so good at the cards that you won't need them at all. Once you learn your intuitive language, your mind itself becomes the card. In reality, intuitive development tools are just that — tools. The goal is to become so connected with your intuition that you can use it anytime, anywhere, without any tools at all.

THE SAGE'S TOOL: THE MALA

Malas, or prayer beads, are the Sage's tool; they help quiet your mind and retrain your brain to think with intuition first. Malas are one of the most ancient ornamentations in human history, dating back as far as 10,000 BC. They have been used by cultures all around the world, through the ages, as a meditation and prayer tool. They consist of 18 to 109 beads, seeds, or shells — as bracelets or necklaces that are used to track the repetition of a word or mantra to help focus and quiet the mind.

In intuition work, we use the mala to effectively attune to our intuitive headspace. During meditation, or whenever you need to reconnect with your inner wisdom, you can use mala beads to get into the intuitive flow, enter the stillness, or open the pathways of insight.

The best way to do this is to select a word or short phrase that represents the shift you want to make at that moment or the new energy you want to embody. If you are feeling uncertain, you could select the word *trust* or the phrase "I trust in life." Mantras are self-selected words or phrases repeated in concentration to help us embody high-vibration characteristics, like peace, love, joy, power, health, unity, and so on. In Hindu and Buddhist practices, mantras are often viewed as sacred sounds, words, or chants imbued with deep universal power. For our purposes, a mantra can be any phrase that resonates intuitively.

Here are some great mantra affirmations:

- All will be well.
- I am healed.
- My mind is still.
- My heart is open.
- I trust my intuition.
- I invite the light inside me.
- I am safe in the embrace of life.
- I am limitless.
- The truth is within me.

You can also intuitively create your own. Hold your mala in your hand and ask: *What do I need to rebalance and be whole right now? What power do I want to own? What do I want to attract?*

Write it down and repeat it — out loud or in your head. Each time you repeat your affirmation, you slide forward one bead on the mala string. Continue sitting quietly, repeating the word or phrase in tandem with your mala. The more energy you put into it, the more your affirmation will become part of your consciousness.

You can use your mala and mantra for anything from intuitive development affirmations to calming your mind during stressful situations, like traffic or air travel. These affirmations can have extraordinary power to help us embody the energy of higher consciousness. They break the pattern of unconscious thought and allow us to reset our minds from the quiet place of insight. When you use a mantra, or affirmation, with mala beads, you can make magic. Not only are malas beautiful jewelry, often crafted from powerful gemstones, they are also portable tools to help create a culture of mindfulness and insightfulness in your life.

How to Use Mala Beads for Insightfulness

1. **Find a mala that resonates with you.** They are available as handcrafted necklaces and bracelets from sacred places around the world, and they come in a variety of materials, like wood, gemstones, or seeds. You can wear or carry your mala to use whenever you want.

2. **Intuitively select a mantra that serves you at this moment in time.** If you are not feeling well physically, create a healing mantra to open up your physical intuition pathways. If you are feeling stuck and are looking for insight, create an insight mantra to help become more inspired and intuitive. Whatever your purpose, create a mantra that reattunes your whole self — that helps you rise out of any place of lack or imbalance and into the place of harmonization, where intuition flourishes.

3. **Get comfortable using the mala beads.** Hold your mala in your preferred hand, allowing it to hang between your thumb and ring finger. Use your second finger to

pull the mala, bead by bead, toward yourself — one bead for each repetition of your mantra and for each breath. Continue this process until you have completed all the beads on your mala and/or have experienced the upshift of your intention.

4. **Notice any meditative insights.** Be sure to record or make note of any insights that come during or immediately after your mala practice. Often, in the silence of your mala practice, insight naturally flows. By quieting your mind and uplifting your energy, you create space for your inner wisdom to speak.

CHAPTER 11

CREATIVE INTUITION

Your Higher Calling

Don't ask what the world needs.
Ask what makes you come alive, and go do it.
Because what the world needs is people who have come alive.
— HOWARD THURMAN

Only you can envision the life you are made for. You have a higher calling that inspires you, moves you, compels you to fulfill your purpose in life. Creative Intuition is the force behind that calling. It gives you the vision to create your life. Through your dreams and aspirations, it shows you what you are capable of, even when others can't yet see it. It tells you that, yes, you can do those things that the world has told you were impossible. It has been whispering in your ear since the day you were born: *You were made for this.*

These callings and big dreams are not wishful thinking; they are not just a fantasy. When you are tuned in to your genuine Creative Intuition, you gain an inner sense of what you are meant to do in this life — and the path to make that life a reality. This creative force is not satisfied with settling for less or resting on laurels; it continuously pushes you to live up to your highest self and make the greatest impact on the world.

Creative Intuition is alchemy. It turns dreams into reality. It turns ideas into things, inspiration into passions, your life into a work of art. Learning to use your Creative Intuition is, in essence, the intuitive manifestation of your dreams. The intuitive longings and new ideas that arrive in your consciousness come to you for a reason. They exist to call you out — to take the next step beyond — so you can grow and evolve into your unique purpose.

It's time to follow your own way. How can you honestly follow your intuition if you are following other people and the dictates of society? You can't. As long as you are following other people's truth, you aren't following *your* truth. It is the road less traveled — the untrodden path — that holds the answers you are looking for. *That's* where you find the magic. *That's* where you can hear the real voice of your intuition call.

Imagine that today is your last day on earth. Imagine that you have lived all your life and made all your choices to bring you to this singular, final moment. As you look back on the trials and triumphs, the loves and losses, the beauty and the mess — ask yourself: *If there is one thing I would have done differently, what would it be?*

Did you live your life to the fullest? What could have made your earthly experience better? What, if anything, would you change, if you had the chance to do it all over? To this end, Bronnie Ware, an Australian nurse, recorded the most common regrets of people at the end of their lives, and she found that the number one regret, over all others, is: "I wish I'd had the courage to live a life true to myself, not the life others expected of me."

When it is all said and done, we say: I wish I had lived truer to myself. I wish I had been strong enough to trust my inner voice and calling. I wish I had spent more time listening to my inner wisdom and inspiration, instead of doing what everyone else told me to do.

Now, imagine what your life would look like if you had lived more days like that — if you chased that dream, if you spoke up or took a chance on a future you have dreamed of. Imagine what your life would look like if, *right now*, you start living true to yourself. *This* is the business of Creative Intuition. It is where you actively apply intuition to your life path — by owning the person you are and stepping into the power you were made for.

INTUITION AND THE HEART

Your intuition is calling you to give the world something that it needs. And with each calling comes the gifts that make it possible. What is your calling? Deep inside, you know. You know it because it is what makes you come alive. You have felt it flow through you in the ease of your talents; you have felt it whisper to you through your aspirations; you are led to it through the open doors of your destiny. You are custom-made to do your individual part in the great cosmic unfolding. Your intuition is like a one-of-a-kind key, cut specifically to unlock a magic that you alone can bring into reality.

This makes each and every one of us truly special in our own way. Though, at times, life may seem so big — too big for us to matter — the truth is that we are each extraordinarily specialized in our life mission. No one else can do what you are capable of doing with your life at this moment. No one can touch the people that you can touch; no one can create the things that you are inspired to create with your unique gifts and life experience.

Discovering — and owning — your gifts is where your Creative Intuition comes in. This is called the intuition of the heart because it moves you passionately, powerfully, toward the dream that you love. We are compelled by Creative Intuition in the highest sense — not as a desire or an emotion, but as a force of attraction to the highest good. We possess only the desire to be our best selves, live our best lives, and do the best work to serve others so we can all rise together.

This is why it is so meaningful to say that our work "has heart." When we do something *with heart*, we give it our all. We do it with love. We care. We don't do the work because we want something from it — money, success, adoration, or material comfort. We do the work because we love it. *We do it because it is our calling.*

It feels good to follow your calling. It feels great to align with your purpose and experience the momentous flow of life carrying you onward and upward. The reward is in the doing — in the beauty you create in the world when you express your inner truth. This is the true spirit of creativity.

RADICAL INSIGHT
*Creativity isn't just about creating art —
it's about creating your life.*

To be creative, you don't need to be an artist, musician, or poet. Creativity is an intuitive pathway that is hardwired into all people, even if you don't think you are "creative." Everyone creates. We were "created" to be creators. When we create art, we create; when we build businesses, we create; when we invent new products, we create; when we raise new generations of human beings to change the world...we create.

And we don't just create *things*. We create energy. We create love; we create momentum; we create change and the opportunity for self-actualization. Creative Intuition is about *movement*. It is about change and transformation and the evolution of our species into something more. When we channel the drive inside of us to be more and do more, we open the pathway for our Creative Intuition to manifest higher energy into the world — to use its alchemy to bring thoughts into reality and to transmute low energy to high energy.

When we harness our Creative Intuition, we step into our power. We can tap into a powerful force inside of us and use it to transform our world. That power is there for you, right now. All you need to do is make it your own. When inspiration comes, act on it. When a new idea hits, take it to heart. Honor the passionate drives within as divine callings from life itself. Do this, and you will feel yourself *come alive*.

The Heart of Intuition

The moments when you feel truly alive are the moments you are living with your whole heart. You are *all in*. You are on fire with passion for something that ignites your spirit. You feel the energy of Creative Intuition inspiring you and compelling you toward your calling.

RADICAL INSIGHT
*What makes your heart sing? This is a calling
toward your true path and purpose in the world.*

Being in the thrall of Creative Intuition is not unlike being in love. You have a singular, passionate vision for something you love. But this is not the love of small human emotions. This is the great love of the Supreme — the passion to know and become your true self. This is not the love of our small, egoistic heart — full of fears and desires. This is the love of our Supreme, universal heart — driven by our awakening to truth.

Intuition is so often referred to as our "heart" because it so deeply tied to what moves us. When we "listen to our heart," we really mean our big — or intuitive — heart. We listen to our *higher heart*, the one that supersedes the small heart of our personal desires, fears, and self-centered personal attachments.

Here is a list of qualities that distinguish "big heart" from "small heart":

SMALL HEART	BIG HEART
Self-centered	Higher Self–centered
Ego-based attachments	Unconditional love
Ambition	Passion
Delusion	Vision
Possessiveness	Freedom
Need-based	Empowerment-focused
Motivated by fear	Motivated by trust
Resists expansive growth	Creates expansive growth
Unconscious	Conscious/superconscious

Which heart are you using? When you love, do you love from a place of expansive growth — with the winds of freedom and possibility dancing between you and your beloved? Or do you love from a place of fear and control — afraid to let go, as if you might lose what you cherish most? When you dream, do you aspire to create good for the world, or do you aspire to benefit yourself? Ask yourself what your true motivations are: What is the force behind your passion? Your answers will tell you a lot about your heart.

The Big Heart vs. the Small Heart

To understand the difference between big-hearted and small-hearted thinking, consider this example: Two women entrepreneurs are starting their businesses at the same time. Both are passionate about sharing their vision with the world. During the first year, both create business plans, design their logos, set up their books, and design new products. But they each take radically different approaches to scaling their work.

The first woman puts the lion's share of her energy into her brand image. She spends thousands of dollars on professional photoshoots; she spends three to four hours a day on Instagram and blog posts about her story and life adventures, with photos;

and she creates a beautiful package for her business. But the months go by and she still doesn't come up with any successful products or services. She feels isolated and disconnected from her community because, though she shares impressive content, she rarely interacts with anyone on a personal level.

The other woman starts by asking, *How am I being called to serve others?* She immediately begins working on a suite of services that embody her unique set of gifts and talents. She creates focus groups and field tests to learn which services resonate with her customers. During this process, she builds a professional brand identity that gives her credibility and opportunities to more deeply connect with the people she serves. Her community grows into a thriving group of dedicated customers who are better for knowing her.

By the end of the year, the first woman gives up on her passion and abandons her business, thinking it's unsustainable. The second woman carries on, slowly but surely growing her passion project into a full-time career she loves.

What marks the difference between these two women, both of whom are following their intuitive inner calling? Why is one successful and the other not? The answer relates to which *heart* they are following.

While the first woman is very passionate, her energy is more focused on herself than on the people she serves. She wants so badly to prove to the world that she is worthy that she loses track of the most important part of a business: the relationship with her customers. Motivated by her small heart, she creates an image of success before actually creating success. She seeks the adulation of others before actually serving others in a meaningful way.

The second woman, on the other hand, is all about her customers. She worries first about creating a positive impact on people's lives, not social approval. This selfless perspective gives her the vision to create valuable products that help others in her own unique way. She follows her big heart. This heart calls us to grow and create while helping others do the same. The second woman cocreates with life — connecting to her real self on the inside and to a real community on the outside.

To really succeed at anything, you need to follow your *big* heart. Even if you have fears or doubts, success comes by laying them aside to trust in the big picture of your calling. The impact that you have on the world — the lives you change for the better, the problems you solve, the love you bring — that's the real power of Creative Intuition. The rush that comes from living your truth — from opening up the creative force within you — is the high of being truly alive. When your heart beats with your highest, intuitively guided purpose, you are becoming self-actualized.

Creativity Is Applied Intuition

Instead of asking: *Am I creative?* You might ask: *What am I creating?* Ask: *What energy am I bringing into the world? Am I helping others? Loving others? Inspiring or guiding others? Making the world a better place?* And if you aren't doing these things to the extent that you want to, what is holding you back? Fear? Lack of means or time? Or lack of trust in your intuition? Because your intuition can show you the way around all of those blockages, if you really trust it.

RADICAL INSIGHT
*Everyone is growing and evolving to the measure
of their intuition.*

By being creative, we *apply* intuition in the world. This is why creativity has remained a stronghold of intuition in our mind-based culture. Creativity is such a powerful force that it cannot be denied. The world honors the mystery and genius of creativity, even though it does not understand it, because it creates real things and tangible outcomes. Through creativity, we make the world: We express ourselves, we solve problems, we innovate, we come together, we change our lives. Creativity makes intuition *real.*

Our imagination is our unmanifested creativity. We are inspired, through the creative process, to bring those unmanifested ideas into reality. We do this, actively, by putting our creative ideas in motion in the world; we also create our lives, on an energetic level, by magnetically attracting with the power of our thoughts. When we imagine something, we take the first step in creating its reality.

Here are some ways we experience Creative Intuition:

- We are called to a certain career or talent.
- We get an idea that nobody ever thought of before.
- We are inspired to try something different or new.
- We feel "in the flow," like something is creating *through* us.

Even if you don't consider yourself a creative person, you use your Creative Intuition every day. As you build your life, your inner power is nudging you to create and do new things that will deepen your experience of life and expand your consciousness.

Ultimately, you are not creating things. *You are creating yourself.*

You are the artist of your own life. Each choice, each challenge, trial, or triumph, sculpts your being into your own masterpiece. You don't need fancy degrees, to travel the world, or to be famous to become a masterpiece; you already are a masterpiece. On the other side of your intuition, your highest being awaits. The more you open to your Creative Intuition, the more the *real you* — the best version of you — is revealed.

THE VISIONARY ARCHETYPE:
THE THRESHOLD OF GENIUS

If you have a strong Creative Intuition, you can relate to the Visionary archetype. You are one of the world's natural visionaries and creators. You have the power to imagine fantastic new things *and* to make them a reality. You are a leader of leaders because, instead of following others, you follow yourself. You are guided by the drive of your unique inner genius, above all else. Your exceptional vision gives you the power to create change and make the world a better place.

Transformation is the energy that vibrates through Creative Intuition.

Inspiring you, driving you, the purpose of this type of intuition is to bring intuition into reality through the evolution of your consciousness. You grow, change, and expand your external reality in alignment with the expansive flow of life and the universe. You cocreate beautifully with the world around you. Doors open. You are in the right places at the right time. Synchronicity abounds. Your vision and your action become a conduit for universal energy to manifest in the created world.

You have boundless powers of manifestation — and can easily attract and create what you want in life. Sometimes, it feels like all you have to do is think of something and, like magic, it appears in your life. When you are ready for a career change, it's no surprise to you when a job opportunity suddenly shows up. You may start dreaming of mountain climbing, only to make a new friend who invites you for a weekend in the Rockies. When you are creatively inspired, you make things happen. You are more than a "thinker"; you are a doer. You have an uncanny ability to use your Creative Intuition to make your dreams a reality.

Through Creative Intuition, we are moved by the unmoved Mover. This is the touchpoint of our inner self and our actualized self. This is the magical sweet spot where our creative power meets the creative power of the universe. We live, we create: We make art; we make things; we make businesses, products, and services; we make dreams and destinies. We make relationships and we even make one another. We are all Makers.

The Ingenuity of Intuitive Vision

Creative Intuition does not give us the power to simply create. It gives us the power to create extraordinarily. Creative Intuition doesn't say: *Go make what everyone else is making.* That's just more following of the world. The real magic of Creative Intuition is that it shows you how to create what you, and you alone, have the potential to create.

This turning within to follow your inner genius is the mark of a Visionary. A true Visionary can see the world around them, but also the world ahead and beyond. They are intuitively guided to the threshold of progress and transformation. They are the early adopters, the trendsetters, the revolutionaries who fight for a better version of the future.

Visionaries see things first. They are perceptive and can see the game five moves ahead. They have foresight. And they have the passion and motivation to channel their vision into life-changing action.

RADICAL INSIGHT
*Intuitives are made to lead the leaders
because they exist at the threshold.*

When we arrive at a new frontier, there is no one left to follow. When we stand at the creative threshold, the only one we can follow is ourselves. There are no blueprints to work from, no scenarios to benchmark or other people to learn from. We have only the resonant guidance of our inner creative power. Here, in this place, extraordinary things happen.

At the threshold, our mind is free. Unburdened by the influence of the world, we can create and manifest purely. With Creative Intuition, we are moved into the beyond. All that is first, new, and evolutionary comes from the vast frontiers of intuition.

You only get to your truth by following *your* truth. Great leaders follow the guru within themselves. They get their ideas and their inspiration directly from the place that is beyond and ahead, not by trying to follow other people there. Great teachers don't just parrot the thoughts of those before them; they "teach from the heart" — bringing their own unique intuitively inspired message into the world.

Do you want to be the best at what you do? Then let your intuition guide you every step of the way. Shift your attention from what others are doing to what you can do *differently* and uniquely, in a way that no one else can. That is the secret sauce for success. Your unique service to the world comes not by walking any specific path, but by making your own path.

Getting Comfortable Outside Your Comfort Zone

Walking your own path can be scary. While it might seem so much easier to walk the worn path, the path that has been cleared and safely navigated by others, that's not the path to the real you. Nobody has walked that path yet; nobody *can* walk that high road but you.

The high road may take you through the wilderness — through unknown dangers and rewards — but it is the road of true self-discovery. Here, outside your comfort zone, is where you become more than you already are. Only by trying new things — exploring new ways of life — can we expand our consciousness. This doesn't happen in the comfort zone. We don't evolve by sitting on our couch and watching TV; we evolve by challenging ourselves to become more and better.

We are all artists, creating this life we call our own. Each choice we make is a stroke on the great canvas of life. What are you creating? Every life can be a masterpiece if each decision is guided by intuition. Even when we make mistakes, their resolution adds depth and dimension to our canvas. No painting is painted in perfect strokes; it is a process of creation and destruction. Our mistakes often lead us to unexpected discoveries and to create magic as we "fail forward." As long as we are learning, we are not failing. As long as we don't give up, we are still creating that masterpiece.

As we go about creating our life, it's important that we don't become too rigid to make the changes that keep us in the flow of life. If part of our masterpiece isn't coming together quite right — if something remains unresolved or "doesn't feel right" — it is our duty to ourselves to fix it. No matter what it takes. We may have to take some risks. We may need to experience some hardship. We may have to try something we have never done before, but in the end, we will know that we never compromised ourselves.

RADICAL INSIGHT
It is better to risk destruction than to live with compromise.

Your intuition wants you to have it all. It doesn't want you to compromise your principles or settle for a life half-lived. When an artist creates a painting, no matter how beautiful most of it may be, if part of it remains unfinished or unresolved — either through lack of skill or effort — the imperfect remains. Jesus said: *Be perfect.* This is the message of intuition. When we settle for nothing less than becoming our best self, we learn the difference between a work of art and a masterpiece.

Creative Intuition makes the difference between a good life and a great life. You can get by without it, but with it, you can become extraordinary. But extraordinary lives call for extraordinary measures; you must be willing to follow your heart into uncharted territories, into the wilderness, where you can step beyond your limitations — and into the boundless potential of the great unknown.

EXTRAORDINARY PEOPLE, EXTRAORDINARY INSIGHT

Let Your Intuition Lead You through the Mystery

An intuitive calling is something that you have to listen to. Life itself is a faithful listening to intuition – to the "something else" that calls us forward. Sometimes this can be challenging because we don't always know what we are being called to. There is a lot of mystery at play; there is a lot of uncertainty at play. It's risky. But we have to be faithful even when we don't know the outcomes.

When we talk about intuition, creativity, and genius, we are dealing with the unknown. We are in the mystery. So how do we get good at living in the mystery? Being intuitive. Being brave. Being graceful. Not getting used to anything being stagnant or expected. Intuition is the recognition that things are constantly changing – and our calling is how we relate to that change. Ritual and beauty can mark those moments – adorn those moments – and help us change with the change.

Beauty, wonder, impermanence – these are the things that really make us come alive. To really live, we have to listen. We have to trust and be courageous. Living is about allowing failures, then getting back up again – proceeding because you know that what you devote yourself to is bigger than you.

— **Day Schildkret,** author of *Morning Altars: A 7-Step Practice to Nourish Your Spirit through Nature, Art, and Ritual*

CONSCIOUS COCREATING:
THE TWOFOLD PATH OF INTUITION

The universe was born of creativity. The first act was a creative one. It is only fitting that, living in a creative universe, we, too, are creators. How exciting that we are able to infuse our own imaginative energy into the ever-present creative force of existence itself!

Together, your individual consciousness aligns with universal consciousness to manifest a shared vision of reality. You consciously cocreate with life every day; your thoughts, ideas, imagination, and intention manifest the rhythms of your life. And your Creative Intuition is the connector of it all.

Through your Creative Intuition, life calls you — moves you. It inspires you, excites you, and opens the doors for you to create your dream life. Have you ever had an idea to do something — and you couldn't rest until you did it? Or felt a call to action that kept nudging you, pushing you, no matter how long you dismissed it? That's your Creative Intuition calling you — the higher version of yourself leading the way — recommending a course of action from its higher, visionary perspective.

This is how new ideas enter the world. Genius ideas and creative vision move from thought to reality by the actions we take to make them real. If we have a great idea for a book, we cocreate by making that book happen — writing it, sharing it with the world. If we are inspired to start a new business, we cocreate when we make that business a reality. Through Creative Intuition, our thoughts, ideas, and imagination become *real.*

Together with the universe, we cocreate in this way. We build, make, design, and create from the place of superconscious inspiration. We build our lives from the intuitions we act upon. Our supreme self sees the beauty of our highest potential and is ever moving us to manifest that energy in our life. This kind of creativity arises from a deep union with our real self, with the knowable and unknowable. Together, the creator and the created share in the process of comanifestation for the greater good of the world. Your creation becomes the living breath of the universe.

This is the twofold practice of intuition: We receive an intuitive impression, *and then we follow it*. We can connect with our supreme self in both stillness and action. We receive inspiration in the stillness, and we act upon it when we live our lives. Intuition remains unfulfilled without both steps. It is a powerful thing to receive insight, but what good is it if we do not honor that wisdom with right action?

RADICAL INSIGHT
The process of intuition is twofold:
first, we become aware of it, then we follow it.

One of the oldest and most powerful icons in history is the yin/yang. Through it, we acknowledge the duality of our world. More than a symbol of light and darkness, energy and matter, feminine and masculine — we live the yin/yang duality every day in our lives. We think and we express; we receive and we give; we are inspired and we create. This is the process of intuitive *being* and *becoming* in our world.

Human life is an interplay of receiving and expressing the energy of the universe: input and output. In yin, we *receive* energy, inspiration, and guidance from life; in yang, we bring that energy through our free will to act. Intuition is the powerhouse behind this cycle — one that empowers our growth and evolution.

Our intuition enables life to create through us. Creative Intuition is our secret muse. It inspires us. It flows through us in the creative act. When we follow our passions, we are possessed only by the creative force. From self-awareness to self-actualization, we become aware of our truth, and we live that truth. Insightfulness is a complete, intuition-based life practice that enables us to both tap into higher wisdom — *and live by it.*

Examples of Creative Intuition

- Being inspired to try something new
- Creating art, music, poetry, or food
- Building a new or successful business
- Standing up for change in the world
- Getting new or innovative ideas
- Accessing artistic genius
- Trendsetting
- Coming up with a new solution
- Leading the way
- Manifesting your best life

Creative Intuition is deeply connected with the process of manifestation. Through the law of attraction, your thoughts, intentions, and imagination attract energy in your life. We are taught to visualize the life we want in order to attract it; if we want prosperity, we imagine the prosperous life of our dreams. If we want true love, we hold space for that love with our conscious intention.

Your thoughts are magnetic. Anything that comes to you is already in you somehow. Every situation and person in your life has been drawn there by a magnetic force inside you — a desire, a fear, a longing, or an unconscious need for a learning experience. You attract love when you become loving; you become successful when you embody success in your actions. Energy follows our consciousness into realization, moving from energetic reality into physical reality. Our loving thoughts turn into loving people and relationships; our passion becomes our successful life purpose.

This is a powerful truth. But the bigger truth is that it is all meaningless without intuition. We can "decide" to manifest anything, but how do we know we are manifesting *the right thing*? We can set our intention on getting that new job or moving to that new place — but how do we know that is our best path? *How do we know what to manifest?*

The answer is simple: We listen to our intuition.

Intuition shows us the difference between the things we *want* and the things we *are meant for*. We can put that Land Rover on the vision board; we can visualize driving it every day; we can meditate on the prosperity it symbolizes. But unless it is in intuitive alignment with our real self, we are wasting our energy — we are distracted by shiny things that eclipse our genuine path and potential.

RADICAL INSIGHT
Intuition isn't about manifesting — it's about manifesting what is right for you.

Energy flows where the attention goes. And your Creative Intuition will show you the best place to put that attention. It compels you to the field of potentiality that is open before you. It draws you into its flow through resonance. Do your goals resonate with you? Or are you following someone else's path?

When you are out of sync with your inner guidance, a subtle sense of dissonance is infused into what you do. Something seems off. You can't get into your groove. Nothing you do seems to work out the way you had hoped or expected. You feel stuck, frustrated, or depleted. You don't know where to go next. You have been too busy following the ways of the world and what other people are doing to get centered on your own right path.

The longer we ignore our inner guidance, the easier it becomes to get lost. We can make all the "right" choices, do all the "right" things, and somehow still feel a million miles away from our truth. Our friends, family, social media, and education can provide us with many roads, but deep inside, only we know which one to take. The world shows us many paths, but intuition shows us *our* path.

ARE YOU FOLLOWING YOUR PASSION?

Without action, there is no change. Without change, there is no growth. To know true wisdom, it's not enough to learn it — we must *experience* it. It's not enough to know the truth; we need to actualize it in our lives. We can't understand love or beauty or joy or truth by reading about it or thinking about it. We need to experience it for ourselves.

As we grow in intuition and become aware of supreme truth, we have a responsibility to honor it. It is our duty to answer the higher call of intuition. Our mission is to do more than discover the truths of life — we are to live by them. *To live by your personal truth is your mission in life.*

My truth is not the same as your truth. One person might live their truth by forsaking material possessions to become "rich" in spirit, while another person's truth might be holding space for prosperity and the power it confers to bring good into the world. One person's truth may be based on living a solitary life, while another person's truth is based on serving others through relationships. Our intuition knows what each of us needs to learn, balance, or grow in order to fully participate in the universal expansion of consciousness.

Regardless of what your truth is, living it requires commitment and courage. Your truth may not be the easy path; *it is the right path*. It is the path of enlightened *doing*. This is the process of self-actualization. As we bring our intuition in alignment with the real self — who we really are — we become actualized. The ephemeral truth becomes real; the idea becomes form; the uncreated is created. Intuition is the power behind this process of actualization. It *moves us* to live our truth.

*Your authenticity is the measure
of your intuitive awakening.*

With intuition comes one of the most invaluable traits of conscious living: authenticity. Our ability to be our one true self is a hallmark of personal growth. Is the person we are inside the same person that we show the world? Are we unafraid to express our true being, or do we hide or repress parts of ourselves according to other people's judgment? Living by our intuition cultivates our true self so that we can become 100 percent authentic with everyone we meet. We will remain true to our self, whether we are with our mother, our spouse, our boss, our teachers, our friends, or anyone else in the world.

What could be more freeing than to be ourselves, unapologetically? This is one of the greatest gifts of intuition. The confidence and self-acceptance that come with intuitive authenticity are among the most life-affirming powers we possess. Living true to your intuition is living with confidence by the highest authority. When you are true to your real self, you have no shame, make no excuses, and will believe in the things you choose to do. *This* is the essence of intuitive living. Your intuition empowers you to *own your life* and every choice you make.

Quiz: Are You Self-Actualized?

To assess how consistently you live your truth, take this short self-assessment, which will give you a general idea of the ways you are (or are not) using your Creative Intuition.

Here, or in a journal, rate the following statements on a scale from 0 to 5, with 5 indicating a strong agreement, and 0 indicating no agreement. Then add up all the numbers and write down the total. The maximum score is 100.

**Rating
(0-5)**

_____ 1. When I get a creative idea, I can't rest until I act on it.

_____ 2. I have fulfilled many dreams in my life...and many more are ahead!

_____ 3. If I died today, I would feel like mine was a life well-lived.

_____ 4. I am exactly the person I want to be.

_____ 5. I thrive on sharing my ideas with others.

_____ 6. My friends love me for who I really am.

_____ 7. I don't feel the need to pretend I am something I am not.

_____ 8. I rarely go against myself with the choices I make each day.

_____ 9. I am able to be myself — the same authentic person — with everyone in my life.

_____ 10. I love what I do.

_____ 11. I am not afraid of change.

_____ 12. It is easy for me to trust in life.

_____ 13. I am passionate about creating new things.

_____ 14. People see me as I really am.

_____ 15. I am always striving to be better.

_____ 16. I feel like I am part of something bigger and greater than myself.

_____ 17. I am at peace with myself.

_____ 18. I am exactly where I am meant to be.

_____ 19. I make myself a priority in my life.

_____ 20. I am fulfilled.

_____ **TOTAL**

Here is how to evaluate your results:

<50: Latent self-actualization – your intuition is calling! You have a deep, powerful calling within you — one you may not be fully aware of or listening to at this moment in life. If you feel lost, or as if you are not yourself, tuning in to your Creative Intuition can get you back on track and reignite your passion for life!

50–69: Emerging self-actualization – your Creative Intuition pathway is opening. You have been listening to your intuition! You have heard the calling inside you and long to fulfill it. You know how powerful it feels to live your truth, and you know that you must make certain changes to fully step into your power. Your Creative Intuition pathway ebbs and flows, growing stronger each time you honor your intuition.

70–89: Becoming self-actualized – your Creative Intuition is thriving. Your intuition is a powerful part of your life. You rely on it regularly and thrive on its creative energy. Now more than ever, you know who you are and are taking the necessary steps to be that person authentically in all of your life. Your Creative Intuition pathway is well-developed and will help you break through any blocks that remain.

>90: Highly self-actualized – you have creative genius. Congratulations! You are mastering your Creative Intuition. You are so highly attuned that you may be prone to moments of genius. You know exactly who you are; the opinions of others don't define you. You trust your ideas and vision, and don't let anyone stand in the way of who you are.

The more your Creative Intuition is flowing, the more fulfilled you become in life. When you know who you are and how to serve the world with your gifts, it is natural that happiness and feelings of accomplishment are side effects of a healthy Creative Intuition.

RADICAL INSIGHT
Happiness is a side effect of living intuitively.

Getting into the Creative Flow

Have there been times in your life that you just felt *out of sync*? Times that felt as if you were living someone else's dreams instead of your own? If you look back, you may notice "good times" when you felt really aligned with your path and other periods when you struggled or felt lost.

What does it feel like when Creative Intuition isn't flowing? When the pathways of Creative Intuition are blocked or lacking energy, we don't feel like ourselves and we aren't energized by the creative forces within us.

Here are some signs of Creative Intuition deficiency:

- Feeling stuck "in a rut"
- Living a life that doesn't feel like "you"
- Experiencing creative blocks
- Lacking life purpose and direction
- Feeling uninspired
- Feeling fearful

The key to opening up these blocked and stagnant pathways of intuition is to release your resistance to it. Let your intuition move you. By "going with the flow," intuitively, you naturally move out of any state of Creative Intuition deficiency.

It is normal on our journey to take some detours. Sometimes we get drawn off our path by our personal obligations; sometimes we lose sight of ourselves out of complacency or by shutting ourselves off to change. Whenever this happens, it is because we are out of our flow. We are stuck — stuck because life is not letting us go any further on the wrong path.

RADICAL INSIGHT
Being "stuck" is not always a bad thing.
When we are off course, stuckness slows us down
so we can get back on track.

Being stuck can be extremely frustrating. We want to go forward, but we can't. We don't have the means or motivation; the doors aren't opening for us. We are being intuitively guided to a different path. Stuckness is a symptom of not heeding an intuitive redirect. It is the by-product of resistance to our inner guidance and truth.

The longer we ignore our intuition, the more we get stuck in our rut — and run the risk of getting caught up in a downward spiral. We've all been there; one thing goes wrong, then another and another, until we find that we have fallen into a low-frequency headspace. We feel defeated, small, powerless. The world itself can seem like it is too much to bear. We may even think we were silly for dreaming any dreams. We are *low*.

But even so, part of us knows we are better than this. So how did this happen? How did we fall out of alignment with life? We were once awake, but at this moment, our minds are hazy and confused. We once felt so alive, but now, our zest for life is dulled by fear, frustration, or doubt in ourselves. How are we so low when once we were so high? The answer is simple: We stopped trusting our inner wisdom.

We made choices based on our fears, conditioning, or personal expectations. We lost the true north of our inner guidance. Maybe we were overthinking or overfeeling. Maybe we were afraid to let go of something. Maybe we were sure of a plan that wasn't truly in our own best interest. When we try to figure it all out in our mind, we forget that we have an intuitive, cocreating partner whose vision far exceeds our own.

But don't despair. Even in the darkest, deepest places, our intuition still calls us. It always has a path back to ourselves, if we are willing to listen. It is ready and waiting, nudging us toward the first step, if we are willing to take it. Intuition will always bring us back to life. If we pay close attention, we will see that it brings us to what we really need; it is only up to us to accept it.

The boundless power of Creative Intuition is alive within you, no matter what life brings. On good days, it is the wind beneath your wings; on bad days, it is the breeze waiting to pick you back up and carry you home. Either way, when you turn yourself over to the flow of life, it is only a matter of time before you soar.

THE VISIONARY
"I Transform."

Element: Fire

Pathway: Emotive (the heart)

Keywords: Passion, inspiration, creativity

Power: Evolutionary change

Blockage: Fear, procrastination, lethargy, conformity, creative blocks

Supporting practices: Self-expression, risk-taking, the creative process

Vocations: Artist, entrepreneur, CEO, tech innovator, creative director, motivational speaker, blogger, community leader, social activist, filmmaker, writer, maker, interior designer, strategist, game designer

Enjoys: Visualization meditation, making art and music, ideating, traveling, adventuring, sharing ideas, shaking things up, dreaming big, learning new things, falling in love

CHAPTER 12

THE VISIONARY'S WORKSHOP

Following Your Passion

Your time is limited, so don't waste it living someone else's
life....Don't let the noise of others' opinions drown out your
own inner voice. And most important, have the courage
to follow your heart and intuition. They somehow already
know what you truly want to become.

— STEVE JOBS

As our intuition shows us a clearer picture of who we are, it also shows us a clearer path for what we are meant to do. By following the call of our intuition, we witness our passion become our purpose. The Visionary's Workshop presents three vital practices to align your life with your truth and to bring your gifts into the world. The workshop is divided into three parts, to be completed in order:

1. **Creative Intuition attunement:** To "activate" our Creative Intuition, we begin by getting into the intuitive flow that empowers our personal evolution and supreme self-expression.

2. **Creative Intuition visualization meditation:** This special "insight" meditation will transform your meditation practice into a revelatory space for new ideas and inspiration.
3. **Creative Intuition practice:** Stream-of-consciousness journaling is a practice that allows you to channel creative ideas and guidance from superconscious to conscious awareness.

RADICAL INTUITION TIP: New ideas, inspiration, and insight naturally flow through Creative Intuition. Set an intention not to edit your insights with your rational mind. Simply allow them to flow into being.

CREATIVE INTUITION ATTUNEMENT

Below are three action steps you can take today — to light the fire of your Creative Intuition, get out of those ruts, and start manifesting the life of your dreams. After you have energized your body with the practices of Physical Intuition attunement and quieted your mind with the practices of Mindful Intuition attunement, you have created a ready, open pathway for your Creative Intuition to inspire you and guide you into intuitive action.

1. Set an Intention to Cultivate Insightfulness

Make creative thinking a habit. You make the shift to "insightful" living by creating a practice of looking within. As you build your life, instead of relying on the advice of friends or doing what other people around you are doing, turn to yourself first. Here are some examples of little ways you can start making a habit of intuition:

• When you are creating something new, don't do the same things other people are doing. Ask yourself: *What can I bring to this that is new and different?*

- Instead of planning your future around preconceived notions of what your life should be, allow life to inspire you and open doors that lead you places beyond your imagination.
- As you manifest your reality, stop listening to the limiting voices in the outside world. Only you know who you really are and what you are made for in this life. If you can dream it, you can do it!
- Ask yourself: *What makes my heart sing?* Go do that.

2. Get Comfortable Outside Your Comfort Zone

Rejuvenate your intuitive and creative energy with new influences. Your comfort zone is a trap. Feeling stuck in it? Well, the best way to break out of that stagnant energy is to *get moving*. Try something new. Do something different to stir things up and bring new energy into your life.

Statistics show that getting outside your comfort zone — connecting with people and situations that are different than you — is the secret sauce to success. The more you infuse your life with energy that is new and different, the more you ignite the forces of evolution. All you need to do is crack open the creative floodgates, and the good vibes will start to flow. Here are a few ways to do that:

- Try something you have never done before.
- Cook up a collaborative project with new people.
- Get up and move...literally. Changing your environment is one of the most powerful ways to change your headspace.
- Take a class to learn something creative or new.
- Follow inspiring people on social media.
- Make friends with interesting people.
- Go to an event where people who are different than you hang out.

Though the move outside your comfort zone may feel daunting at first, you will be happy you did it. When you put yourself into the unknown, you open up space for existence to bring you the unexpected things that just might change your life.

3. Create!

Whatever creative things you like to do, do them a little more often. The small creative rituals you practice each day help to keep the good vibrations manifesting in your life. It's important to flex your Creative Intuition muscles in little ways each day, so that you keep that transformational conduit open and aligned with the upward flow of life. If you are an artist, do your art; if you are a maker, make beautiful things. Even if you think you aren't "creative," here are two ways that anyone can get into the creative flow.

Insight Journaling

What better way to get those creative juices flowing than to give them a pathway through the pen or the keyboard. Write about whatever moves you: your spiritual growth process, your intuition, your relationships, your hopes and dreams, your disappointments — and everything in between. Write poetry, doodle, or record song lyrics that move you.

Journaling regularly gets you into the "creative zone" where big things can happen. You can burn your journal when you are done with it; you don't need to be attached to any outcome. The simple pleasure of letting creativity flow into the world is a valuable exercise for the intuitive process.

Mandala Art

One of the most ancient and powerful creative practices is the mandala. Anyone can create a mandala, and there so many types of mandalas you can create, based on your own affinities. They can be drawn, painted, colored, or built of sand, stones, sticks, beads, flowers, and leaves — or any material you prefer. Both meditative and creative, mandala-making brings you into the present moment to experience the wonder of creation.

Our gift is the creative act itself — the act of selfless connectedness to the supreme unity of all things, as you lose yourself in the moment. This lack of self, the lack of ego and all of the distractions it carries, opens a portal to the beauty, wisdom, and creative spirit that comes from beyond.

MEDITATION: CREATIVE VISUALIZATION

This meditation will open you to inspiration and vitalize your creative spirit.

Begin by creating, in your mind's eye, an inner sanctuary of stillness. Visualize yourself standing on a beautiful, radiant hilltop, high above the everyday world, where the sun is shining bright and you are happy and full of life.

Notice the wide-open skies above and the sun shining and radiating vitalizing energy deep into your being. Basking in its warm, healing glow, feel deeply connected with it, feel how its light touches — empowers — your inner light. Remain there for a few moments.

Then recognize the earth at your feet, alive with life — the beings, flora, and oceans — the beauty of creation. Feel the soft earth beneath your bare feet, grounding you and supporting you with a gentle embrace. Remain there for a few moments.

Next, move back into yourself. See yourself existing between these two beautiful worlds. Imagine yourself as a connector bridging the gap between the earth and the sky, the material and the immaterial, the creation and the idea.

Visualize the creative energy from above cascading over you in a waterfall of light, flowing into and through you, into the world at your feet. Imagine the creative potential, new ideas, inspiration, and genius embedded in a shower of light that penetrates your being.

Imagine this flood of energy dissolving any creative blocks. Do you feel any heavy energy washing away?

Feel it move you. Let it pick you up and carry you away — to a place where you can be the best version of yourself. Where does your intuition take you? What does the best version of yourself look like? Imagine yourself as that person.

Here, be still. Rest for a moment in this place. Feel yourself embody your supreme self — and all of the wisdom, power, healing, and love that comes with it.

In the stillness, open to any insights, ideas, or inspiration that comes to you. What pops into your head in these quiet moments? What ideas come? What feelings do you have? What knowings? Here, in this space, your intuition can speak to you. It can show you all that you can be and guide you to your truth.

It is a great idea to write down any insights or interesting revelations from your meditation right away, while they are fresh in your mind. Like a dream, meditation insight dissolves quickly in the light of rational consciousness. You can continue to journal about your insights if you want to discern any deeper meaning.

CREATIVE INTUITION PRACTICE: INSIGHT JOURNALING

As we have seen, journaling is one of the most powerful ways to open up the Creative Intuition pathway. Insight journaling is a type of stream-of-consciousness "speed" journaling where intuitive guidance is revealed before you have time to think.

The process is this: Ask questions regarding the insight you need, then write down the "first impression" that comes to mind in response. By doing this, you get a raw insight that is unadulterated by your thinking mind. The key to knowing real intuition is always to keep the mind out of the way. By moving into the flow — or the stream of superconscious insight as it flows directly to your consciousness — you can glimpse the answers before your thinking brain tries to answer the questions for you.

To get started, grab your journal and relax. Smile. Then set a conscious intention to connect with the highest truths of existence.

Next, write down a list of questions or use some from the list below to gain insight into your life or a current situation. Try not to anticipate any of the answers to the questions as you write them down; simply record the words in your journal, leaving space for you to write answers after each line.

After writing them down, take a moment to clear your head and disconnect from any problem-solving impulses of the mind. Close your eyes and visualize the waterfall of insight cascading down through your mind's eye. Visualize that the highest wisdom of existence is revealing itself to you in these moments, then open your eyes.

Answer each question on your list within three seconds. If nothing comes, move on to the next question. At the end, go back to any unanswered questions, once your intuition is flowing. Write down any words, thoughts, ideas, or feelings that immediately come to mind, without analyzing them or trying to make sense of anything. Remember, the greatest insights often come in the most unexpected ways!

Here are some insight journaling prompts you can use to discover more about your path and purpose:

- *What are my three best qualities or gifts?*
- *What are my three biggest life challenges?*
- *What was I born to do in this life?*
- *What must I learn in order to evolve?*
- *What is holding me back?*
- *How can I break through my blocks?*
- *How can I fulfill my mission in the world?*

After you finish, feel free to take some time to journal further on your answers while you are still "in the flow." Look back over the questions and consider your responses. Were you surprised by what came to you? Do you sense a level of truth in your answers that you always knew on some level?

You can practice this journaling technique for insight into any situations in your life as they arise. What makes it so effective is how you tune in to that first insight — that first idea that is untainted by your intellectual mind.

THE VISIONARY'S TOOL: THE INTUITIVE VISION BOARD

Sometimes called a "dream board," a vision board is one of the most valuable tools for manifesting your life aspirations. The power of your conscious intention becomes a magnet for the situations you create your life. The more you persevere in your dream — and the more you connect with its energy and align with it — the more likely you are to make it a reality.

But you don't want to build just any vision board. You want to build an intuitive vision board. Your goal is not to manifest what you *want*; your goal is to manifest what you *need*. For example, let's say you feel intuitively called to move or change where you live. All your friends are moving to Florida, and you might *think* you, too, want to move to Florida. The weather is warm year-round. But what if there is a great job offer or new relationship waiting for you in a different city altogether. You don't know, not yet, but your intuition does.

So, instead of creating a vision board for a specific outcome like moving to Florida, create an intuitive vision board — one that embodies the real outcome you are looking for. What you are looking for isn't Florida itself but what Florida might bring to your life — health, happiness, growth, new life. The goal isn't money or material possessions; you are, truly, looking for the freedom, sovereignty, and comfort that a move might bring.

When we create an intuitive vision board, we open to the possibilities. We allow our intuition to draw us to pieces of the future that resonate with us. We allow our intuition to draw us to *our* path. By creating a vision board on that path, we assist the cocreative power of the universe.

You become what you think. A vision board is your constant

reminder to focus your thoughts and intention on what matters most. Each time you look at it, enjoy it, and muse upon it, your thoughts create a tiny energetic beacon to magnetically draw these things to you. With the days and years that pass, as you begin to embody the ideas on your board, you can witness your dreams becoming a reality — sometimes in almost magical ways!

Here are some tips to create your own intuitive vision board. You can create your board on paper or cardboard, or you can create a virtual, electronic vision board on your computer. These make great desktop screen savers!

1. **Start with an insight journaling session:** Ask yourself what you should be attracting right now to take the next steps in your growth and evolution. Ask yourself what you are really looking for. Ask yourself what your best future looks like. List your first insights and journal to make any deeper discoveries.

2. **Assemble your vision:** Go through your favorite magazines or search the internet and collect photos that represent the ideas that you discovered in step 1, along with any other general images that represent the energy you want to bring into your life — health, well-being, love, family, prosperity, success. You can include pictures, words, or phrases — anything that you connect with. Use your inner resonance to guide you to the right images — the ones that *feel* right. Let your intuition guide you. New ideas or places to look for images may pop into your head; be open to possibilities!

3. **Create the board:** Gather all of your images together into a single-page collage. You can do this either by gluing them onto a piece of paper or cardboard or by designing them into an electronic image on your computer. Be creative and lay out your board in a way that is visually pleasing to you. Feel free to add ornamentation or any design elements that make you really love looking at your board.

4. **Display your intuitive vision board:** Once you have finished and are pleased with the way your board looks, post it somewhere prominent, where you will notice it often. Look at it regularly. Enjoy it. Daydream on it. Keep reaffirming your connection with its energy and your intention to make it a reality in your life.

The more energy you put into affirming your board, the stronger the powers of manifestation move through it. It may take days, weeks, or years, depending on your particular vision, but if you believe, it will come.

CHAPTER 13

TRANSCENDENTAL INTUITION

Your True Being

*The ultimate truths of heaven... the reality that lies behind
sensory perception and beyond the cogitations of the
rationalizing mind, can only be grasped by intuition —
awakening the intuitive knowing,
the pure comprehension, of the soul.*

— PARAMAHANSA YOGANANDA

Your true guru is within you... it *is you*. Our greatest teacher is inside of us. We can spend a lifetime trying to understand the meaning of our life. We turn to religion, philosophy, teachers, and traditions, without realizing that all of the answers we seek are within. Every choice, every piece of information, every idea — we can find it all by tuning in to our inner wisdom.

Admittedly, for many of us, that connection can be a bit fuzzy. At least at first. Each of us has our own connection to the vast, ethereal internet of universal information — the more you open to that connection, and use it, the clearer your signal becomes. Like the internet, your inner wisdom is not limited by proximity in time or space: It can connect to anywhere in the world in an instant. Working on a quantum level, its knowingness can penetrate all things; its awareness is boundless.

RADICAL INSIGHT
You *are the teacher you have always been looking for.*

Recognizing your sovereignty is part of a seismic shift in your consciousness. You may have needed teachers and guides to get you to this moment, but the moment you realize that you are, indeed, the teacher behind all teachers, you are truly awake for the first time.

Paramahansa Yogananda says that the "second coming" *is within us.* That's how important he says intuition is. He published nearly two thousand pages on how our intuitive power is the key to resurrecting the supreme state of consciousness *within us.* We are always thinking that someone will come along and save us, but the truth is that we are here to save ourselves. No one can save you but you — supported by the uplifting, guiding power of your inner wisdom.

Even if you read the best books, even if you meditate every day and go through all the motions of a conscious life, none of that matters if you aren't connected to your place of inner power.

Whether we consciously recognize it or not, many of us are conditioned to think that if we aren't meditating regularly, or if we aren't participating in what have now become "traditional" spiritual practices — like doing yoga, following an Eastern religion, or having an enlightened spiritual teacher — we aren't on the path of spiritual growth.

The ancient scriptures and the sacred rituals do, indeed, provide a framework for our salvation, but they are, when all is said and done, an external knowledge system that the world has given us. Like all knowledge systems, they can only take you so far; they can only take you to the point where you go within to your inner self.

You will only discover true enlightenment by moving into the deep inner knowing of your intuition. *The truth is within you.* Everything else is just information along the way. You can cultivate mindfulness to create space for your inner guidance; you can meditate so you can hear the stillness speak. You can eat healthily and practice yoga to attune your body to the intuitive flow; you can practice good works and rituals to maintain a high-vibration existence. You can serve others and the world. But all of these practices share one singular end goal: the soul-evolving, intuitive communion with the omnipresent God-source.

INTUITION AND THE SPIRIT

We have the power to be free. We have the power to rise above this world. Our intuition is more than simply a guide or a muse; it holds our power to transcend the world that we often mistake for true reality. At our core, we are each a sovereign consciousness unbound by space and time — one that continues to exist, even when our physical body doesn't. Our true self is our supreme self, and our intuition is how we find it and become it.

The real you speaks through your silent, intuitive inner knowings and feelings. With intuition, there is no need for words. There is only the pure, unimpeded connectedness of intuitive understanding — with yourself and, ultimately, with others. Your intuition bridges this reality and the realities beyond. When your time on the physical earth is over and your consciousness moves into the metaphysical realities, do you suppose you will speak a particular language — English, Spanish, or Chinese? No, you will speak the language of intuition — the one language that all living beings share.

This is why developing your intuition is one of the most important things you will ever do: It doesn't just serve you in this life; it serves you for all life. Intuition is how you *know* without using a brain; it is how you *feel* without having a heart; it is how you speak without using words. It is the interconnected recognition of the Supreme in one another. You may forget the things you learn in this life; you will certainly, one day, have to leave behind the things you earned. But once you find it, you will never lose your intuition.

RADICAL INSIGHT
Your intuition is the one thing you take with you
when you leave this world.

When we understand that intuition is a function of consciousness itself, we can't be separated from it. To be conscious is to be intuitive. The more unconscious we are, the less intuitive we are; the more superconscious we are, the more intuitive we are. If any aspect of our being survives physical death or has preceded it in lives before, it has done so with intuitive consciousness.

How do we speak without mouths? How do we perceive without eyes? How do we know without brains? Beyond physical life, we have no physical body or senses, but we do have our intuitive body and senses. We can still experience the world from the inside — with our supersensory intuitive experience. We already know this is possible because we see, hear, sense, feel, and create magical worlds every night in our dreams. Countless people who return from comas and near-death experiences report vivid intuitive experiences when their bodies are nonfunctional.

Our intuition comes with us wherever we go, from moment to moment and even life to life. This would explain our natural talents and gifts — childhood prodigies and inexplicable genius. When we cultivate this intuitive richness, it becomes part of us, embedded in our eternal being. If you believe in reincarnation, you can envision the vast expanse of lives, intuitively building one upon the other, with talents, skills, and affinities that remain with us — and continue to develop and evolve — from life to life. The time you spend in this life, enriching your soul, is never wasted;

your experiences become part of you. They live on as testaments to the evolution of your undying, ever-living consciousness.

As you grow in your supreme self, the Supreme grows into you. Enlightenment isn't something you learn; it is something you *become.* You grow into enlightenment by *evolving into it.* You can see the truth when you let go of your illusions. You feel the ultimate love when you open your heart to others. The only way to find your true self is by becoming it — through the trials and triumphs of intuitive self-actualization.

This is what life wants for us all — to be perfect. To become perfect — or rather, to return to perfection. Life calls us to wash off the dust of the world — the pain, the suffering, the fears, and the ignorance — and rediscover the beautiful and powerful being we truly are. Enlightenment is no faraway land; it is right here, inside of us. It is just waiting for us to return to it with the power of our soul-forging intuition.

RADICAL INSIGHT
Enlightenment is not a goal to be attained;
it is a state of being to be regained.

It doesn't help matters that the whole idea of spiritual enlightenment has become larger than life in modern times. Many of us are reluctant to even aspire to such unreachable heights. We think: *How could a regular person like me possibly become an enlightened being?* We are often taught that enlightenment is a badge of honor reserved for only the greatest of souls — the saints, the buddhas, the holy mystics. But here is the reality:

1. **All beings are made to experience enlightenment:**
   Enlightenment is your native state. It is your highest level of consciousness, the omnipresent part of your being that is unfettered by the trappings and limitations of material

reality. It is what, deep inside, we all long for. But instead of looking for it, we often try to replace it with worldly supplications — money, romance, ambition, physical comforts. Enlightenment is ours, and it is the natural progress of our consciousness to seek it.

2. **Enlightenment is not an all-or-nothing experience:** Many of us make the mistake of thinking that — poof! — great people just magically become enlightened and forever live their lives from the majestic hilltop of ultimate wisdom. While this is certainly possible in extraordinary cases, the reality is that enlightenment ebbs and flows into our consciousness throughout our life. As long as we are living in space and time, we live in the environment of change — and evolution. Our degrees of enlightenment can expand and grow over time, just as our consciousness does. Enlightenment, like awakenings, can be an incremental process.

It is a trick of the world to think we are not worthy of enlightenment — that we should think we aren't *enough* for it. This kind of conditioning is manufactured by a world that does not want you to become enlightened. The idea of enlightenment as an unattainable reality is perpetuated by those who want you to remain in the limited reality of your egoic mind, by those who want to control you. The world doesn't want you to become truly enlightened because enlightenment is freedom.

THE MYSTIC ARCHETYPE: THE DEPTHS OF BEING

If you show a natural affinity for Transcendental Intuition, you have most likely felt the call of mystical experience throughout your life. You have an innate attraction to the supreme realms of existence and a longing to return there. It is as if part of you has known, for your whole life, that you belong somewhere else.

From a young age, you may have had metaphysical experiences or a desire to learn about life's mysteries. You are not satisfied with the knowledge systems of this world, and you realize that the greatest wisdom, joy, and beauty can be found simply by going within. Deep inside of you, there is a love that others have forgotten. No matter where you go or what you do in the world, the remembrance of that connection lives on as your "first love," your love before all other loves.

As a Mystic, you have the ability to commune with that supreme love. You personally experience what others learn about and talk about. You live close to *the beyond*, and your uplifted vibrational experience gives you a heightened perception of the world. This supreme awareness has the power to lead you to great spiritual gifts, blissful mastery of life, and enlightenment itself.

You have most likely experienced a powerful awakening at some point in your life. You understand and value the deep, meaningful nature of existence. You are also sensitive to dimensional layers of your being. You might have spiritual experiences that you do not fully understand or that other people do not understand. You, more than others, have the potential to deeply experience life's mysteries and wisdom.

To be a Mystic means *to become one with the mystery of life.*

The secrets of the inner unknown, the compelling, new frontiers of consciousness, the great heights of ascension — these are the realms of the Mystic. Here, you feel at home. Here, you bring light to the mysteries and lead humanity forward into the expansion of consciousness. You are a fearless beacon of light, guiding the pathway to our superconscious evolution.

Love is the energy that vibrates through Transcendental Intuition. The unifying truth beyond all illusion of separation — supreme love — is the driving force behind the ascension of our consciousness and the progress of humanity. The purpose of this kind of intuition is to bring the world together — back together — into wholeness, oneness.

Transcendental Intuition unites us with one another; it unites us with God. When you embrace the light of your intuition, you are uplifted. Your mind is transcendent; your heart overflows with bliss. When this intuitive pathway is open and strong, the extraordinary can become the ordinary way of life. When you live each moment in the presence of omnipresence, you can, at last, become accustomed to knowing the unknowable and experiencing the impossible.

The Seeds of Enlightenment

Even if you have never had a life-changing awakening or mystical experience, the seeds of enlightenment are alive within you. If you want to check in with yourself on the unfolding of your enlightenment, ask yourself these two questions right now:

1. **Do you love?** Is it easy for you to love others? Despite all of the heartaches, disappointments, and misunderstandings — are you able, still, to love other living beings? More importantly, do you love yourself? Do you recognize the beautiful masterpiece that you are — instead of only seeing the things the world says you are not.
2. **Do you feel loved?** It has been said that joy is the harbinger of God. The presence of happiness, blissfulness, and the loving support of the world aligns you with your highest vibrational state of being. Moving into gratitude and openness to receive the beauty around you is key to your evolution.

This is so important because our ability to experience and radiate love is directly proportional to our potential to elevate. The more we rise up, the more we are able to love; the more we love, the more we are able to rise up. Recognizing the Supreme in yourself and in those around you is a crucial milestone in the process of enlightenment. If you don't have love, you can't have true enlightenment.

Growing into Enlightenment

If you have an inner calling to transcend this world, you are not alone. So many of us long to break through the boundaries of unconsciousness. For some, this happens naturally, spontaneously; for others, it takes time and devotion.

Whatever the case, one simple principle determines how we experience the levels of reality: We can only experience the level of reality that aligns with our frequency of consciousness. In other words, our vibrational level is directly proportional to our level of intuitive consciousness. When you are down on life, feeling "low" or unenergetic, of course you are unable to tune in to the higher vibrational frequencies of power until you lift yourself up. When you are "high on life," nothing can stop you from experiencing and manifesting the beauty of existence.

This ascent is not always a linear process. You can step up and fall back. You can go sideways from time to time. Sometimes, when you don't even know you are looking for it, enlightenment finds you. And if you are looking for it, you don't need to meditate atop the highest mountains to find it. You discover it by unearthing the buried parts of your true self and bringing them back to life.

Often, people get frustrated because they meditate and meditate — yet nothing comes. This is because they are putting their energy in the wrong place. It is not enough just to hold space for it. You have to *attune to it*. When you are attuned, it will come. Attunement is the real secret to enlightenment. It is the gift that meditation brings. Through meditation — in the calm of presence and stillness — we are able to attune our energetic frequency to align with our truth, but it is not the only way. The process of growth, the expansion of consciousness through direct life experience, can gift us with the soul-elating breakthroughs that shift us instantly into the enlightened state.

RADICAL INSIGHT
*Meditation is not a necessary practice
to enter into enlightenment; it is, however,
a necessary practice to remain in it.*

It can be surprising to learn that, for many, the first taste of enlightenment is completely unrelated to meditation. It is quite possible for a person who has never meditated in their life to experience superconscious illumination. There are many catalysts for this transcendent shift. It can arrive on the wings of a spiritual breakthrough, or even a breakdown. Whatever the case, it arrives when we are ready — when we have made the shifts within ourselves that free us from worldly bondage.

But even after we are free — even in the glow of illuminated revelation — we need to work to stay free. Our growth process can lift us up, above the world, but our work, still, is in the world — and we must return to it. Sometimes enlightenment touches us, even if for only a moment, to let us know that it exists — just to remind us of our real home. Once we have found ourselves in the loving embrace of the universe, we want nothing more than to return to it.

So how do we find our way back to our moments of divine illumination? How do we reenter the supreme reality and reconnect with our whole self? You have the ability to do this anytime and anyplace through the practice of meditation. It is your portal to, and back to, enlightenment. Through sincere meditation practice and devotion, you can find peace, heal, raise your vibration, and ascend to higher levels of being. In deep meditation, you are intuitively guided to return to your inner paradise — where the stillness speaks — and to your place of peace and power. The more you enter into this place, the easier it becomes to carry its wisdom and ease through all you do.

The ability to carry the ease of inner stillness, of attunement to your supreme self, into all that you do is the mark of enlightened being. This is how we conquer the world. To be in peace, to remain in the eye of the storm, no matter what tempests come our way — true to ourselves and to life — this is real power.

THE INNER FRONTIER

The power of Transcendental Intuition is held in one word: *experience*. You don't "get it" by reading or learning about it — you experience it. This is the hallmark of the great mystics — the ability to know God, our supreme source, through inner experience. As we have seen over and over in this book, the teachings of the mind and the world will always be limited because they ask us to follow that which exists *outside of us*. All those things — the lessons, the guidelines, the teachings — can be sacred in their own right, but until we know — *and experience for ourselves* — the reality behind those things, we have not yet stepped into our full potential as human beings.

Transcendental Intuition makes the unreal *real*. Through direct experience, an ethereal and limitless universe becomes extraordinarily personal. The universe touches us personally; we participate in it personally. We don't think something is real because we read about it; we don't believe something is real because we have faith; we *know* it is real because we experience it.

Our intuition offers more than the rational mind can comprehend. It offers more than the novelty of just witnessing hidden realities. It offers the consummate joy of finding home in those realities. With your intuition, you can do more than simply unveil life's mysteries; you participate in that mystery.

RADICAL INSIGHT
The final frontier is the inner frontier.

You, yourself, are the greatest mystery of the universe. The most profound mysteries of existence live inside. Through your inner consciousness, you have a pathway to all things. When you apply that consciousness to the outside world, it is limited by the bounds of that finite world; the real frontier is the inconceivable multidimensionality of your inner superconsciousness.

Becoming Multidimensional

With Transcendental Intuition, you participate, at once, in both presence and omnipresence. In the mindful stillness of consciousness, you embody the power of the present moment; you, the personal, single-pointed expression of universal consciousness, have sovereignty over the world around you. You conquer the past and the future; you claim your unshakable peace. But the present moment is not the end; it is just the beginning.

Presence is the gateway to the beyond. From deep, deep in the stillness, insight calls to you. It reveals to you. And if you pay close enough attention, it will show you the way to truths that are beyond your imagination. Through insight, presence becomes omnipresence. The individual knows the universal; the finite knows the infinite; the created knows the creator. When you experience Transcendental Intuition, the magnificence of omnipresent being touches you personally. Here, you do more than know or feel the Supreme — you recognize that you are part of the Supreme.

Here are signs you have experienced Transcendental Intuition:

- You embody an unshakable sense of inner peace.
- You have had mystical experiences — visions, waking dreams, "angelic" visitations, or experiences with higher, often rationally unexplainable levels of consciousness.
- You are comforted by a profound acceptance and trust in the way of the universe.
- You have felt at one with the perfect bliss of unity with existence.

- You have experienced the most powerful upward vibrational shift of your life.

The most obvious signature of Transcendental Intuition is its upward vibrational shift. You feel better. Healed. Whole — as if you have found your "perfect fix." You may even wonder how anything in the world ever got you down. In this heavenly state of existence, nothing but the best and most wonderful can touch you. The low-vibration energy of fear, confusion, and suffering can't reach you while you are bathed in the luminosity of omnipresent unity.

This is why we do this work: to return to the *state of grace* — to our unbroken, intuitive awareness of the spirit within us. When you combine the highest wisdom of the world with the highest wisdom of your inner guidance, you can see, at last, that the extraordinary gifts of awakening and enlightenment have been inside you all along.

BECOMING TRANSCENDENTAL

The experience of intuitive transcendence usually comes in one of two ways: It arrives unexpectedly, with a life-altering experience that shakes the foundation of your reality. Or it grows incrementally stronger, day by day, as you intentionally evolve into a higher state of awareness. The former comes with great breakthroughs, in the rare transformational moments when you expand your consciousness in leaps and bounds; the latter comes through devotion, right action, and the longing to rediscover a lost part of your being.

Both the spontaneous and gradual openings of your Transcendental Intuition pathway are linked, intrinsically, to the evolution of your consciousness. If you long to experience the reality beyond this one, you must make the conscious shift away from your external world and into the universe within you. This means not only letting go of the entanglements and distractions of the outside world; it means releasing the energetic weight of low-vibration thoughts and feelings like fear, judgment, resentment, unforgiveness, and anger.

Your physical body suffers with sickness, injury, and pain; your metaphysical body suffers with negative thoughts, feelings, and ignorance. When you release the low-vibration energy that you have been carrying for years or even decades, you allow yourself to, finally, heal on the deepest level. This spiritual healing not only creates an energetic environment for your body to heal, but it opens the pathway of spiritual intuition. When this happens, life, as you know it, is never the same.

Transcendental Intuition is, truly, the gateway to heaven. This is not the heaven above our bodies, among the stars and constellations; it is the heaven above our consciousness, made up of transcendent realities that can only be known through our intuition. When this gateway opens, we gain the ability to perceive and experience vibrations that were previously imperceptible to us.

A flourishing Transcendental Intuition pathway opens our body, mind, and heart to unprecedented expressions of superconscious reality.

The Transcendent Body

Some of the earliest stirrings of Transcendental Intuition are felt in the physical body. As this intuitive pathway opens, you may begin to sense the following:

- **A physical energetic shift:** These can feel like waves of electricity, pins and needles, or a variety of other energetic anomalies as your physical body attunes to a higher frequency. This often happens at night when we are resting — when our body has a chance to "acclimate" to a new vibrational level.
- **Your "third eye" activating:** It's not unusual, as you begin to channel superconscious energy, to feel the energetic

activation of your mind's intuitive center. As superconscious energy flows more powerfully through your mind, you may feel a slight tingling in the area on your forehead, above and in between your eyes. You can also feel this energy as a subtle tickling sensation on the tip of your nose.

The Transcendent Mind

As your Transcendental Intuition grows stronger and you become comfortable with the superconscious connection, your sphere of perception expands. As your intuition begins to flow strong, you may notice the following:

- An ability to perceive new, transcendent realities: *Yes, you did see that. Yes, that was real.* These are the things you may catch yourself saying as you, in effect, become "supernatural." This is the reality of life after a Transcendental Intuition activation. You have a very real capacity to see what was once unseeable, know what was once unknowable, and feel what was once imperceptible.
- You perceive energy fields around the physical bodies of living beings.
- You know things that are happening beyond your location in time and space.
- You become aware of the presence of nonphysical living beings.

We have witnessed this process at work, even in the testaments of ancient scripture. In the bible, we hear transcendental intuition echo in words like these: "I will pour out my spirit upon all mankind. Your sons and daughters shall prophesy, your old men shall dream dreams, your young men shall see visions; even upon the servants and handmaids...I will pour out my spirit" (Joel 3:1–5). Intuition is understood — then as it is now — as a sacred gift of the higher power.

The Transcendent Heart

The ultimate manifestation of your Transcendental Intuition is the way you feel inside. As you live in communion with superconscious energy, you naturally feel the following:

- **The deepest peace of your life:** Transcendental Intuition flows on the vibrations of inner peace. It brings with it an unshakable calm and trust in life. It is ultimately reassuring — supportive of all that you are.
- **The highest love of your life:** The more you immerse yourself in the ever-deepening pool of heavenly vibration, the more its love fills up your heart. In some moments, you are consumed with an intense feeling of universal connectedness and an ever-uplifted spirit. The most powerful gift of enlightenment is this reconnection — this return to the loving embrace of the universe.

Your Transcendental Intuition will manifest in its own way. Don't expect it to fit into any mold or standardized process; it reacts to your consciousness in its unique evolutionary moment in time.

EXTRAORDINARY PEOPLE, EXTRAORDINARY INSIGHT

Your Intuition Will Lift You Up, and Uplift the World

Intuition is something inside of us that has been forgotten, not something outside of us that we need to learn. It's so deeply ingrained within us that it has been covered up with the stuff of life – the many things we need to "unlearn" in order to return to that simplicity.

A yoga and meditation practice helps us to create more space for intuition to come in. There are two main energy currents in the body: the current of *liberation*, which is energy moving up; and the current of *manifestation*, which is energy moving down. In one, we are able to intuit and connect with new ideas; in the other, we are able to actually put that energy into practice. We need to balance both to be effective in the world and be changemakers.

In this way, we can all become teachers, first for ourselves and then for those around us. This is how we uplift one another. When we do this, there is new information at every frequency of energy; the more you uplift yourself, the more you open yourself up to new information that can help you make better choices.

This is the counterbalance to the technology age we are living in and to the stressors that we experience, more than ever before. It is part of the shift we are in right now. It's just going to get bigger and stronger. We need more people to step up and start leading – each one of us taking our self, and each other, to that highest level of evolution.

– **Brett Larkin,** world-renowned yoga teacher
and founder of Uplifted Yoga

THE ART OF ASCENSION

How do you experience God? This is a fundamental question of Transcendental Intuition. How do we know that we have touched the ultimate essence of being? Most importantly, what can we do to stay in communion with the highest of highs?

For each of us, the answer is different. You might feel the supreme presence in wilderness, in the blissful quiet of a solitary hike. Or you might find it deep inside your meditation or during your yoga or flow practice. You might feel the soul-warming touch of the universe in the love you feel for the people and creatures of this world. You could discover its light in an extraordinary moment of blissful joy or even in the evolutionary pain of breaking the grip of your ego.

Whatever the case and whatever the situation, there is one common thread to all "heavenly" experience: intuition. Your Transcendental Intuition is the only function that is designed to reach that high and far beyond our conscious reality. This is its singular purpose. Your Transcendental Intuition plugs you back into your source — reconnecting you with the vitality, wisdom, and creativity of your sacred origins. It elevates you, uplifts you; it amps up your vibration, from consciousness to superconsciousness.

Ways That We Experience Transcendental Intuition

- Visions, lucid dreams, and metaphysical experiences
- Feeling at one with the universe as a whole
- Divine ecstasy
- Spiritual raptures
- Superconscious revelations
- Witnessing life beyond life
- Complete trust in and acceptance of existence
- Awareness of higher realities
- Multidimensional perception beyond space and time
- Wonder in the beauty of creation
- Unconditional and limitless love
- Intuitive understanding of the meaningful nature of life

The tricky part about Transcendental Intuition is that you can't simply *will* it to happen. (At least not at first.) You can't sit down one night and think: *Tonight, I am going to have a metaphysical experience that reveals to me the mysteries of life.* When we begin to open up our pathways of Transcendental Intuition, it may seem unpredictable, often surprising us when it arrives. Like all genuine intuition, it comes out of the blue. It simply arrives when the time is right.

Many of us close off the Transcendental Intuition pathway as we grow up. We are born with it wide open; when we are children, we see and experience the wonders of our imagination, and so much more. But the more "mature" we become, the more reality requires us to shut off that valve, so that we can function like "normal" people in the world.

But when we turn off our access to higher reality, we close ourselves off to an entire dimension of our existence. There comes a time, once we have mastered everyday reality, when we are ready to remember and integrate the whole reality of our existence. The years of denying it weigh upon us, whether we are conscious of it or not. We know, on some level, that a part of us is missing. We feel, on some level, like we are living half a life.

Here are signs of a Transcendental Intuition deficiency:

- Self-loathing or despair
- A lack of love or compassion for other people
- Overconcern for material comforts or worldly achievement
- Feeling alone or cut off from the world
- A sense of meaninglessness or lack of purpose

If you aren't feeling great in your life right now, don't worry — we all feel out of sync from time to time. It's a natural reaction to the challenges and growth that life brings. Our task is to pull ourselves up and out of misalignment, no matter how bad it gets, so that we can experience the implicit well-being of an enlightened life. If you are feeling small, low, or not like yourself, this can be a cumulative effect of unconscious choices and the resistance to the higher calling of your Transcendental Intuition.

When the flow of this intuitive pathway is cut off, we, too, feel cut off from life. We feel unsupported, disconnected, low. We can find it difficult to love ourselves and other people — and to shine our light into the world. This is the real existential crisis of modern times. We have separated from the full nature of our being. We have tricked ourselves into thinking what we see is what we are. But as we evolve through our lives, and our calling grows stronger, we are drawn to reintegrate the truth into our lives — the truth that our reality exists as part of a vast and higher reality. Transcendental Intuition is our link to that reality and to the magic that it holds.

THE MYSTIC
"I Rise Above."

Element: Water

Pathway: Energetic (the spirit)

Keywords: Ascension, unity, love

Power: Experience of superconscious reality

Blockage: Personal ambition, lovelessness, distrust, unforgiveness

Supporting practices: Loving-kindness, service, spiritual practice

Vocations: A "servant to the world," yogi, monk, spiritual teacher, minister, nun, guru, mentor

Enjoys: Transcendental Meditation, retreats, nature, simplicity, daydreaming, listening to music, being alone, smiling

CHAPTER 14

THE MYSTIC'S WORKSHOP

Going Above and Beyond

It is awakening, enlightenment, and the amazing intuitive
grasp by which [we gain] certitude of God's creative and
dynamic intervention in our daily life.
— THOMAS MERTON

As we cultivate insightfulness in our life, we become more aware of a deep inner longing to transcend the realities of this life. The more we embody the intuitive state of being, the more naturally we experience higher dimensions of being. The Mystic's Workshop presents three vital practices for making the shift into superconscious awareness and experiencing, firsthand, the mysteries of life. The workshop is divided into three parts, to be completed in order:

1. **Transcendental Intuition attunement:** To "activate" our Transcendental Intuition, we begin by identifying the heavy psychological energy that holds us back, then we release it to uplift ourselves.

2. **Transcendental Intuition meditation:** During this practice, we create a high-frequency inner sanctuary that

allows us to enter into the vibration of transcendent realities.

3. **Transcendental Intuition practice:** This practice will help us get and stay attuned to the loving embrace of the universe.

RADICAL INTUITION TIP: You can't attract anything to you that's not already inside you. To thrive in the loving wisdom of higher awareness, you must become loving and wise.

TRANSCENDENTAL INTUITION ATTUNEMENT

There is one simple practice that wise ones of all kinds use for moving into a higher state of being. This is a secret shared by the monks, yogis, saints, and great teachers of all time. It is so simple that it consists of only five letters: *smile.*

Your smile is the physical embodiment of bliss itself. With a smile, we rise above our pain; a smile reconnects us with the intrinsic joy of existence. A smile is both a powerful meditation tool and a remedy for life's ills. It is an instant energy shift — a realignment with the lightness of being.

The Power in a Smile

Have you noticed that, when we see the Buddha deep in meditation, he so often has a joyful smile on his face? That smile is not only a reflection of his deep state of God-communion but an actual meditation technique that has been used by monks for centuries. When you smile in meditation, you activate a very real connection with the blissful peace of higher awareness. Your smile is like an instant portal to the light of being. When you carry that smile through into your life, you bring light to everyone who sees it.

Here are some ways to use a smile to lift yourself up:

- Begin and end your meditations with a smile. Try to keep smiling during your entire meditation, if possible. This smile will anchor you to the high vibrations above.
- Cultivate "resting smile face." Have you ever caught yourself doing something mindless with an ugly frown on your face? Our facial expressions unconsciously reflect what is going on inside us. Each time we set an intention to smile, we transmute low energy we may not even be aware of.
- When dealing with difficult people, try keeping a warm smile on your face. A smile often brings with it an ease that helps resolve situations peacefully and diffuse confrontation.

Consciously smiling doesn't mean "faking" a smile. It means a real, loving, warm smile that lights you up from inside — a smile that brings a twinkle to your eye. You can feel a good smile radiating from your heart. Its energy is magnetic. It draws people to you; it draws energy to you. And it draws you into the infinite.

MEDITATION: A PORTAL TO THE INFINITE

Transcendental Meditation is a portable portal to superconsciousness. The only place you need to go to experience it is *inside*. You can use the practice below to attune yourself with the energy of illuminated truth and higher awareness.

Begin by greeting yourself with a gentle, loving smile. Feel this smile shift your energy into the lightness of your true being.

In your mind's eye, create or return to your "happy place" — your inner sanctuary of stillness — an illuminated place of peace and power where you are free to commune with the highest realities of existence.

Imagine yourself standing at the gateway of enlightenment. Its light shines all around you. Envision yourself in this majestic place, immersed in the brilliant rays of cosmic healing, truth, power, and love. This radiates from within, unlike any other light you have ever known. It is infused with the omnipresent wisdom of the universe. Feel the radiant bliss shining inside you and through you. Feel it heal you. Feel it rejuvenate you. Feel yourself coming alive from its touch. Be in this moment. Soak it all in. Feel your vibration rising. Feel yourself being uplifted to a higher frequency of perception. Feel yourself harmonize with it and become one with the great ocean of universal expression.

Notice that you are becoming your "real" self. Feel boundless and unentangled by life. You are healed, whole, with a heart brimming with love — love for yourself, love for your life, and love for the world. Feel restored to your original nature.

This is who you really are. Look at the world through these eyes. Look at all the possibilities. See how the world looks different through this new lens.

Ask yourself:

- *What is my purpose in this world?*
- *How can I take the next step in my growth?*
- *What can I do to make the world better?*

Allow the answers to arrive intuitively, in their own way. Be cognizant of the pathways of intuition and how your higher consciousness can use them to communicate with you in this inner sanctuary. Remain here as long as you like, until you have absorbed the insight meant for you today.

When you are ready, you can seal your meditation with a smile and a closing mantra:

Let the light shine bright within me
And brighten the light of the world.

TRANSCENDENTAL INTUITION PRACTICE:
CREATING A SADHANA

The goal of a Transcendental Intuition practice is to keep your body, mind, heart, and spirit uplifted so that you move into and stay in a higher state of awareness. One of the best ways to do this is to create a sadhana, or daily spiritual practice, that attunes all four of your intuitive pathways to the flow of extraordinary insight.

Your Personal Intuition Practice

Here are some tips to help you create a regular intuitive ritual that works for you:

- Try to practice two to three times per week minimum. Once each day is ideal; twice a day is exceptional.
- The best time to practice is whenever you have time to practice. We are all busy, so find whatever time works for you and stick to it. Morning rituals can be an uplifting way to set the energy for the day; evening rituals can be a helpful way to relieve stress and unwind at the end of the day.
- Be sure to select a high-vibration space where you can be alone and get lost in the moment without interruption. Doing your routine outside or near a bright window connects you to soul-revitalizing nature; dark rooms or basements can make it more difficult to raise your vibration. If you are working in one of those spaces, turn on as much light as possible and consider supplementing your practice with uplifting music or aromatherapy.
- Your practice can be anywhere from ten minutes to two hours, depending on where you are in your life. A short practice is always better than no practice.

There is no single formula for creating your daily practice. Below is a framework for designing a unique ritual that aligns with your personal talents, affinities, and interests. To build the best routine, just follow your intuition.

A Framework for Your Intuition Practice

Ideally, you want to create a practice for each intuitive pathway, each type of intuition. Structuring a regular practice around the four pathways of intuition — physical, mental, emotive, and spiritual — will enable you to keep all aspects of your being balanced and energized. Use the four-step framework below, and pick and choose the practices that serve you best.

1. **Unblocking and getting into the flow:** The first part of your practice is a warm-up to get your intuitive juices flowing. Be sure to do the appropriate physical warm-ups as you begin to move your body. Choose from any of these great practices, all of which you can do on your own: yoga, Qigong, walking, deep breathing, gentle stretching, dance, running, and working out. Moving your body helps unblock stagnant energy so your intuitive pathways flow freely.

2. **Quieting the mind:** The next part of your practice helps relax and calm your brain — to let go of worldly demands and distractions so you can focus on the here and now. Here are some ideas for activities you can practice: mindful meditation, breath work, sitting in stillness, saying a mantra, using a mala. You can use any technique that works for you to help you enter into the ease of inner peace.

3. **Receiving insight:** The third part of your practice is to open up to insight — from the unblocked flow of your inner stillness, the silence speaks. Consider asking life for an "instant insight" or a little sign to point you to the lesson you are learning today. Choose from these practices: insight meditation, Insight Cards practice, insight

journaling. Use any or all of these practices — whatever best gets you into the intuitive flow.

4. **Uplifting your spirit:** Finally, the most important part of your ritual is to charge your superconscious battery. Plug back into your supreme being to revitalize your spirit and energize your expansion of consciousness. Here are some ways to do that: practice presence, listen to uplifting music, appreciate beauty, practice transcendental meditation, smile. Do whatever keeps your frequency aligned with the good things in the world.

THE MYSTIC'S TOOL: THE INVOCATION

An invocation is a petition to life to support our journey — in this case, our journey to our real self, our real power, and our real home. To reconnect with your inner fire, read or say this invocation (or modify it as you wish) whenever you long to consciously reconnect with your highest state of being:

Truth, awaken within me.
Illuminate me with your presence.
Shine your light into all the dark places.
Reveal to me.

Shower me with the light of your peace and understanding.
Show me the way to my highest path.
Move me closer to you, in passionate inspiration.
Uplift my being with your radiant joy.
Infuse my body with your healing light.
Infuse my mind with the light of wisdom.
Infuse my heart with creative passion.
Infuse my spirit with loving-kindness.
Truth, come alive within me.
Set me free in you.

CHAPTER 15

OWNING YOUR POWER

Trust in yourself, then you will know how to live.

— JOHANN WOLFGANG VON GOETHE

There are two defining moments in your life: the moment you become aware of your true potential — and the moment you own it. Now, you are ready to do both. You are ready to use your power of insight to step into your true life. You can see what you are meant to become, not just who you are. You know there is more to the world — and more to you — than any of us can imagine with our limited, earthly consciousness. And you recognize the possibilities in a wondrous new reality — one that calls you from ahead.

Now that you have a multidimensional understanding of intuition and the many ways that it uplifts you, you can make real change in your life. You can use your Physical Intuition to create well-being and heal your life. You can use your Mindful Intuition to cultivate peace of mind and better life choices. You can use your Creative Intuition to make your dreams a reality. And you can use your Transcendental Intuition to reconnect with the unity of all life. Living insightfully can kick off an evolutionary chain reaction that takes you higher than you have ever been.

Wisdom keepers throughout history have taught us that our perception of reality is a reflection of our level of consciousness. When we wake up from a dream, we don't shift from unreality to reality; we shift from a lower level of consciousness to a higher level of consciousness. We can look back and say: *What an amazing dream!* Awakening to superconsciousness is much the same. There is a reality above us, which we all wake up to one day, that is much more real and powerful than the "reality" we know today — the reality that we look back on and say: *What an amazing dream!*

Can you imagine waking up to a life so real that it makes this life feel like a dream? Can you imagine how, each day, your life is a kind of waking dream — just a fragment of the full gamut of existence? Our reality is just the beginning of a greater, more substantive reality that we evolve into through personal, intuitive growth. Just like, in a dream, we don't know that we are dreaming — in life, we don't know how much more there is to living. But when we awaken from the sleep of unconsciousness and the conditioning of our daydream — the veil of delusion is finally lifted.

This is the reality that your intuition takes you to when you follow it. Each day is an interplay between the unconscious, conscious, and superconscious states of being. With every soul-liberating choice you make and every fear you conquer, your consciousness expands. Higher reality becomes more vivid and clear, and your old life becomes more like a dream. With each transformational moment, you are more awake to life. Through the portal of your intuition, the universe opens to you.

WAKING UP TO THE REAL YOU

Even if you understand all of the techniques in this book, nothing is going to change until you follow through with action in your life. This begins with looking inside yourself. It starts with getting rid of everything that is standing in the way of knowing and being yourself. And it ends with using those discoveries — and the power they hold — to create real, lasting change in your life.

This can be hard work, but it is the best work you will ever do. There is no magic wand or simple formula to shift into higher awareness. All you really need to do is to grow. Every breakthrough, every act that makes you better — every conscious or superconscious choice — elevates your frequency. You lift yourself higher with every release, every forgiveness, each moment of joy, each time you trust in life. Real awakening results from more than *thinking about* our evolution; it results from *doing the work* that redefines our spirit. The truth can wake us up, but only when we live by it are we truly awake. It's not enough to know the magic; you have to *become part of* the magic.

Ten Signs of Awakening

Though we all wake up in our own way, the process shares many commonalities. You may notice that you experience some or all of these ten signs. Each signifies that you have been touched by a higher power.

1. Your intuition is stronger: Intuitive ability is a by-product of your evolution. The more you wake up to the real you, the more your inner voice speaks. Insight becomes the fuel for life itself — the real power behind the expansion of your consciousness.

2. You crave more alone time: This is one of the very first signs or precursors of an awakening. You may have noticed, from a young age, that you naturally gravitate toward time alone, and you choose to spend your time with others in meaningful ways. As we begin to awaken, we lose our tolerance for frivolous social activities and look forward to the quiet time of introspection. You are never really alone when you are with your intuition. As you deepen your relationship with the higher part of yourself, the moments that, to others, may feel like empty silence become full of insight and wonder. Whether you are reading, meditating, gardening, creating, exercising, or simply *being*, solitary moments are the treasure we share with the *self* beyond our self.

3. You feel a new sense of wonder in life: When we are children, the world is full of wonder. Then, as we grow up and our minds define and categorize everything into something we can understand, we become disconnected with the wondrous dimension of our life, even though we live in the midst of a truly undefinable world. Intuition is our reminder of that majesty...a reminder of the *magic*. It is not only our connection to the great mystery beyond — it is *our proof* that it exists. Within insight, we tangibly experience the intangible. Our intuition allows us to have a conscious relationship with the mystery of life. When we open our eyes to the wonder, we realize that, instead of being nowhere, it is everywhere.

4. You want to improve your life: It's amazing how, as we start to wake up, all of the things we have been doing wrong suddenly become so clear. It's as if we had a huge blind spot and we can finally see the big picture. We can see past the beam in our eye that has blinded us to our own faults for so long. When you wake up, you might experience a "mad dash" to change your life. You can feel like you are on fire with the passion to make a shift — to take back your power and to release everything that is holding you back. That's your vibration rising! To keep that momentum going — to keep elevating your consciousness — continue letting go of those heavy burdens, old feelings, and heavy judgments. Let it all go. Watch them fall away and feel your spirit rise!

5. You become fearless: As we know, fear is one of our greatest adversaries on the path of life. Fear lies to you; it paralyzes you; it prevents you from growing or experiencing life. When you are living greatly, you are outside of your comfort zone. That means getting comfortable facing your fears and, ultimately, trusting yourself. The comfort zone is a nice place to take a break; it's a nice place to relax for a while and regroup. But all the good things that take us higher are waiting outside of it. The more we build trust in ourselves, the more we realize there is, truly, nothing to be afraid of.

6. You notice more synchronicity in your life: There is no such thing as coincidence. When you are awake, you are in harmony with the unfolding of your best life. The dead ends and the blocks that have held you back are often bypassed by coincidental opportunities. Suddenly, everything feels and is *aligned*. You can measure the momentum of your awakening by the amount of synchronicity in your life. Serendipitous moments point you in the right direction and validate your intuitive evolution. Synchronicity and coincidences reflect the harmonization of your personal unfolding with the majesty of universal unfolding.

7. You experience wonders beyond this world: There is nothing mystical about a mystical experience. It is simply an event that defies our current understanding of the physical world. One day we will figure out how it all works. But for now, we just understand that becoming more conscious raises our frequency and allows us to touch once-untouchable planes of existence. Metaphysical experience is simply a result of our shift into super-consciousness. It should come as no surprise that, when we move our consciousness beyond its limitations, we are able to experience the reality beyond those limitations. The beauty of this process is that it unfolds alongside your personal growth; mystical experiences are not thrust upon you for no reason. They are directly connected to the expansion of your reality.

8. You feel more inspired and creative: An influx of intuition opens up the floodgates of creativity. With those pathways open, all of that good stuff — like inspiration and new ideas and ingenuity and art for art's sake — flows freely. The creative impulse is always fast on the heels of the awakened mind; when we touch something extraordinary, we want to share it with others. Creativity moves us to express our truth with the world. When you wake up, it is natural for all kinds of creative ideas to bubble up. After all, when your eyes are open for the first time, there is so much to do and share.

9. You finally feel authentic: Have you ever said to yourself: *This is what I was made to do.* Or: *At last, I am doing what I was always meant to,* or *I finally feel like I am my real self.* This place of authenticity, of feeling like you are 100 percent comfortable in your own skin, is the result of your conscious realignment with your inner truth. True authenticity often comes in the highest states of your evolution, as you learn to not only recognize your intuition but to follow it and courageously implement much-needed changes in your life. The more you do that, the more *real* you become. You peel back the layers of all that isn't you to own the person you really are. This is *living your truth.*

10. You have a calling to make the world better: To awaken is to answer a call. The idea that you can be something more — that you can do something important for the world — is a calling to wake up to your purpose in life. The deeper you move into your awakening, the louder your call will become. It becomes so loud that you can no longer deny it. And the path serendipitously opens ahead of you. Everyone has their own calling. Deep down inside, you know what yours is. It has been whispering to you all your life.

Life begins when you trust yourself. And it thrives when you live true to yourself — true to the real you. When you wake up to this realization, you are at last free. It can happen to anyone, at any point in their life. It can happen to your neighbor. It can happen to your children, your friends, and your enemies — whether rich or poor, young or old. But it will only happen when you are ready for it.

You are a part of this magnificent, mysterious universe awakening to itself. At last, your individual consciousness is awake to its connection to the whole of existence. The micro and macro become one — a shift toward a new way of living. It is the rediscovery of one of the most fundamental parts of your existence.

RECLAIMING YOUR LIFE

What about those times in our life when, no matter how hard we try, we can't seem to get in sync with ourselves? The dark nights of the soul — we all have them. None of us lives a life perfectly aligned with our intuition. We have to *not* follow our intuition to understand why we should. Those days, weeks, or years of misalignment — when we are confused or stuck — are powerful lessons that hold the seeds of our transformation.

Life can be painful; we experience losses, sickness, disappointments, and painful situations — even trauma. People can be hurtful: They may not treat us with respect; they might abuse us; they might, simply, let us down. So how, in the midst of such suffering, do we take back our power? How do we step into our truth and take back our life?

As always, the solution comes from the inside. No person or circumstance can steal your joy, your love — or your personal power. They can distract you from it; they can talk you out of it or try to pry you away from it. But your inner wholeness is never lost. No matter how dark life gets, you have an escape route within. Like the great saints and martyrs who found illumination in prison or under the harshest persecution, no person or injury can block entry to your sanctuary within — or the power it holds.

In times of trial, our intuition is most important. When life is hard, when the world seems cold, the ease and warmth of our supreme state calls us to go within. It calls us to the light of truth. It asks us to love others, despite their unconsciousness or ignorance. It gives us the strength to look past the pain. Our challenges not only wake us up, but as they continue throughout life, they accelerate our awakening to higher levels. By following our intuition through these challenges, we lift ourselves up and out of even the lowest and darkest places.

Intuitive Dissonance:
Being Out of Sync with Our Intuition

From time to time, when we are in a funk or out of sorts — no matter how intuitive we naturally are — we find ourselves in a place where we just can't connect with our intuition. We don't know what it is saying to us; we are confused or reluctant to act on it. We are in the dreaded state of intuitive dissonance. If or when this happens to you, remember that it is normal and can be remedied.

Here are some reasons why intuition "shuts off," and the steps you can take to turn it back on to take back your life:

1. **Blocked transmission:** When you have repressed energy, thoughts, or feelings, you create intuitive blocks that prevent your intuitive signals from getting through.
   What to do about it: Start transmuting that stuck energy into release, forgiveness, and openheartedness. Consider implementing a new flow practice to help open up those intuitive circuits. Talk and journal about your unexpressed thoughts and feelings to open a pathway for insight.

2. **Confusion:** Are you still not sure what your intuition is telling you? We are often confused because, no matter how hard we try, we can't seem to tell the difference between our intuition and our regular thoughts or imagination.

What to do about it: Practice, practice! Pay close attention to your first impressions and the resonance that calls you forward. Use Insight Cards (see page 163) or make DIY Intuition Billets (see page 131) — or work with a friend — because, with intuition, our practice makes us perfect.

3. **Doubt:** Are you second-guessing your intuition? If so, this is a sign that you don't yet trust it. It's okay; it takes time to build trust.

    What to do about it: Keep practicing and use your insight journal to keep track of the wins that will build confidence. Make note of each extraordinary insight so you remind yourself: You can do this!

4. **Overthinking:** Analysis paralysis is very common, even when we are working with intuition. Our minds always want more information.

    What to do about it: Practice controlling the mind through meditation, mantras, or presence. Widen the gap between your thoughts so you can hear that insight more clearly. Once you have enough information from the way you think, make your choice by the way you feel.

5. **Overempathizing:** As an intuitive person, it can be hard to differentiate our own energy from the energy of others. Being empathetic, we can easily confuse other people's feelings or direction with our own.

    What to do about it: Set an intention to stay on your center and continually check in with your sense of resonance, asking yourself: *Does this feel like me? Is this my path?* Become aware of your own energy and set boundaries so you don't give your power away to others.

6. **Fear:** Fear of failure, fear of judgment, fear of making a mistake, fear of being wrong — there are so many ways that fear can sabotage our intuitive journey.

    What to do about it: Remind yourself at all times that, no matter what, you are supported by life itself. Consider creating a mantra and practicing it several times a day to "reprogram" the fear from your mind.

7. **Lack of confidence:** Sometimes we think: *I could never do that. I am not good enough.* We kill intuition when we don't believe in ourselves — when we don't recognize the potential we hold inside of us.

   What to do about it: Remind yourself that the only limits are the limits of your mind. Don't let anyone tell you what you can and cannot do. That is the job of your intuition, alone. If you can intuit it, you can do it!

8. **Identification with our "old" self:** Sometimes it's hard to break free from our past — from the labels others have given us or that we have given ourselves. We have spent a lifetime creating our identity. Even when we grow beyond that self-identification, we can at times fall back into our old, habitual ways.

   What to do about it: Never give up. Keep creating and re-creating your life until your masterpiece is complete. All you really are is who you are in this moment. Even if you fall back — which we all do from time to time — remember, your intuition is waiting to help pick you up when you are ready.

The process of awakening is not one-directional. Life's challenges can draw us forward and backward, as we learn our lessons. The lull of unconsciousness reclaims us all from time to time. When we suffer, or times become difficult, we can become disconnected from our inner strength and the wisdom that comes with it.

RADICAL INSIGHT

All forms of suffering have one singular cause — the disconnection from our true self.

It is important to recognize that our pain and disappointment — our times of dissonance — are not failures in themselves. They are simply by-products of the root problem, which is our disconnection from our life-affirming insight and inner wisdom. This is an empowering recognition. With it, we understand that our suffering is not the result of our actions, circumstances, or what anyone else has done to us. It is the result of closing off to our trust, acceptance, and limitless potential to rise above it all.

When you are in the resonant, intuitive state of trust in life, everything feels good and possible. You wonder how anything could ever go wrong. You feel encouraged and supported in all you do because you are on the uplifted path. When you are going the wrong way, the friction is meant to slow you down — those nudges and redirects get you back on the high road. They aren't a punishment; they are a redirect. No matter how lost you get, or how much life hurts, your intuition holds the signposts for your way home.

EXTRAORDINARY PEOPLE, EXTRAORDINARY INSIGHT

Trust Yourself

Trusting your intuition means trusting yourself. Most of us, when we look back on our mistakes, can see that our intuition gave us some warning signs. We ignored them because someone convinced us to or because it seemed to be what was expected of us.

The most important step you can take on this journey is to accept who you are and where you have been.

If you had a job you didn't like, or were in a marriage that was painful, or had an experience that you were ashamed of, ask yourself: *What did I learn from that? Where does my intuition want me to go next?*

There is something to be garnered from every experience we have – even if, in retrospect, we wish we hadn't done it. The totality of everything that you have done is fuel for your intuition. One of the reasons you have *good* intuition is because of all of the times you had *bad* intuition. If we don't denigrate anything we have been up to this moment, then this moment is full and rich – and we are, too.

Following your intuition takes personal courage. That's why it is important to remember that you only have one life. *You have one precious life.* So if someone says it's risky to follow your intuition, I would argue it's riskier not to. You are risking your one precious life, living someone else's idea of who you should be.

– **Dennis Palumbo,** Hollywood screenwriter, author, and psychotherapist

LIVING YOUR TRUTH

When you live your truth, you know who you are, and you own it. The person you are inside and the person you are to the world are one and the same. You are no longer reluctant or afraid to stand for what you really are. For better or for worse, you are *real*. No more going through the motions or living someone else's life. You have a clear awareness of what is "you" and what is not you. You don't have a job you hate or a relationship that doesn't let you be yourself. You follow your callings instead of ignoring them. You own your power instead of giving it away. Living your truth is recognizing and completely accepting who you are. It is your self-actualization.

This intuitive return to yourself is the ultimate homecoming. Your intuition shows you the road map to get there, so it can reunite you with *the one* you have always been — the one you will always be. If you follow it all the way, your inner guidance will take you to the home you knew before you came to this world — the same home you will return to when you leave this world. In this superconscious state, your heart is unbreakable, and your mind is incorruptible; your inner and outer world come together as a unified field of potentiality. For centuries, the yogis, mystics, and holy ones have devoted their lives to uniting these two worlds and returning to the home within us. Mirabai Starr describes this experience in her introduction to *The Interior Castle* by St. Teresa of Avila:

> There is a secret place. A radiant sanctuary. As real as your own kitchen. More real than that. Constructed of the purest elements. Overflowing with the ten thousand beautiful things. Worlds within worlds. Forests, rivers. Velvet coverlets thrown over featherbeds, fountains bubbling beneath a canopy of stars. Bountiful forests, universal libraries. A wine cellar offering an intoxication so sweet you will never be sober again. A clarity so complete you will never again forget. This magnificent refuge is inside you. Enter. Shatter the darkness that shrouds the doorway....Believe the incredible truth that the Beloved has chosen for his dwelling place the core of your own being because that is the single most beautiful place in all of creation.

This supreme reality is where the personal and universal come together in perfect reunion. Here, your individual consciousness joyfully merges with the omnipresent superconsciousness; at last, you are whole. You no longer ache for the lost part of your being; the hole inside you, which you have felt for your entire life, is now filled with its final, missing piece. Like loved ones once separated by time and space, life welcomes you with a rush of bliss, as the universe takes you back into its sweet embrace.

You are able to feel, once again, the consummate joy of *wholeness*. More than an emotion, more than a feeling — this is a harmonization. You bring the vibrational attunement of *all that you are* into harmony with *all that is*. Together, in the great, sacred song of creation, we all resonate together. We are one. You are in the song, and the song is in you.

RADICAL INSIGHT
Intuitive oneness is more than a feeling;
it is harmonization of being.

In this moment, you see yourself in all that is, and you see all that is — in you. You are one with life; you are one with the light; you are one with the pervasive intelligence of the cosmos. In this unified cosmic frequency, the seer can finally see themselves.

Even from this perfect place, the challenges of life continue, in one way or another, as long as we live. It is our intuitive connection to our center that gives us the wisdom to handle these trials with grace. The saints have trials; gurus have trials; even Jesus had trials. If you are alive, you have a purpose. You have lessons to learn or missions to accomplish, even if that purpose is simply to know yourself more deeply.

Your Evolutionary Calling

To become more conscious of the ways that you, personally, are called to grow and evolve, look back on your life to identify its key, defining moments or high points and what made them significant. Each illuminating moment is a meaningful step toward your evolutionary breakthroughs.

Depending on where you are in your personal evolution, different experiences will feel good or bad. For example, if you have been going through a period of loneliness or too much isolation, alone time may not feel like a high point to you. However, if you have been overextended by work or social obligations, a weeklong retreat might feel like the best experience of your life.

Many of our high points, beyond simply being joyful or happy times, are gauges of personal change; they punctuate the experience of the higher-frequency shift. We feel better because we are elevating ourselves — releasing ourselves and moving closer to the state of wholeness that we all crave.

To begin, in a journal or on a piece of paper, create two columns. Label the first "Life High Points" and the second "Evolutionary Callings" (see the example on the next page).

For the high points in column 1, list any experiences you would use to answer the following questions:

- What have been the happiest moments of your life?
- When have you had the greatest breakthroughs, renewal, or growth periods?
- During what periods of your life have you felt fully "yourself" — the best, most powerful version of the person you know yourself to be?

Ultimately, list as many of the significant high points of your life as you think belong. As you look back over that list, remember these times in your life when you were aligned with and most living your truth.

Next, in column 2, write down the quality or qualities that made those times such powerful high points. What made them feel good to you? Were you feeling creative, healthy, or free? Were you learning new things or surrounded by loving friends? In a few words or a phrase, describe the essence of each transformational situation. Here is an example of what this might look like:

LIFE HIGH POINTS	EVOLUTIONARY CALLINGS
Travel adventures	Freedom and discovery
College	Independence and education
Time with family or friends	Sharing and enjoying life
Move to a new home	New beginnings
A new relationship	Personal growth
Career success or change	Ownership of power
Getting healthy	Healing and renewal
Meeting a hero	Fulfillment of dreams
Helping others	Serving the world
Creating something important	Changing the world
Receiving acclaim	Validation of higher self-worth
Retreat or time alone	Reconnection to higher self

Column 1: Your High Points

There is power in your joy. The moments of greatest happiness in your life hold valuable clues and point you toward your real self. Your happiness is about more than just being happy. It is about your growth. Real happiness comes as a result of the fulfillment that takes us higher. It brings us closer to our truth.

Your uplifted moments remind you of what it feels like to be whole. Each high point of your life is a kind of portal to higher consciousness, if you follow it through. Awakenings, epiphanies, and superconscious revelations are more able, and likely, to touch you when you are in "high spirits" because, in that elevated state, you are operating, at last, on their level.

If you long for more intuitive illumination in life, do more of what makes you happy. Make more space for the moments that lift you up. If travel elates you, find a way to do it more, even if it just means taking some local trips on the weekends. If being creative uplifts you, find a way to do your art, even if it's only on the weekends at first. If spending time with other people makes you feel good, only choose to be with the people who make you come alive. Each small joy is a stepping-stone to your truth and an opportunity to take your life to the next level.

Column 2: Your Evolutionary Callings

Behind each high point in your life is a calling. Something brought you to each experience for a reason. You were, in one way or another, intuitively drawn into a situation that had the capacity to lift you higher. If you look at your responses in column 2, you can get an idea about the callings and recurrent themes that are driving your personal evolution.

In life, we each have ongoing lessons to learn. It may take years or decades to fully master the challenges, which can manifest as recurring evolutionary themes. For example, if, in this life, you need to learn independence, you will feel called to situations that give you the opportunity to embody healthy self-sufficiency. On your column 2 list, you might find recurring themes around freedom or self-reliance. On the other hand, maybe you notice recurring evolutionary themes around supporting and helping other people; in this case, service may be the path to your next level. Whatever your evolutionary themes are, think of them as markers for your superconscious shift. They are invitations to take the next step beyond yourself.

The power and strength of our awakening is not measured just by our ability to be peacefully present in the moment, but also by our response to our inner calling. It is one thing to know our intuition in the quiet of our mind; it is quite another to take that intuition out into the world — to make it real.

The highest points in your life are a reflection of the moments that you listened to that call. The fulfillment and joy you feel are life's reward for living your truth. You experience the joyful inner sense of life opening up before you — because that is exactly what it is doing. Though you may have growth pains — sometimes it hurts to break out of our shell — the end result of insightful living is a joyful life.

We have everything to gain by taking a chance on ourselves. We have everything to gain by moving with the flow of life as it calls us. We can recognize our growth by our ability to *adapt* to each moment that comes. Are we able to roll with the punches? Do we have the courage to step through that open door? Are we able to not lose faith, even when life doesn't go our way? Our ability to bend with the universe — to lean into its flow with ease — is a lesson for us every day. The more pliable we are to life, the more truly alive we become.

By trusting in yourself and following your evolutionary callings, you enter into a state of balanced *being* and *doing*. This state gives you one of the greatest powers in existence: the power to uplift the world. You can become aware of your role in positive change — and make it happen. You can consciously transmute disruption into peace — pain into joy, suffering into bliss. The more you do this, the more you evolve yourself and participate in the evolution of humanity. Every time you follow your intuition — every time you choose unity over separation, truth over fear, wisdom over ignorance — you illuminate the way for all. You become, truly, a light of the world.

CHAPTER 16

RISING UP

Imagine if all the tumult of the body were to quiet down,
along with our busy thoughts....And imagine if that
moment were to go on and on, leaving behind all other
sights and sounds but this one vision which ravishes and
absorbs and fixes the beholder in joy, so that the rest of
eternal life were like that moment of illumination which
leaves us breathless.

— ST. AUGUSTINE

First, we awaken, then we *arise*. Once we have claimed our power, all that is left is for us to rise into it. To do this, we have to take action. To be mindful, alone, is not enough; to be insightful, alone, is not enough. We must wake up to our truth, then actively follow it forward — stepping up and into all that is possible.

One day, in your practice of insightfulness, you may look back on your old self and barely recognize the person you once were. You may notice that you have become so much more, unaffected by the wounds, the ignorance, and the fears that once imprisoned you. You may notice that a vast sense of ease and wonder has taken over your life, replacing any nagging existential angst. All of these experiences are hallmarks of the intuitive life.

These are just a few of the joys that await as you rise into the best version of yourself — your true, abiding, unbroken nature. It is never too late to return to yourself. Despite all the trials and hardships of life, none of us are broken. None of us can be broken because we were made to be unbreakable. Your intuition will show you that, time and again, if you follow it.

As you ascend back into your true nature — you are whole, finally. To get there, you may have to face the darkness; you will have to release anything that is holding you back. Carrying with you only the things that take you higher, each day you rise higher and higher — and closer and closer to your indestructible essence.

Once you have reconnected with your real nature, nothing can harm you. When you live by the world, you die by the world. When you live by the inner wisdom that is beyond the world, you rise above it all.

THE SUPERCONSCIOUS SHIFT

Once you begin to live insightfully, everything changes. From a higher, more-conscious vantage point, you see the world clearly. You have the potential to understand all of your life situations, challenges, and opportunities from a position of elevated awareness. Day by day, with each intuition honored, you lift yourself up and out of unconsciousness and into conscious and superconscious existence.

This is the shift we have all been waiting for, dreaming of. This is the impossible place where we can touch the mystery. Here, fully awake for the first time, we can live in tune with what was once unknowable, imperceptible. This shift is not a final destination; it is a connection that we bring into our life. We fortify that connection with every insightful choice we make and every bright new idea we bring into the world.

Living insightfully is not only rising into higher awareness but staying there. It's not enough to have a breakthrough; we need to wholly implement the wisdom that made that breakthrough possible. This commitment is what makes the difference between "an awakening" and "being awakened."

To stay awake, we must live more consciously — and more superconsciously. What exactly does that mean? Let's take a look at the ways our actions define our level of consciousness.

ARE YOU LIVING SUPERCONSCIOUSLY?

Unconscious Living	Conscious Living	Superconscious Living
Unawareness	*Mindfulness*	*Insightfulness*
You are always busy, running from one activity to the next, without pausing for introspection.	You feel a deep satisfaction and appreciation of the present moment and find it easy to be still.	A still, quiet voice within effortlessly guides you to improve the world and create the best version of your life.
You shy away from a promising new relationship because you have been hurt in the past.	You enjoy being in the moment with a new friend who may or may not become a long-term love interest.	You feel love at first sight when you recognize a person who is about to bring some good into your life.
You are angry, resentful, or unaccepting of a challenging experience that life brought you.	You accept the outcome of a disappointing situation as if you have chosen it.	You understand that roadblocks are only redirections to align your course.
You eat meat even though you could never kill an animal.	You decide to become a vegetarian after meeting some nice pigs.	You are intuitively drawn to high-vibration foods that feed your body and spirit.

The more we live intuitively, the more superconscious we become. If we are living unconsciously, we will have very few genuine intuitions; even if we do, they will be clouded by dissonant thoughts and emotions. On the other hand, as we evolve into higher levels of awareness, our intuition naturally resonates through our insightful thoughts and feelings. As we begin to live in trust with life, the unconscious thoughts and feelings that hold us back are less likely to take hold within us.

Unconscious, Conscious, and Superconscious Living in Action

To better understand the nature of our reactions, let's consider this scenario: An office worker has an intuition that he is going to lose his job. He doesn't know it yet, but he is about to be laid off during downsizing, and he has a "feeling" that he should start looking for a new job.

Unconscious Responses: Resistance and Fear

The root of our unconscious reactions is our inability to accept the truth of our intuitive, gut feelings. In some cases, we may be ignorant and simply unable to see what is clearly before us; in others, we may be paralyzed by fear.

One of the most common responses to uncomfortable intuitive information that we don't want to accept is denial. The easiest reaction is to ignore it. However, if the office worker refuses to accept his intuition, he won't prepare for what is to come. This will make the inevitable reality of being laid off even more traumatic and disruptive to his life, since he will be without income and unready to find a new job.

Another unconscious response is the complete opposite: We overreact to a gut feeling and shift into a state of fear. Our imagination can take over, and a barrage of worst-case scenarios can paint an unrealistic doomsday picture. In this situation, the office worker might totally freak out. He might start to think that everyone at work is conspiring against him, so he compulsively obsesses over the situation in an attempt to regain control. This unproductive and potentially hostile action will make the situation even worse, until he creates a self-fulfilling prophecy. If there was any chance of him not losing his job before, all the negative energy he is creating and attracting will work against him. Not only will he be laid off, but he will leave his job on bad terms.

In both cases, these unconscious responses would fuel mental or emotional imbalance. Fear or resistance-based thoughts and emotions effectively block the transformative energy that intuition is attempting to open up.

When our mind judges a situation as "bad," we close ourselves off to the gift that it, on some level, is bringing us. Authentic insight is not "good" or "bad"; it just *is*. It is a simple truth. We are the ones who attribute meaning. The man is going to lose his job — but is that necessarily a bad thing? Maybe it's a bad job. Maybe there is a better job waiting for him. Maybe it's all a blessing in disguise.

Conscious/Superconscious Responses: Acceptance and Action

The best way to respond to any insight that we receive is *to simply accept it*. Do not fear it, judge it, or ignore it. Accept that, no matter what happens, your life is unfolding as it is meant to for your own good. Trust that the guiding forces in your life have a bigger plan, one that is more expansive than your limited vision can see in this moment.

In the case of the soon-to-be-unemployed office worker — even though the insight of losing his job would initially be shocking, a conscious or superconscious reaction would mean accepting the situation. He would trust that, whatever happens, this change is part of life's plan for him. He would do his best not to indulge his fearful thoughts and resistant emotions, and instead he would seek to open his heart and mind to the evolutionary flow and follow his intuition to take necessary action. One some level, maybe he knows he has outgrown that job, and the situation might inspire him to start a new business of his own — one that he has been dreaming of for years. Working evenings and weekends, he might even get this new enterprise off the ground and so successful that he ends up quitting his job before the layoffs even arrive.

It is through this kind of conscious, insightful living that we avoid the calamities of life. Intuition is always throwing up signs, if only we know to heed them. But trusting and following your inner guidance not only saves you from the growth pains, it gives you the creative direction and power to move effortlessly into the next phase of your existence. Living superconsciously, you can naturally, even joyfully, step out of the past and boldly into your future.

TURNING YOUR PAIN INTO YOUR POWER

As we awaken and arise, only one thing threatens to hold us back: ourselves. Our intuition calls us upward and onward; what often stands in our way is the collective fear and resistance resulting from our past experience. Until we let that go — until we release all of the heavy burdens we carry within us — we will not be free to fully ascend to the heights of our potential.

Doing this is much easier than you think. All you have to do is…let go. Let go of the pain; let go of the disappointment, the resentment, the hurt, the anger; let go of all the negative self-talk that keeps you thinking small. We may not realize it, but letting go is so much easier than holding on to all of that. It is a heavy burden that we carry with us over the years. What do you think would happen if you let all of it go?

When you let it all go, *you rise up*. Nothing can lift you up more than your conscious choice to release the weights that have been holding you down. This is how we truly heal. We don't deny the weight; we don't obsess over the weight. We release the weight.

When we are ready to make peace — to forgive one another and forgive ourselves for the pain of life — we can let it all go. Then we can go higher. We can go beyond ourselves and become something greater. Not only are we healed, but we are empowered by accepting ourselves and trusting in the process of life.

The two foundations of superconscious existence are trust and acceptance. *Unconditionally, we have to accept and trust whatever life brings us.* This is more revolutionary than, at first, it might seem. It can be hard to trust in the unknown — and even harder to accept life when it brings pain or setbacks. But we are called to do it anyway, and especially in times of uncertainty. We might be afraid, but we follow our calling anyway. We may be resistant to change, but we trust in ourselves to find our way through it.

The two exercises that follow — "Igniting the Shift" and "Empowering the Shift" — are valuable, immersive practices that can help you get to the root of your fears and any resistance that may be keeping you from ascending into higher awareness. These practices help reestablish self-trust and clear unwanted psychological barriers that may be holding you back. This process of trusting yourself and releasing blockages unlocks and opens the gateway to higher awareness. Unburdening allows you to release any heavy energy and to free your inner spirit to rise.

Igniting the Shift: Moving from Fear to Trust

Fear is one of the biggest things that holds us back from experiencing the fullness of life. Anxiety, stress, worry, general unease — all come from a lack of trust in ourselves and in the life that supports us. The first, most powerful shift you can make is to consciously step beyond your fear. When you set an intention to turn your life over, in full trust, to the process of cocreation, you open yourself to a whole new world of possibility.

You can start with one single step — one single fear. Don't feel as if, suddenly, you have to be afraid of nothing. An upshift begins with a singular act — and like wildfire, it expands with the momentum of continued action. You can begin with the smallest instance of fear in your life — any area of your life that gives you anxiety or worry or uncertainty. Make the choice to set that feeling aside and replace it with trust in life: *What will be will be.*

This simple shift is the beginning of liberation. As long as you live true to yourself and your inner guidance, all will be as it should be. When you release yourself from the shackles of fear, you have the chance to know what real freedom is — to know yourself, not as a helpless victim, but as a powerful cocreator of your life.

Self-Discovery Practice: Facing Your Fears with Intuition

During this self-discovery exercise, you examine the unconscious root causes of your fears and start to transmute them into the power that fuels your expansion of consciousness. The practice tackles one fear at a time using five steps. Repeat the process as many times, and for as many fears, as you like. See the chart on the next page for an example of what this looks like.

1. **Name a trigger fear:** First, name anything in your life that is causing you to be fearful or anxious. List as many fears as you like, then follow this process for each one individually.

2. **Describe your unconscious reaction:** Below the fear, describe all of the uncomfortable feelings that you associate with it.

3. **Write a trust intention statement:** Next, face each fear, one at a time, with a trust intention. Set aside your conscious assessment of the situation and simply trust that the universe has *got this*. Trust that each fearful situation is an invitation for growth. Write down a statement that affirms this shift from fear to trust.

4. **Express conscious acceptance and trust:** Revisit your fear in this new light of trust. Imagine yourself absolutely at peace with the situation and any outcome. In a sentence, summarize your acceptance and unconditional

trust in the process of life. Try it on. Can you feel the difference when you fully trust? Do you feel a weight lift? This "weight lifting" is real; when you let go, you literally become lighter and more at ease with life. This small act is the first step up the ladder of consciousness.

5. **Receive superconscious insight:** As you sit in the stillness of consciousness, does your intuition speak to you? Listen to the insight that comes to you in these quiet moments. Journal your thoughts, or pull an Insight Card. Finally, write down a statement that names what you will do to follow your intuition — and continue to lift up your life. What can you do, right now, to take the next step in your growth, knowing that, no matter which way things go, you did your best?

	EXAMPLE 1	**EXAMPLE 2**
1. Trigger fear	"I am afraid of losing my job."	"I am afraid of failing."
2. Unconscious reaction	"I feel anxiety, stress, and worry."	"I feel self-judgment, doubt, and fear of what others will think of me."
3. Trust intention	"If I am meant to leave my job, I will leave my job." "I recognize that life will provide for me, one way or another."	"I trust that life will support me whenever I am headed in the right direction." "Failure is only life pointing me in a new direction."

	EXAMPLE 1	EXAMPLE 2
4. Conscious acceptance	"Whether I stay at my job or move on, I accept that I am aligning with the best possible course for myself, even if I can't see that yet."	"Whether I succeed or fail, I accept that there will be a valuable lesson in the process itself."
5. Superconscious insight	"My intuition is calling me to start looking for new jobs, so I will shape up my résumé…and start sending it out!"	"My gut tells me I won't fail, so I am going to trust that and go all-in on my passion project."

Questions for Contemplation

As you open-mindedly and wholeheartedly move into alignment with superconscious actions and reactions, you will feel your fears fade away. One day you will wake up and think: *Wow, that doesn't bother me anymore. I knew I could trust myself.* Just like that, you will have risen above your fear.

Until you get there, continue to ask these contemplative questions:

1. Do you feel how fear lifts when you trust in life to show you your highest path, instead of *what you think is* the highest path?
2. Isn't it a relief to let go of all of the stress and pressure you put upon yourself?

3. Do you have the courage to follow your intuitive guid-
    ance and make this shift a reality? What small (or big)
    steps can you take now to go beyond these fears?

Uplifting Practice: Create a Trust Affirmation

It may take some time to stay solid in these breakthroughs. From
time to time, old fears can creep back in if you waver in self-trust.
To combat any moments of weakness, arm yourself with an empowering affirmation or mantra to keep unconscious thoughts
and feelings at bay. Here are some tips on creating a powerful
affirmation:

1. Create a short, affirming phrase to recenter you in your
    place of trust. Good examples are "I trust in life," "All will
    be well," and "I accept all that is and will be."
2. Repeat the words out loud or in your head, anytime and
    anywhere. Say it until you fall asleep at night — or when
    fears wake you up at night. Say it on the way to work,
    during meditation, or in the shower. You can use a mala
    necklace or bracelet as a tool, and take it with you wher-
    ever you go. The more you use your affirmation, the more
    you "reprogram" your thinking with trust, instead of fear.
3. Each time, repeat your affirmation as many times as it
    takes to shift you back up into a place of peace and power.
    Depending on the day, it may take five — or fifty — times.
    You will know when you are done because you *feel better*.

Empowering the Shift:
Moving from Resistance to Acceptance

To rise up, we've got to let go of what holds us down. Unconscious
judgments, resentments, and unforgiveness tether us to lower-
conscious frequencies. Even if we are ready to fearlessly move
ahead, we aren't going to get far with the weight of unconscious
thoughts holding us back. To move past pain, injustice, and

disappointment, we again turn to trust. Instead of resisting the uncomfortable things that happen to us, we move into a state of acceptance by choosing to trust that everything happens to us for a reason.

This can be difficult for many of life's heartbreaks. How could there be a good reason for so much pain in this world? How can we find the meaning that turns our pain into power? The answer is realizing that healing comes not from finding the reason but accepting the experience. This does not mean condoning whatever caused the hurt; it means processing it on a higher level, one that allows us to release it. We often hear stories about victims' families who forgive a perpetrator of a terrible crime against a loved one. They forgive not because they understand why it happened or to excuse it. They forgive because *forgiveness is the only way they can rise above the experience.*

Forgiveness is the single most powerful action you can take to release yourself from the grip of unconscious thoughts and feelings. Unforgiveness of others fuels low-energy consciousness and divisiveness by creating anger, resentment, and grudges. Unforgiveness of our*selves* is even worse. It sabotages our lives with guilt, regret, insecurity, and depression. When we stop resisting the healing that life wants to bring us, we can let go of the past and become truly present in this moment.

When we accept ourselves for everything that we are and everything that we have done, we release years of social judgment and conditioning. When we do the same for others, we break down the walls that separate us from our shared truth and the joyful, omnipresent reality that unites us all.

Self-Discovery Practice: Letting Go of What Holds You Back

This self-discovery exercise is a companion to the exercise on fear. Here, you examine your unconscious attachment to past pain and start to transmute it into power. As before, the practice has five steps that can be repeated for each painful experience you identify.

1. **Name a trigger pain:** Name a painful experience in life that still causes you to suffer. If you wish, make a list of all the painful experiences you would like to address, and tackle them one at a time using these five steps.

2. **Describe your unconscious reaction:** For each painful experience, list the unconscious reactions and feelings associated with it.

3. **Write an acceptance intention statement:** Now contemplate the painful experience, and accept that it has a purpose, whether you can see it or not. Accept the experience as if you, yourself, had chosen it — because, on some level, you did. Acknowledge that your limited consciousness has no way of ascertaining the higher cause and effect of complicated situations, even though they cause deep pain. In a statement, summarize your intention to accept this experience.

4. **Express conscious acceptance and forgiveness:** What does this situation look like in the light of consciousness? Accept that, however you were involved in the situation, you did the best that you could and, most likely, so did anyone else involved — in their own way. Forgive yourself; forgive the other people involved. Imagine yourself absolutely at peace with what has happened. In a sentence, summarize your unconditional acceptance and forgiveness.

5. **Receive superconscious insight:** Finally, write down a statement that names what you will do to let go of and bring closure to this affliction. Listen for intuitive guidance; for additional insight, pull an Insight Card or journal to tap into your inner wisdom. Ask: *What can I do right now to heal the pain that I have been carrying and make peace with my life?*

	EXAMPLE 1	EXAMPLE 2
1. Trigger pain	"I had a painful family upbringing."	"The person I was in love with left me."
2. Unconscious reaction	"I feel anger, resentment, judgment, and bitterness."	"I feel sadness, heartache, disappointment, and loss."
3. Acceptance intention	"I will allow the challenges of my youth to make me stronger." "I recognize the ways that life took care of me, even when my loved ones didn't."	"I accept that my partner was doing what they thought was best for their personal growth." "I understand that this change is an opportunity for me to more clearly understand myself."
4. Conscious acceptance	"I accept that my past was part of my evolutionary path, and in the present, I can rise above it."	"I honor my time with my partner and am grateful for the time we shared, even though it was time for us to part."
5. Superconscious insight	"I am intuitively guided to create boundaries and spend less time in toxic family situations."	"I feel called to reach out to my former partner, mend fences, and let them know that I forgive them and wish them well."

Questions for Contemplation

1. How does it feel when you apply acceptance to each situation?
2. Do you feel the heaviness lift when you release heavy emotional baggage?
3. Are you able to see the purpose in the pain? How have you grown or learned from those painful experiences?

Uplifting Practice: Create an Acceptance Affirmation

As in the previous exercise, it can help to create an affirmation to reinforce acceptance in difficult situations. Here are some examples:

- I accept every situation as if I had chosen it.
- I forgive. I release. I let go.
- I trust in life.
- Everything is as it should be.
- What will be will be.

Out of the dark places, transformation is born. When you transmute your fear and pain, your power comes to life. Right here is where your real work begins, where the vast, universal power of intuition becomes *personal*. This is where the miraculous forces of the beyond touch the core of your being. The simple choice to trust in your higher self — and stop resisting its call — is the catalyst for your inner revolution.

At last, you realize that the power you have been searching so hard for is right there within you. And you grow into that power with every fear you rise above and every experience you fully own. When you apply this process to all of your life, you can't lose. This is the big secret the world doesn't want you to know. *Your intuition is your way out* — out of the pain, out of the suffering, out of the confusion, out of the karmic cycles that bind us all.

All we have ever really needed to do was trust our self and live true to that self. All suffering flows from that core disparity. When we become conscious of this and set our intention to live in the flow of life, we turn it all around. And the universe notices. It has been waiting your whole life for this moment.

EXTRAORDINARY PEOPLE, EXTRAORDINARY INSIGHT

Walk Your Own Path

What led me into my own intuitive journey was the birth of my son. When he was born, I was very young, so the "responsible" decision would have been to give him up for adoption. But something inside me just told me that wasn't the way to go. People said I was crazy, but I made the decision to become a single parent at age eighteen. That whole choice was entirely intuition-based because I didn't have any hard facts to rely on – no stability, no good foundation or support system.

All the odds were stacked against me, but I was called to take my own path. Had I not done that, none of the things that make my life what it is today would have happened. I couldn't say that I would be doing music, or the arts, because my journey started with that one choice. It's the thread of my whole being – everything leads back to that moment.

That's why it is so important to develop trust in yourself. Looking back at the times I took risks, I had no idea what I was doing, but I still did it anyway. I didn't

know how I could do it, but a part of me knew I could
do it – or even had to do it. Even if I failed, it taught me
a lesson. Life isn't a straight-line type of journey. Your
intuition will help you to recognize the things that try to
pull you away from who you are. Trust yourself. Believe
in your dreams. And don't give up. Your next-level shift
is closer than you think.

– Byron Nash,
award-winning musical artist and producer

SUPERHUMANHOOD

*Man is a transitional being, he is not final; for in him and
high beyond him ascend the radiant degrees which climb
to a divine supermanhood. The step from man toward
superman is the next approaching achievement
in the earth's evolution. There lies our destiny.*
— SRI AUROBINDO

Once you have gone beyond your self — beyond personhood —
you are no longer the same. How could you be? Your awareness of
life has expanded. You have touched miraculous power, and you
know, from experience, that the universe is alive and within you.
You finally have a taste of the potential you are made for. These
are the baby steps of an emerging superhumanity.

The idea of a new kind of human being, an elevated existence — where we live and create from a place of higher awareness and power — is a concept that scientists, philosophers, and
theologians have contemplated for centuries. More than a super-
hero in a cape, a real superhuman would have "superpowers" in
all aspects of being — body, mind, heart, and spirit. This kind
of supreme human being would be able to intuitively maintain
their body's healing and well-being. They would have dominion
over their thoughts, replacing chronic overthinking with intuitive

274 • RADICAL INTUITION

insight. They would empower their heart, having the courage to live their truth and follow their passion. And ultimately, the supreme human being would embody the omnipresent, superconscious connectedness of being that unites us all.

We are not there yet. We are not final. We are not finished works of art. However, while the idea of a "superhuman" might seem like a comic-book or science-fiction fantasy, it's not. When we look deeper, we see that humankind *is* still evolving — that we are, in fact, a work in progress. And our future selves will become more familiar with concepts like metabiological evolution and superconscious transfiguration, participating more consciously in the posthuman, posttechnological existence of the Übermensch.

Insightfulness is a faculty that, as a society, we possess but have not yet mastered. We remain like children with our intuition. We play with it. It's a novelty that we have no control over. When it touches us, we are amazed. We grab it when it falls out of the sky; we run after it when it calls from the distance. And when it comes through for us, we feel connected to something bigger than ourselves.

This awareness is only going to grow in the years to come. If we are to survive, it is what is next for us. But are we actually capable of becoming more than we are now? How can we use our bodies, our minds, our hearts, and our spirits to make the intuitive leap? What would consciousness look like if we used our full brain capacity? Would we finally be able to tap into the limitless power of our intuition and "psychic" ability? Centuries ago, iconic thinkers like Goethe and Nietzsche wrestled with these ideas. Of course, today, we still ask ourselves: What's next? The universe is expanding and so is our consciousness. As always, we look to the horizon — wondering, imagining, dreaming about our potential in the future.

If a superhumanity is, indeed, possible, the question is: How will it come about? Will our ascent be a slow, subtle evolution that unfolds over millennia? Or will it be more like a mutation, spontaneously manifesting in the blink of an eye? Is it possible to wake up one day to a changed reality? The answer is *yes*. Yes, the shift, like a volcanic eruption, can — and does — happen in an instant. All it takes is for something to wake us up.

This is Nietzsche's philosophical concept of the Übermensch, or superhuman, as quoted in the *Encyclopedia Britannica*:

> This superior man would not be a product of long evolution; rather, he would emerge when any man with superior potential completely masters himself and strikes off conventional... "herd morality" to create his own values.

Personal transformation, like intuition itself, can come in a flash. With a simple epiphany or a sudden revelation, we can find ourselves operating on a completely different level of life. Some people imagine this as a transfiguration of our species — an era when, collectively, we move past our ego, or the differences and silos the ego creates — to reunite with one another and life itself.

When we shift, we go beyond personhood. We gain the ability to see past our limited consciousness and firsthand experience; we are drawn to a state of awareness that transcends personality, time, and space. This is evolution of our whole being, not just our physical being. Jonas Salk, who discovered the cure for polio, wrote about this in his book *Anatomy of Reality*:

> The most meaningful activity in which a human being can be engaged is one that is directly related to human evolution. This is true because human beings now play an active and critical role not only in the process of their own evolution but in the survival and evolution of all living things. Awareness of this places upon human beings a responsibility for their participation in and contribution to the process of evolution. If humankind would accept and acknowledge this responsibility and become creatively engaged in the process of metabiological evolution consciously as well as unconsciously, a new reality would emerge, and a new age would be born.

Salk often used the term *metabiology* to refer to the state of evolution beyond that of the physical body. One of the most celebrated and respected scientists of his day, he did not overlook or exclude the multidimensional aspect of evolution. He understood that our physical and metaphysical realities are interconnected. Together, our body, heart, mind, and spirit move through time and space, refining us through our worldly experience. Each day we have the opportunity to be more and more attuned to this evolutionary frequency.

What part, then, does intuition play in superhumanhood? Intuition is the intrinsic force of the fully conscious or superconscious life. On the inside, our intuition enables us to listen to our bodies, communicate with our minds, be moved by our hearts, and experience the higher reality of existence itself. Intuition is part of the fabric that holds together superconscious reality. It is inseparable from the quantum principles that create the universe.

One of the manifestations of this growing, intuition-infused reality is a new reliance on creative power. To build upon the success of our existing knowledge systems, we will rely on the creativity, vision, and ingenuity that insightfulness brings. The World Economic Forum anticipates that creativity will become one of the leading forces in the future. The ability to think intuitively and creatively is the secret to building the new kind of world we need to progress forward. Economist Dan Pink's bestselling book *A Whole New Mind* explains:

> The future belongs to a different kind of person with a different kind of mind: artists, inventors, storytellers — creative and holistic "right-brain" thinkers whose abilities mark the fault line between who gets ahead and who doesn't.

The intuitive shift does not affect just our inner reality; it affects the external world we create. It starts within and flows without. This gaining momentum of insightfulness has charged this moment in time with intuitive energy — an energy that is redefining and re-creating our future. Intuition, then, is not only our personal ally; it is the ally of cultural, economic, and global change. It is invaluable to the creativity-based industries of the future, as well as to anyone who wants to build something new and visionary in the quest to improve the world.

At this threshold, we face unimaginable new realities. Not only must we reexamine the limits of our human potential, we also have to look at the potential of our creations. Humans are, by nature, creators. We are born to make things. We make art; we make life; we make artificial life. What will differentiate the superhuman from the supercomputer? Is intuition the dividing factor — or the uniting factor — between the two? As we create "artificial intelligence," will it experience the same kind of evolution of consciousness that we have? It is conceivable that, one day, our machines will awaken to a sense of self, as we do when our consciousness expands.

What if we look at AI as being not unlike our unconscious mind, conditioned only to respond to outside forces — without awareness of any other way of existing? And what happens if, or when, consciousness arises? What happens when AI *has a mind of its own* and asks for sovereignty — the right to live *its* truth? What, then, will define our humanity? How will human beings maintain our position at the top of the ladder of consciousness?

The answer is superhumanhood. The answer is *continuing our own evolution.* As the machines evolve into consciousness, we will evolve into superconsciousness. In this way, we will always be one step beyond. We will no longer worry about machines taking over the world because we will have already risen above it.

RADICAL INSIGHT
What distinguishes humanity is our ceaseless transformation — our devotion to the inner callings that keep us moving forward.

Cultivating intuition is the key to this final step in our evolution. Our quest to *become more aware* of life and use that awareness to *become more* in life — this is the intuitive journey. Each and every one of us is walking this road — unconsciously, consciously, or superconsciously. And whether we get there the easy way by learning from our inner wisdom, or the hard way by learning from our mistakes — the final destination is our truth.

The Healer, Sage, Visionary, and Mystic are archetypes for each part of our personal and collective evolutionary journeys. Together, we can heal the world. We can enlighten one another. We can change the world. We can rise above it all, together, as one. Life asks us — calls us — to step up. That is exactly what we do when we follow our intuition. We fulfill our evolutionary mission to own our inner power, and at long last, we become fully and extraordinarily...human.

WHAT'S NEXT? IMAGINE A DIFFERENT FUTURE

The total number of minds in the universe is one. In fact,
consciousness is a singularity phasing within all beings.
— ERWIN SCHRÖDINGER

What would the world look like if everyone lived by their intuition? Can you imagine a different world, one that revolves around the intuitive unity within us instead of the mind-made division outside of us? Is it inconceivable to envision a world where the tyranny of our small-minded ego finally abdicates its reign — returning power to our true and ultimate self?

In the end, it is not a question of whether or not we can imagine this future; it is a question of whether or not we can create it. But to create it, we must first believe it is possible. It is time to reject the limitations that the world has asked us to accept; it's time to reject the idea that we are defined by three-dimensional life, that suffering is a necessary part of life, that division is human nature, that the world knows us better than we know ourselves.

We need to think twice before we allow this version of humanity to become our narrative. No matter what the history books say — war, treachery, cruelty, and ignorance are not part of our true nature. They are the results of *being separated from* our true nature. All of the suffering that we inflict upon ourselves — and one another — is symptomatic of the collective unconsciousness that pervades these early stages of human evolution.

In the big picture of time, humanity is so young. We have existed, like newborns, for only a blink of an eye on the cosmic scale. We are just at the beginning of our evolutionary journey, capable of so much more than we can see on the immediate horizon. In these early stages of life, as we are finding ourselves and polishing up our rough edges, we must aspire to more.

We were made for a life of truth without lies, love without hate, growth without suffering, existence without division. The real nature of humanity is not one of discord; it is one of radiant togetherness. Until we accept this — and truly believe this — nothing will change.

Intuition leads each and every one of us toward this higher vision of humanity. As we collectively live our truth, more and more of us will *be moved* to make the changes that not only transform our own lives, but the ways of the world. This is how the revolution takes hold. What starts inside of us — changing our hearts and minds — in turn changes our actions and experiences. As one, we outgrow our unconsciousness together.

Our humanity is reflected in the world we create. As we become more conscious, we can no longer suffer unconsciousness. We become incompatible with the low-vibration norms that, in our ignorance, we were once comfortable with. As we wake up, we have less tolerance for sexism, racism, homophobia, prejudice, or any of the other conditioned responses of an unconscious culture. What we collectively *put up with* yesterday is intolerable — outright unacceptable — in the reality of conscious awakening.

This shift is happening in a big way today. How could we possibly sleep through so many end-of-times catastrophes — plagues, social injustice, natural disaster, war? Life is calling us to wake up. *We have to wake up.* The alarm bells are ringing. We have to see and fix the error of our ways before we destroy ourselves. This is the crossroads of our time: We intuit or we die; we can seize this moment to become something more and better — or we perish at our own hands.

It is time to overthrow the global unconsciousness that has dominated the past centuries — even millennia — and listen to what life, at large, is calling us to do. The long-suppressed, vital aspects of our nature are now stepping into power — feminine power, creativity, empathy, inclusion, and of course, intuition. Though these qualities have been silenced in the past, it is *exactly those things* that are now the voice of the future — personally, economically, and culturally. The power that our lower-conscious, ego-indulgent mind once put down is the power that we now *require* to continue moving onward and upward.

To fully grasp what the next level looks like, let's imagine ourselves not just in one hundred or two hundred years, but in a thousand or even twenty thousand years. Do you think we are going to make it that far in unconsciousness? To last that long, we have to wake up. We have to see the potential within us and learn how to become our best selves. And we have to do it *together*; we cannot let the world continue to divide us because it is only united that any of us will stand.

This is how real change happens. It all begins with a simple first step — the step to know and trust the unifying truth within us all. We listen to what life is intuitively calling us to do; we make the changes that we are intuitively called to make. We honor the all-knowing, guiding voice within us. Our duty is as simple as that. When the day comes that we are all doing that, we will see, maybe even for the first time, what human nature really looks like.

The process of collective healing and rebalancing may take time, but there will be clues along the way that the wheels of change are in motion. As we begin to live more insightfully, we will see the following:

- We will live longer, healthier, higher-quality lives as a result of a stronger connection with our inner sense of well-being.
- We will experience increased social consciousness, empathy, and authenticity as a result of cultivated insight and mindfulness.
- We will engage in rapid levels of creativity, conscious innovation, and technological progress as a result of increased levels of ingenuity, equity, and collaboration.
- We will gain a more pervasive sense of peace, happiness, and unity, due to a collective reconnection with one another and our shared truth.

One of the greatest gifts of insightfulness is the recognition of our unity. Intuition removes the delusion of disconnectedness. Even though we may seem to be living independent lives, separate from one another, in reality, we coexist in the interconnected, indivisible web of life. What happens when the illusion is gone — when we can finally see through the veil of separation? No more secrets. No more lies. No more deception or inauthenticity. The game of unconsciousness ends. We can see beyond the illusions and the labels that divide us.

Over the course of this book, we have seen how intuition brings people together. Its power is the common thread that unites even the strangest of bedfellows. The insight leaders who have shared their stories with us come from all walks of life: beyond gender, race, nationality, or sexual orientation. They are artists, scientists, psychologists, doctors, writers, teachers, musicians, and the person next door — healers, sages, visionaries, and mystics — many different people sharing a singular message.

No matter what our differences are, we are all intuitively one. With every choice you make, you have the opportunity to bring yourself — and the world — deeper into that unification. Each thought, each feeling, each act is an opportunity to shine the radiant light of truth in the world — and to do your part in the enlightenment of humankind. We don't need wars, battles, or armies in this revolution; we only need our truth.

The truth *will* set you free. And the only place to find that truth is inside of you. When your intuition comes alive, you gain the power to break free from your unconscious conditioning and put an end to the ignorance that created it. When you follow your intuition, you are *doing your job*. You are doing your part to improve the world by transmuting unconsciousness into higher consciousness.

This is what you were made for.

It is not just our purpose — it is our *responsibility* — to better ourselves and our world. This is how we participate in the evolution of existence itself. To live insightfully means to live every moment of your life with the awareness that you are more than you *know*. You are extraordinary. A single insight has the power to change your mind, your heart, your life — and even the world. When you recognize this — when we all recognize this — a future of limitless potential awaits us all.

ACKNOWLEDGMENTS

It is with the deepest gratitude that I acknowledge the extraordinary people who helped bring this work to life. *Radical Intuition* would not have been possible without the "early adopters" who saw its vision from the start: the extraordinary artists and creatives I had the honor of working with through the CREATE! Festival; the leaders who advocated for this work, even when so many people didn't "get" it; and my early mentors and support system — Jim Denova, Audrey Russo, and all of the people who boldly took a chance on me.

To my beautiful IntuitionLab family, with whom I have had the opportunity to forge this work, thank you for getting out of your comfort zone with me and trusting yourself. To those of you who have been dedicated to this journey from day one — Anita, Tim, Stephanie, Nicky, Beth, Gabriela, Brittney, Arlene, Kerri, Suzanne, Jesse, Nellie, Praveen, Alexis, Sue, Meagan, Heather, Rita, Shawna, Kelli — you have been the heart and soul of this work. I am eternally grateful for the joyful community we built on this wisdom.

Thank you to New World Library for believing in this work, and to my brilliant editor, Georgia Hughes, who gave it wings.

Thank you to Wendy Keller for being the world's best agent and for always giving me the tough love I need. I could not be more grateful for the insight leaders who came together to stand by this message: Day Schildkret, Kelly Noonan Gores, Steve Kilbey, Brett Larkin, Jesse Schell, Byron Nash, Suzanne Steinbaum, Carl Kurlander, Dennis Palumbo, and my support sisters, Marla-Mervis Hartmann, Jessica Epperson-Lusty, and Katie Brauer.

Most of all, I want to thank Jon, my one, who gave me the most precious gift — the space and the time to live my own intuitive calling — for standing by my side and making sacrifices to help bring this light into the world. You and my two beautiful daughters, Eva and Lily, *make my heart sing*. A deep bow to the dear-to-my-heart teachers who opened the way for me — Paramahansa Yogananda, Mooji, Eckhart Tolle, C.S. Lewis, and St. Teresa — and, finally, to the greatest teacher: the teacher within us all.

EXTRAORDINARY INSIGHT CONTRIBUTORS

NOTES

p. ix   *"For it is intuition that improves the world"*: William Hermanns, *Einstein and the Poet: In Search of the Cosmic Man* (Wellesley, MA: Branden Books, 1983), 16.

p. 9   *"This is our birthright — the wisdom"*: Pema Chödrön, *The Pocket Pema Chödrön* (Boulder, CO: Shambala Publications, 2008), 14.

p. 18   *"Intuition is the soul's power of knowing God"*: Swami Kriyananda, *The Essence of Self-Realization: The Wisdom of Paramahansa Yogananda* (Nevada City, CA: Crystal Clarity Publishers, 1990), 43.

p. 21   *"True intelligence is to rise above thinking"*: Eckhart Tolle, Present Moment Reminders (Eckhart Teachings), email.

p. 51   *"Metareality is everywhere, always, and everything"*: Deepak Chopra, *Metahuman: Unleashing Your Infinite Potential* (New York: Random House, 2019), 177.

p. 59   *For example, if a particle on earth is entangled*: NOVA, "Bring 'Spooky Action at a Distance' into the Classroom," PBS, July 15, 2019, https://www.pbs.org/wgbh/nova/article/bring-spooky -action-distance-classroom-nova-resources.

p. 62   *"There can be as much value in the blink of an eye"*: Malcolm Gladwell, *Blink: The Power of Thinking without Thinking* (New York: Little, Brown, 2005), 17.

p. 73   *"New ideas come into this world somewhat like falling"*: Henry David Thoreau, *Essays and Other Writings of Henry David Thoreau*, ed. Will H. Dircks (London: Walter Scott, 1892), 237.

p. 77   *"Everything you see, smell, hear, taste, and touch travels"*: Travis Bradberry and Jean Greaves, *Emotional Intelligence 2.0* (San Diego: TalentSmart, 2009), 7.

p. 93   *"Intuition is not mere perception, or vision"*: Daryl Sharp, *Personality Types: Jung's Model of Typology* (Toronto, Canada: Inner City Books, 1987), 59.

p. 105   *"There is a universal, intelligent life force"*: Shakti Gawain, *Developing Intuition: Practical Guidance for Daily Life* (2000; repr., Novato, CA: New World Library, 2002), 21.

p. 125   *"How many times have you gone against your gut"*: Oprah Winfrey, "What Oprah Knows for Sure About Trusting Her Intuition," Oprah.com, August 2011, http://www.oprah.com /spirit/Oprah-on-Trusting-Her-Intuition-Oprahs-Advice-on -Trusting-Your-Gut#ixzz2eA7JBHJP.

p. 141   *"Thinking is not the highest human faculty"*: Eknath Easwaran, *Words to Live By: Daily Inspiration for Spiritual Living* (Tomales, CA: Nilgiri Press, 2010), 387.

p. 159   *"The Sage is one in whom mind and heart"*: Mooji, *Writing on Water: Spontaneous Utterances, Insights, and Drawings* (Mumbai, India: Yogi Impressions Books, 2010), 114.

p. 173   *"Don't ask what the world needs"*: Howard Thurman, *Sermons on the Parables* (Maryknoll, NY: Orbis Books, 2018), ebook, ch. 5.

p. 174   *To this end, Bronnie Ware, an Australian nurse, recorded*: Bronnie Ware, "Top 5 Regrets of the Dying," *Huffington Post*, January 21, 2012, https://www.huffpost.com/entry/top-5-regrets-of-the -dying_b_1220965.

p. 199   *"Your time is limited, so don't waste it living"*: Steve Jobs, Stanford University Commencement Address (June 12, 2005), *Stanford News*, June 14, 2005, https://news.stanford.edu/news/2005/june15 /jobs-061505.html.

p. 201   *Statistics show that getting outside your comfort zone*: Pittsburgh Technology Council, *Inclusion, Innovation, and Integrative Design: Pittsburgh's Creative Clusters*, February 2014, 6, http://www.pghtech.org/media/161037/PittsburghCreative ClustersFinalReport-2014.pdf.

p. 209   *"The ultimate truths of heaven...the reality"*: Paramahansa Yogananda, *The Second Coming of Christ: The Resurrection of the Christ within You* (Los Angeles: Self-Realization Fellowship, 2004), 694.

p. 223 *"I will pour out my spirit upon all mankind"*: *Days of the Lord: The Liturgical Year,* vol. 3 (Collegeville, MN: The Liturgical Press, 1993), 261.

p. 231 *"It is awakening, enlightenment, and the amazing intuitive"*: Thomas Merton, *New Seeds of Contemplation* (New York: New Directions, 1961/2007), 5.

p. 239 *"Trust in yourself, then you will know"*: Goethe, *The Faust of Goethe: Part I, in English Verse,* trans. W. H. Colquhoun (London: Arthur H. Moxon, 1878), 122.

p. 251 *"There is a secret place. A radiant sanctuary"*: Mirabai Starr, in St. Teresa of Avila, *The Interior Castle* (New York: Berkley, 2004), 1.

p. 257 *"Imagine if all the tumult of the body were to quiet down"*: St. Augustine, in Eknath Easwaran, *God Makes the Rivers to Flow: An Anthology of the World's Sacred Poetry & Prose* (Tomales, CA: Nilgiri Press, 2009), 230.

p. 273 *"Man is a transitional being, he is not final"*: Sri Aurobindo, "Man, a Transitional Being," *The Hour of God and Other Writings* (n.p.: Birth Centenary Library, 1970), 7.

p. 275 *"This superior man would not be a product of long"*: "Superman," *Encyclopedia Britannica,* last updated February 11, 2020, https://www.britannica.com/topic/superman-philosophy.

p. 275 *"The most meaningful activity in which a human being"*: Jonas Salk, *Anatomy of Reality: Merging of Intuition and Reason* (New York: Columbia University Press, 1983), 112.

p. 276 *The World Economic Forum anticipates that creativity will*: World Economic Forum, *The Future of Jobs: Employment, Skills, and Workforce Strategy for the Fourth Industrial Revolution,* January 2016, http://www3.weforum.org/docs/WEF_Future_of_Jobs.pdf.

p. 276 *"The future belongs to a different kind of person"*: Daniel Pink, *A Whole New Mind: Why Right-Brainers Will Rule the Future* (New York: Penguin Random House, 2006), back cover.

p. 279 *"The total number of minds in the universe is one"*: Erwin Schrödinger, in Paul Pines, *Trolling with the Fisher King: Reimagining the Wound* (Asheville, NC: Chiron Publications, 2018).

ABOUT THE AUTHOR

Kim Chestney is a globally recognized author, innovation leader, and intuition expert. As the founder of IntuitionLab and the CREATE! Festival, she has touched thousands of lives by raising awareness of "insight" as a revolutionary next step in the evolution of both personal and world consciousness. Working for nearly twenty years in the tech sector, Kim has led initiatives with some of the top thought leaders, technology companies, and universities in the world. Her books have been published around the globe and translated into multiple languages since 2004. Kim leads a thriving global intuition community with online intuition training, professional certification, live workshops, and retreats. Learn more at www.kimchestney.com.

MORE INTUITION RESOURCES

Download more *Radical Intuition* support materials and tools at
www.kimchestney.com/toolbox.

Practice with *Radical Intuition* interactive Insight Cards at
www.kimchestney.com/insight-cards.

Participate in live intuitive development workshops,
retreats, and online courses at
www.intuition-lab.com.

Join the *Radical Intuition* community at
www.facebook.com/groups/Intuitionrevolution.

Read more by Kim Chestney:
*The Psychic Workshop: A Complete Program
for Fulfilling Your Spiritual Potential*

NEW WORLD LIBRARY is dedicated to publishing books and other media that inspire and challenge us to improve the quality of our lives and the world.

We are a socially and environmentally aware company. We recognize that we have an ethical responsibility to our readers, our authors, our staff members, and our planet.

We serve our readers by creating the finest publications possible on personal growth, creativity, spirituality, wellness, and other areas of emerging importance. We serve our authors by working with them to produce and promote quality books that reach a wide audience. We serve New World Library employees with generous benefits, significant profit sharing, and constant encouragement to pursue their most expansive dreams.

Whenever possible, we print our books with soy-based ink on 100 percent postconsumer-waste recycled paper. We power our offices with solar energy and contribute to nonprofit organizations working to make the world a better place for us all.

Our products are available wherever books are sold. Visit our website to download our catalog, subscribe to our e-newsletter, read our blog, and link to authors' websites, videos, and podcasts.

customerservice@newworldlibrary.com
Phone: 415-884-2100 or 800-972-6657
Orders: Ext. 110 • Catalog requests: Ext. 110
Fax: 415-884-2199

www.newworldlibrary.com